The Honeycomb of theWord

Interpreting the Primary Testament
with André LaCocque

In hommage
André LaCocque

The *Honeycomb* of the *Word*

Interpreting the Primary Testament with *André LaCocque*

Edited by W. Dow Edgerton

Exploration Press, Chicago

Exploration Press
Chicago Theological Seminary
5757 University Ave.
Chicago, Illinois 60637

ISBN: 0-913552-64-X

Library of Congress Catalog Card Number: 2001012345

Contents

Introduction
W. Dow Edgerton

vii

Quelques Souvenirs
Robert Martin-Achard

xi

Unconventional, But Feminine
Diane Bergant

1

Culture and Religion in Hellenic Judaism
John J. Collins

17

The *Life* of Study
W. Dow Edgerton

37

My Dinner with André
Robert M. Grossman

51

**The Question of Idolatry:
A Formal or Material Principle?**
Theodore W. Jennings, Jr.

56

Debate Concerning a Heritage
Bernard Keller

71

**Three Biblical Portraits
of the Divine-Human Encounter**
Vernon Kurtz

88

Contents

A Preacher's Teacher: Lessons on Ministry from One Who Proclaims the Word
Craig Mousin — 104

Toward a Post-Holocaust Practice of Biblical Criticism
Daniel Patte — 122

An Overlooked Double Entendre in Jonah 2:5
Shalom Paul — 155

Christology After the Shoah
John Pawlikowski — 158

Fides Quaerens Intellectum: Biblical Antecedents?
Paul Ricoeur — 179

Genesis 1-5 as Matrix of Jesus' Mission
Wolfgang Roth — 209

God of the Future
Herman Schaalman — 228

Understanding Scripture and the Holocaust
Byron Sherwin — 236

Publications by André LaCocque — 249

Introduction

W. Dow Edgerton

In these pages the reader will find honey from the honeycomb of the Word. Yet the Word itself is sweeter, says the psalmist, as these essays also bear witness, and whatever sweetness these pages offer flows from the sweetness of the Word which precedes them, accompanies them, and endures beyond them forever. The work of André LaCocque, in celebration of whom this volume is presented, is an unwavering testimony to this truth.

The honeycomb, however, is not only sweet but also complex, intricate, many-faceted. This, too, is true of these essays and must be, because the work of André LaCocque is itself complex, intricate, many-faceted. The list of contributors includes biblical scholars, theologians, philosophers, lawyers, teachers, rabbis, pastors, preachers, Jews, and Christians. As broad as it is, the list could be broader still, because the breadth of Dr. LaCocque's investigation, passion, commitment, and friendship exceeds even so broad a community.

It is tempting to offer the reader a framework of interpretation, but any such framework would inevitably diminish and distort the work of the person honored here. It is similarly tempting to group the essays according to theme or focus, yet this too would be distorting. The essays here find their real collective center in their relationship to André LaCocque. We shall use, instead, the juxtapositional logic of the alphabet to guide us, and in so doing perhaps the reader will discover links and affinities no synthesis could hope to find.

We begin, therefore, with an essay by **Diane Bergant** of Catholic Theological Union, "Unconventional but Feminine." Dr. Bergant draws inspiration from LaCocque's *The Feminine Unconventional: Four Subversive Figures in Israel's Tradition* to explore the Song of Songs and its surprising celebration of sexuality and gender roles. Next comes the University of Chicago's **John Collins** and his essay "Culture and Religion in Hellenic Judaism." Here he examines the interpretation of Judaism to Hellenic culture as it is found in the *Letter of Aristeas*, and Book Three of the *Sybelline Oracles*. This is followed by **W. Dow Edgerton** of Chicago Theological Seminary with "The *Life* of Study", a meditation upon Psalm 19 as an evocation of hermeneutic experience.

Next, **Robert M. Grossman**, an attorney, contributes a personal memoir, "'My Dinner with André'", with special reference to the experience of teaching together with Professor LaCocque. **Theodore Jennings**, Chicago Theological Seminary, follows with "The Question of Idolatry: A Formal or Material Principle." Here the author offers arguments founded upon Jeremiah that theology's formal principle for distinguishing idolatry (the difference between the unconditional and the conditioned) needs also a material principle: the doctrine of God as a critique of all forms of injustice. **Bernard Keller,** formerly of the University of Strasbourg, comes next with "Debate Concerning a Heritage", a consideration of the relation between the Jewish Passover and Christian liturgy, including a rich dialogue with Andre Neher which illustrates the delicacy and difficulty of such comparative work.

Rabbi **Vernon Kurtz**, of North Suburban Synagogue Beth El in Highland Park Illinois, contributed the essay which follows, "Three Biblical Portraits of the Divine-Human Encounter." Here Rabbi Kurtz examines transformative episodes in the lives of Abraham, Jacob, and Moses, with particular reference to the interpretations of medieval Jewish commentators. The Reverend **Craig Mousin** (also an attorney) of DePaul University's Center for Church/State Studies, then follows with "A Preacher's Teacher—Lessons on Ministry from One Who Proclaims the Word". This is an open letter, reflecting upon the challenge of Professor LaCocque's teaching and its impact upon the author's work as an advocate for refugees.

Daniel Patte, Vanderbilt University, then presents "Toward A Post-Holocaust Practice of Biblical Criticism". Professor Patte argues that following the Holocaust any biblical interpretation which claims to be critical must include an assessment of how it affects Jewish communities and individuals, but even more, to grasp what it means to be confronted by the "*tremendum* of the abyss". **John T. Pawlikowski**, Catholic Theological Union, takes up a related question in his chapter, "Christology After the Shoah". The author considers important Jewish and Christian perspectives and their implications for what he terms a "Christology of witness" by which one could take up a fundamental responsibility as a post-Holocaust Christian. **Paul Ricoeur**, professor emeritus of the University of Chicago, and a long-time friend and colleague of Professor LaCocque, contributes the next chapter, "*Fides Quaerens Intellectum*: Biblical Antecedents?", bringing together an examination of Anselm's famous argument with reflection upon the name and self-naming of God in the Hebrew Bible. **Wolfgang Roth**, professor emeritus from Garret-Evangelical Theological Seminary, focuses his essay upon a reading of Jesus' mission as it is presented in John's gospel through a construction of Genesis 1-5: "Genesis 1-5 as Matrix of Jesus' Mission."

Rabbi **Herman E. Schaalman**, Rabbi emeritus of Emanuel Congregation, Chicago, Illinois, contributes to the volume's discussion of Jewish and Christian understanding in the face of the Shoah with his chapter, "God of the Future". Finally, **Byron L. Sherwin** of Spertus College of Judaica offers a consideration of the Holocaust's influence upon understanding of Scripture and Jewish tradition's understanding of Scripture's influence upon understandings of the Holocaust: "Under-standing Scripture and the Holocaust".

As much as this collection of essays offers, the reader will also find something speaking between the lines. Beyond respect and admiration for André LaCocque's work as a scholar and teacher can be heard the voice of gratitude for the witness of his life.

The late **Robert Martin-Achard**, professor emeritus of the University of Geneva, contributed a personal memoir for this volume shortly before his death, which expresses this gratitude both professionally and personally. For this reason it is included as a preface to the other contributions.

A final word before turning to the rich essays presented here. To choose one quality is inevitably to neglect others, so it is with some apprehension that I offer to characterize so full a witness as André LaCocque's with a single word: integrity. Yet this is, indeed, a quality so frequently named by those who know him. His word is his deed; his deed is his vocation; his vocation is his life; his life is his faith; his faith is in the God of Israel—and his delight is in the Word which is sweeter than the drippings of the honeycomb.

Quelques Souvenirs

Robert Martin-Achard

Dear André,

It was first through your father, Jean LaCocque, that I met you, at the Theological Seminary of Montpellier. Several things had taken him there in 1946: the discovery of Kierkegaard, the Exodus of 1940, the charge of a Protestant parish in Belgium—and of course, his passion for Israel. He was my room-mate and repeated every morning all the Hebrew verb forms to get them in his head. We spent long hours exchanging our ideas on the reading of what one called in Christian circles, the "Old Testament," and in particular its Christological understanding, so honorably reclaimed by Wilhelm Vischer (pastor from Basel, great friend of Karl Barth) who had just been called to occupy the chair of Old Testament at Montpellier. One year later, you came to join us, after having undertaken theological studies at Strasbourg, where in the sixties you returned and obtained successively the degrees of Doctor of Philosophy and Doctor of Theology. Your father, at whose pastoral consecration I had the honor to participate, bequeathed to you a profound love for the people of the patriarchs and prophets. But if your vocation of teaching and research was thus oriented at the outset, it quickly became evident that your theological and scientific work would unfold in a freedom of sympathy and lucidity all its own. It is not insignificant to recall that the last time I met Jean LaCocque, it was at the turning of a street in the oriental part of Jerusalem where we were permitted a rapid, providential, and final exchange in this city so dear to millions of believers of yesterday and today.

In my memory now I place you between Brussels and Strasbourg, and I remember particularly your thesis defense at the latter place. You appeared before a specially chosen ecumenical areopagus: professor Edmond Jacob (Protestant), Andre Neher (Jewish), Joseph Schmitt (Catholic), presided over by Marcel Simon (Anglican), the author of a minute inquiry on the relations between Jews and Christians in the first centuries of our era, entitled *Verus Israel*. There you presented and commented upon a text of Jewish tradition, *The Fathers According to Rabbi Nathan,* vigorously defending the midrashic reading of Israel, hardly known and appreciated in our Christian setting at the time. Your interest in Israel and its hermeneutical tradition showed itself already in this inaugural work as it would become evident through all your writing to this time.

You invited your students and readers to approach the Old Testament texts, not only in the accustomed manner of a Protestant theological faculty, but also in the manner of the people by whom they had been elaborated, heard and interpreted through the centuries. It was thus that your teaching at Brussels introduced your listeners to a world until then ignored, and, despite the difficulties of the time, your teaching rang out clearly.

It was from the same perspective that you participated as a professor from Brussels, in a colloquy convened at Bièvres (near Paris). The colloquy was concerned with the teaching of the French-speaking Protestant theological faculties on a burning theme of the time, that of Tradition. In a clear, rich, and pertinent presentation you treated "The Tradition in Low-Judaism". There you showed that following the experience of the Exile, the synagogue responded by reorganizing its canon, the list of works recognized as holy, and appealed to tradition. This Tradition did not merely fix the scripture, but offered also a way to interpret it, and permitted it to live dynamically, avoiding the hardening that menaces every institution, even in its way of reading. You declared, "Thanks to the Tradition, the Bible will participate in the living reality of which it testifies...going beyond every fixation, every stasis...". This Tradition's purest expression, you said, is the Midrash, which finds its origin in the Old Testament itself. You concluded your remarks on the Tradition, Scripture, the Christ, and their interrelations by this significant statement: "This is why, in order to know Christ and to let his stature become fulfilled in me, I turn toward Israel, Israel of the Old Testament, Israel of the Talmud, Israel of the Church and the Synagogue, that it may teach me to listen, to see, and to believe."

In an article published in 1962 you returned to the problem of the Tradition in Israel by way of a study dedicated to the "insertion of the 'Song of Songs' in the Canon". (Here is another theme you took up very early, the importance of which appears afresh today!) You recalled there that the Old Testament was not made in a day but by stages. The last of these stages was linked to the synod of Jamnia (90 c.e.), following the disastrous Jewish war against Rome. It was a synod marked by a care you termed *pastoral*, and which concerned in particular, the canonicity of the "Solomonic" books, whose authority was the object of secular discussions. The rabbis understood well that their interpretation in the midst of Israel must be directly linked to the tradition that had introduced them into the Jewish canon. That is, the text recognized as canonical is inseparable from the traditional interpretation that made it acceptable among the Jewish books and which, according to the hallowed expression, "stain the hands" (because they are holy). With such canonicity, a certain kind of reading is given, a view imposed on the holy writing. You indicated that the 'Song' was admitted into the canon because one reads it *there* as an allegory of the love of YHWH toward Israel, and that this interpretation could guide us in the exegesis of the text, an idea which you developed in another study.

But it is above all upon Israel, its vocation, its *raison d'être* among the nations, that you focused your attention, and I discern there a second main period in the unfolding of your work. I note first an article appearing in 1958, in *Verbum Caro,* during a very "ecumenical" time, an article which unfortunately did not have the impact it merited. Entitled "Israel, Touchstone of Ecumenism", it put into evidence the bond which exists between the first schism within the Church (between the Jewish Christians and the pagan Christians), and the situation of division in which through the centuries communities that claim the same Christ found themselves. In breaking with its Jewish origins Christianity let itself be carried into a Platonic ideology which led it to numerous theological derivations and finally to the rejection of Israel and its Bible. You invited the ecumenical movement, then, to a return—not to Rome, Moscow, or Geneva—but to Jerusalem! That is to say concretely, to a total conversion to the apostolic witness, under the gaze of the mother-church of Jerusalem, "The bishop of which all the pagan churches are children." You wrote, for example, "In brief, Israel is the priest of the nations, in whom the Creator gives himself to the creature...Israel, come from the loins of Abram the non-Jew, miraculous child of a dead couple, people a hundred times killed and a hundred times resuscitated, is the word of God for all the world, the presence of God, the concretization of God's grace in the created universe." You then concluded by citing an orthodox writer: "The theology of the Body of Christ must be rejoined to a theology of the mystical body of Israel. This is one of the most profound and beautiful bridgeworks between Judaism and Christianity," for it implies the resurrection from the dead, following Paul (Rom 11.25).

You followed through this urging in your message concerning the overture of the Vatican Council. You proposed that a Jewish representative attend the debates not only as an observer but as moderator, that the Church renouncing its Greek idealism which distorted it, might return to the school of Judaism, realist and unifying. You recalled the vocation of Jerusalem, "center of gravity of the people of God, holy mountain where all the peoples throng and say to the Jew: 'Your God will be my God' " (*Foi et Vie,* 1964).

You returned to these points at greater length in a work entitled *Pérennité d'Israël* which appeared the same year. You developed there in a hundred pages a theology of the people of God, of which the rabbis (as you tell it) pushed back election to the creation of the world recounted in the beginning of Genesis: "In view of Israel, God created!" Among the humans Abraham said 'yes' to God and became the elect of the Lord." This choice, however, was never preferential, exclusive—you insist on this point—it includes all of humanity; its perspectives are universalist, they envision the salvation of the world. In the chapters which followed, insisting upon a passage in Exodus (Exodus 19.4–6), you explained how to understand the vocation of Israel: "the priestly people" is called to exercise a mediating function among the nations, to teach them, to intercede for them, and at the same time to attest God's sovereignty and holiness before them.... Thus Israel is therefore a revelation to humanity of an objective fact. Israel is Humanity in its becoming." You continued in showing how Jesus of Nazareth accomplished the mission of Israel and permitted the gathering of humanity, then completed your reflection by treating the difficult problem of the relation between church and synagogue, historically separated and hostile to one another, and yet fundamentally unified and complementary, called together by pure grace, to belong to the Kingdom of God.

In 1967, appeared *Le Devenir de Dieu*, a rich commentary on the first chapters of Exodus. There you extended and completed your reflection upon Israel, dwelling most notably upon the One who calls to freedom and life, and whose name may not be spoken in Hebrew tradition. You drew upon not only current scholarship on Exodus, but also upon the traditional Jewish readings of these decisive passages. You explained verse by verse the biblical text, which you characterized as an "historical polemic" which opposes YHWH to the forces of nature exalted so greatly in the Egyptian cults. In especially important pages you pondered the famous declaration of Exodus 3.14 which you translated "I will become with whom I will become." In taking account of the particular construction of the phrase, the verb forms used and its context, you concluded "God inaugurates here the accomplishment of a particular action, that of 'becoming with'. God makes the story of God's People in Egypt God's own story," and a little later: "God pledges not only to Moses, but to all the People. The relationship never rests easily. The story will be a long confrontation with the God who gives all that he is, and at the same time claims all of his partner, for he is a jealous God."

A new stage began with your departure for the United States after a first contact with the Protestant world of that continent. Since 1966 you have found yourself in Chicago where you teach at Chicago Theological Seminary; you created there, with your characteristic dynamism, a center of study for Jewish-Christian dialogue, "The Center for Jewish-Christian Studies." You enlarged your horizon through contact with such internationally renowned colleagues as Mircea Eliade and Paul Ricoeur, and in the 70's you led with others an action on behalf of Jews detained in the Soviet Union.

These diverse responsibilities never took away from your scientific work: the time of great commentaries came, which appeared both in French and in English. You carried forward through this period your great interest in apocalyptic Judaism, which appears as such a special phenomenon within Hebrew tradition. In 1976 you published in the collection "Commentaire de l'Ancien Testament" an interpretation of the book of Daniel with a preface by Paul Ricoeur. There you took on with care the various problems raised by this late work, composed undoubtedly in the time of Antiochus Epiphanes, this tyrant, whose death was so fervently awaited (which finally arrived in the autumn of 164 B.C.E.). The book of Daniel emanates from "hasidic" milieus, that is, pious and faithful Jews (called also the "Poor of Israel"), dedicated to a rigorous observance of the divine Law. It is among them that the resurrection of the just was affirmed with clarity, of which you said with good reason: "For Canaan, survival was a fact of nature; for Israel, it is a historical phenomenon...it is a cry, an invocation, a prayer, a wager." The seventh chapter naturally commanded your attention; it evokes, you said, a new creation. And the Saints to whom the kingdom is finally given constitute the True Israel.."an eschatological community which exists already in the heavens."

In 1981 you presented another commentary on Zechariah 9-14 (*CAT # 11c*) in which you acknowledge its unity—a complex unity—and lift up again the apocalyptic traits. You situate this difficult and anthological collection in the first part of the fifth century in a time when the priestly party triumphs at Jerusalem and imposes its narrow view of a restorative eschatology. "Second Zechariah" protested against this seizure of official power by resituating its readers before an event to come, due to God himself, of which the principle elements relate to the feast of Succoth. You complete your commentary with these lines: "Thus II Zechariah appears as devoured by a deep discouragement concerning the prevailing conditions of his time and in his City...yet he has complete faith in the eschatological intervention of the Lord of history, but this intervention will be typically apocalyptic. What II Zechariah awaits is a universal cataclysm. For everything is to begin again at the beginning..."

Decidedly, apocalyptic held all your attention in those days: you presented a 1983 work (which I prefaced), *Daniel et Son Temps: Recherche sur le Mouvement Apocalyptique Juif au IIème Siècle Avant Jesus-Christ*. This work permitted you to examine further certain questions treated in your commentaries: bilingualism in the book of Daniel; the Hasidic milieu hostile to the theocratic party at Jerusalem and from whence came the "apocalypses"; the symbolic language utilized by them; the reinterpretation of messianism linked to David by the image of the "Son of Man" attested in Daniel 7; the theme of the resurrection (which was originally concerned only with the martyrs). You wrote a solid study, well founded, animated by a spirit which allowed us to better enter into this thought, so unsettling in its language, which is Jewish apocalyptic.

I do not forget that during these years (1965-1975) you participated actively in the venture which a hundred francophone biblical scholars (Protestant and Catholic together) undertook, "The Ecumenical Translation of the Bible". This doubtless required much effort, but its happy completion has inaugurated a new epoch in the relations between separated Christians.

I distinguish another stage in the trajectory of your more recent works, a stage marked by the originality of approach as much as the themes approached. I mention them all at once (without pretending to be exhaustive). There was a psychological study undertaken with your son upon the strange character of the Bible called Jonah, and which happily linked a double approach to the "prophet" (*Jonah: A Psycho-Religious Approach to the Prophet*, 1990). There was also an audacious study on a passage of the "Song of Songs" ("La Shulamite et les chars d'Aminadab: Un essai herméneutique sur Cantique 6.12-7.1") in which you took up in a new way the thesis of symbolic interpretation of this scroll. Here you saw "a polemical composition in reaction against the civil and religious "establishment" at the time of the Second Temple. The author of the "Song", you proposed, was a woman poet who sang of erotic love against traditional prophetic approach and imagery of amorous relations, but symbolically between God and Israel. She pleaded in the "Song" for fleshly eros against a spiritualized and disincarnate agapé (1995).

In the following year appeared your work on Job which was destined to receive special attention following the events lived by our generation; you insisted so notably in this long and beautiful writing, upon the diversity of divine names used in the biblical text which disclosed despite its complexity, a single composer, and non-Israelite besides. The book of Job contests, you said, the idea commonly granted by "homo religiosus", even outside Israel, of a retributive justice which exercises itself in an automatic and unchanging way in the name of an all-powerful divinity, passive and far away. The situation of Job was changed radically with the intervention of a God, bearing precisely a name—YHWH—which was also a commitment, and whose creative work in its fullness and variety attested precisely to God's overflowing compassion: before the "Deus otiosus" Job declared himself innocent, but before YHWH he discovered his lack of love, confessed it, and in this new relation, knew himself justified by his God (Job 38 ff.).

The same year, in an ecumenical review, you evoked a question from which no one can escape: "God After Auschwitz: A Contribution to Contemporary Theology." You recalled in gripping strokes what Nazism was in its brutality, in its intention, its methods and results—you characterized its processes of dehumanization as the triumph of a "functional rationality"—and you deduced that after the Shoa both Jewish and Christian theology must be radically rethought: it can no longer present itself as a closed, abstract, and traditional system as orthodoxy would want: Auschwitz is a sheer cry. It teaches us nothing else but the destruction of all illusion. It has no teaching significance. It deconstructs. But paradoxically it sends us back, Christians and Jews alike, to the grace of God alone and invites us to speak not about the sex of angels or the two natures of Christ, but of the concrete problems of our century such as racism, sexism, injustice. For the first time in two thousand years, Jews and Christians link arms instead of ignoring and despising one another. As it was once said by Rabbi Hillel, "If not now, when will it be?" Thus the Shoah opens, through its vital plea, onto a new state of relations between Judaism and Christianity.

Without pretending to be complete, I wish to mention yet one more of your recent works published in French in 1992 and entitled (in English) *The Feminine Unconventional: Four Subversive Figures in Israel's Tradition*. It is a piece of astonishing research, which testifies both to your own unique perspectives and at the same time responds to shared real-world issues, as found in the feminist movement. After the introductory chapters in which you bring forward the situation of women in the Near East and in Israel or, indeed, a celebrated page of Genesis about the human couple, you present a vivid and subtle portrait of five heroines of the Jewish tradition: Susanna, Judith, Esther, Ruth, and the Shulamite woman who appears in the Song of Songs. What a tableau, at once learned and charming you offer us, on the basis of several biblical and post-canonical themes, for our pleasure and our edification, which testify at the same time to the continuity of your fundamental theological orientation and to the profundity of your works through the course of all these years!

But there is a memory which I wish to recall here in particular, that of the academic year which we spent together in Jerusalem, that city which we hold so dearly in our hearts, in 1962/63. Thanks to your and Claire's gracious hospitality, I benefited so richly from those months of study and discovery. Together we visited Yemenite synagogues at the beginning of the Sabbath to hear the "Song of Songs" read; together we visited the holy places of Israel, the Church, and Islam; together we discussed the past of the People of God, the future of Zionism, peace in the Near East, and especially we together shared an unforgettable experience, that of a reading of the Psalms undertaken in common by two Jewish thinkers, two Dominicans, and we two Reformed theologians.

It was André Chouraqui, adjunct mayor of Jerusalem, who took the initiative to bring us together in his home. His name is well known by all those who are interested in the heritage of Abraham, since he has, beyond the many works about Israel, its past and present, translated in succession the Hebrew Bible, the New Testament, and the Koran. We commented in turn on the Psalms that Chouraqui chanted for us to close the evening in the peaceful atmosphere of the Holy City, and I remarked then how much the same text sustained different interpretations. As Protestants in the line of Karl Barth, we sought above all to receive the "kerygma" which Scripture both transmits to us and imposes upon us; our Catholic colleagues invited us to go beyond an interpretation "close to the text" in order to enrich it through the contribution of the Tradition; our Jewish friends found themselves right at home in approaching the Hebrew Bible and simply joined their own commentaries to those, varied and innumerable, which the midrashic reading furnished them and which through the centuries nourished the faith of Israel. In the encounter between the canonical text and the faithful who, as we understood, questioned the Church, its preaching and its behavior, we were thus confronted not only by a hermeneutic emerging from the doctrine solidly built by Rome, but also a kind of reading so evidently delicate and supple, which accompanied the Jewish people through its sorrowful destiny and kept its hope alive. That was 1963; since that time Jews and Christians have taken some steps to meet one another, in accord with your deep desire. It is on this positive note that I conclude these lines and assure you of all my friendship and best wishes for you and yours.

With affection,

Robert Martin-Achard, Genève

Chapter 1

Unconventional, But Feminine

Diane Bergant

This study[1] follows the lead of André LaCocque's work in *The Feminine Unconventional*, wherein he showcases four biblical women who were quite unconventional for their times. Susanna, Judith, Esther, and Ruth all acted in heroic ways usually expected of the men of their times. Whether they were historical or fictional women is not the issue. The fact that a fundamentally patriarchal society with a clear androcentric bias[2] developed and preserved narratives recounting unconventional exploits of women is itself remarkable.

Another unconventional biblical figure is the woman portrayed in the Song of Songs. She is neither a national heroine like Judith or Esther, nor a faithful ancestor like Ruth, nor a model of Jewish orthodoxy like Susanna. However, she is like them in that she acts in ways that do not always conform to the customs of her day. All five of these woman do have one characteristic in common: they are all remembered for some aspect of their sexual behavior. Susanna steadfastly resisted the sexual advances of two lecherous old men; Judith enticed the Assyrian general Holofernes in order to kill him; Esther used her beauty to convince her husband King

Ahasuerus to save her people; Ruth charmed Boaz, the kinsman of her mother-in-law, Naomi. Among these, only the woman in the Song candidly pursued her passion for its own sake. The fact that her behavior is not censured by the author of the book is precisely what makes her depiction unconventional.

The Holy of Holies

The Song of Songs is one of the most intriguing books in the First Testament. Its unabashed sensuality has captured the imagination and has endeared it to those who appreciate passionate human love. More demure readers have frequently cloaked its erotic character under the guise of metaphor. The history of the book's interpretation demonstrates the longstanding endorsement of both perspectives. Down through the ages, both Jewish and Christian interpreters have delighted in the profligate imagery of the book's songs, but they have also frequently reverted to allegory in their interpretations.

The early rabbinic writings reveal a controversy surrounding the canonicity of the book. Why did the Song of Songs 'defile the hands'? (Why was it too sacred to touch?) Rabbi Akiba championed its canonicity by arguing: "Heaven forbid! No one in Israel ever disputed that the Song of Songs defiles the hands. All the world is not worth the day that the Song of Songs was given to Israel; all the writings [*Ketûbîm*] are holy but the Song of Songs is the holy of holies" (Mishna Yadaim, 3:5).

Akiba also condemned the practice of using the Song as a common drinking ditty: "Whoever trills his voice singing the Song of Songs in a banquet hall, regarding it a common song of praise, has no part in the world to come" (Tosefta Sanhedrin, 12:10; see Babylonia Talmud Sanhedrin, 101a). This latter statement shows that the Song was originally understood literally, as a collection of love poems.

Though initially disputed, there was eventual agreement about the sacred character of the Song of Songs;[3] its meaning and religious value remained enigmatic. Several ways of interpreting the Song have been advanced, each one clearly dependent upon the literary classification to which the book is assigned. Most of these interpretations can be classified in one of four basic ways: as a dramatic performance;[4] as an allegory;[5] as a cultic reenactment;[6] or as a collection of love poems.[7] Each of these approaches reveals distinctive facets of the Song and opens up corresponding possibilities for understanding its multidimensional message.

Although the earliest Jewish readings seem to have been literal, both the Jewish and the Christian groups soon espoused an allegorical approach that reflected aspects of the covenantal relationship between YHWH and Israel, or God and the Church.[8] The Jewish approach was a kind of historical allegory, recounting Israel's story from the experience of the Exodus to the advent of the messiah (e.g., the Targum Canticles Rabbah).[9] The Christian allegory was either ecclesiological, describing the relationship between Christ and the church, tropological, with moral implications, or Mariological, seeing the Virgin Mary as the preeminent type of the church. A recent study interprets the book as a program for bringing back Davidic rule after the exile.[10]

As early as Origen (c. 240 C.E.), Christians began to read the book with devotional eyes that saw the relationship described there as one of spiritual marriage between God and the individual soul. This view was endorsed by such influential authors as Gregory of Nyssa, Jerome, Ambrose, Theodoret, and Cyril of Alexandria. It took on added significance in the mysticism of the Middle Ages with the writings of Gregory the Great, William of Saint Thierry, Venerable Bede, Bernard of Clairvaux, as well as the sixteenth century writers Teresa of Avila and John of the Cross.[11] A comparable allegorical approach is also found in Jewish writers such as Philo of Alexandria and Maimonides.

Critical scholarship has brought us back to a literal reading of the Song. The book is now regarded by most scholars as a collection of love poetry. Its sensuous imagery and its depiction of an erotic affair celebrate the passion of heterosexual love. Solomonic legitimation found in the superscription (1:1) places the book in the category of Wisdom Literature, the primary interest of which is instruction in the proper ways of living. It would seem that the love poetry in this book is intended for some kind of instruction.

Contemporary biblical interpretation is indebted to theorists such as Hans-Georg Gadamer and Paul Ricoeur. Gadamer's identification of the world behind the text, the world of the text, and the world in front of the text,[12] as well as his explanation of the fusion of horizons of meaning,[13] along with Ricoeur's notions of distanciation and surplus of meaning [14] have freed interpretation of the Song from any servitude to the past. Thus the book can yield an array of different meanings without compromising its literary integrity.

Gadamer has been criticized for his uncritical presumption of the benign character of the received tradition. He did not consider the biases that it can contain and project. Ricoeur, on the other hand, agreed with Freud that the force and meaning of language can conceal a false consciousness.[15] Refining Freud's 'hermeneutics of suspicion,' he went on to develop a way of constructing meaning that is open to the possibilities of the future while aware of the limitations of the past.

The insights of such theorists, especially Gadamer's 'fusion of horizons' and Ricoeur's 'hermeneutics of suspicion' and 'surplus of meaning,' encourage contemporary commentators to be self-conscious about their respective social locations, to uncover both the texts' and their own biases, and to be open yet critical of the various readings that a text seems to yield. This particular study reads the Song of Songs with eyes sensitive to gender biases. Without presuming that the author or final editor of the Song shared the gender concerns that are so prominent today, it is correct to say that the woman portrayed in these romantic poems is clearly unconventional.

My Love, My Dove,
My Beautiful One

First, let us consider the terms of endearment used by the man to describe the woman: "My love" (*ra'ya*, a loving term used only for women and used quite consistently by the man [1:9,15; 2:2,10,13; 4:1; 5:2; 6:4]), "my dove" (2:14; 5:2; 6:9), "my beautiful one" (2:13). The terms may sound demeaning to some readers. However, this is probably due more to contemporary connotations than to their implications in the Song. These are pet names denoting intimacy rather than frailty. The description of the woman found in the poems refutes any image of the withdrawn and passive damsel who, like a shrinking violet, retreats into some protective place of safety. This woman is bold and forthright in the pursuit of her love. She is not intimidated by the earthiness of life nor by the very natural desires that she experiences. She relishes human emotion, but is not a captive of it. Rather, its intensity is a gauge of the depth of her admiration of the marvelous qualities of the man she loves.

The delicate pet names used by the man are balanced by very strong imagery describing the woman's sexual attractiveness. He compares her to a mare let loose among the stallions of the Pharaoh's chariotry, whose tantalizing presence could throw these well disciplined horses into total confusion (1:9–11). This comparison may seem foreign and even offensive to contemporary sensitivities, but the innovative imagery is striking,[16] and the equine frenzy that it suggests aptly illustrates the man's perception of the sexual irresistibility of the woman he loves.

The point of this metaphor shifts slightly, concentrating now on the mare's adornment. The bridles of Pharaoh's horses were often extravagantly decorated with tassels, fringes and trappings of ivory or precious metal, all of which added to the horses' grandeur. Since ancient Near Eastern women frequently wore jewelry on their faces and around their necks, the similarity lends itself to the comparison. Ornaments only enhance the splendor of what is already magnificent in appearance. According to the man, the beauty of his loved one is anything but frail. Rather, it is every bit as dramatic as the awe-inspiring display of the Egyptian chariotry.

The man further describes the woman's beauty in two other poems (4:1-7; 7:2-6 [Heb]). In each case the poem is generally classified as a *wasf*,[17] an Arabic poem that, with exaggerated metaphor and in an orderly fashion, describes the body of the loved one part by part. Like other metaphorical constructions, a feature of an otherwise unrelated object represents a person's physical characteristic.

Frequently metaphors function not only in a representational but also in a presentational manner, where the association of ideas is based on an emotional response rather than physical similarity. Since the *wasf* most likely grew out of the experience of being captivated by someone's physical charms, and served as a way of arousing these same emotions at a later time,[18] it is best understood from both a representational and a presentational point of view.[19]

The first poem begins and ends with a declaration by the man of the beauty of the woman he loves (4:1,7). Each of the various elements of description highlights one aspect of the remarkable beauty of the woman's upper body. Her eyes are compared to doves, her hair to a flock of goats, her teeth to a flock of ewes, her lips to a scarlet thread, her cheeks to pomegranates, her neck to the tower of David, and her breasts to fawns. While the imagery may seem strange, even crude, to the modern reader, it must have been easily understood and considered complimentary to the original reader.

The emotional responses evoked by a presentational understanding of the metaphors in this *wasf* are all highly erotic. The intensity of a fixed look, which can capture the eye of another and hold that person under a spell without making a move or speaking a word, and the fluttering movement of eyelids, which can also exert a mesmerizing influence over another, are not only engaging but are also very seductive. The sense of mystery that such eyes are able to cast can be accentuated if they are partially concealed behind a veil as is the case here.

Rippling black hair cascading down a woman's shoulders is not only attractive, it can also be quite suggestive. The woman's warm smile and her pleasant manner of speech imply a certain degree of intimacy. The color of her cheeks and the ornamentation around her neck both tantalize and inspire awe. The description of her firm, shapely breasts is probably the most provocative image of all. The strength and sensuality depicted in this poem is undeniable.

The man unabashedly uses these sensual figures of speech in his praise of the beauty of his beloved. The visual imagery is robust, and the movement depicted is energetic. Despite this sensuousness, there is not even a hint of disapproval. One never gets the sense that he is considered too graphic in his portrayal, or that he is describing physical characteristics that should not be mentioned. He is censored neither by the poet nor by anyone within the poem itself. On the contrary, both the subject of the characterization (the woman's sensuality) and the provocative imagery used are in keeping with the nature of the rest of the poetry. The sexual attractiveness of the woman and the erotic attraction of the man are as natural as the nature-sensitive comparisons that comprise the poem. The very use of this particular literary form of praise (the *wasf*) shows that the sexual nature of their relationship is highly esteemed.

The second *wasf* (7:2-6) begins its description with the feet and moves upward to the head. The woman's dancing feet probably caught the man's attention and his gaze moves up her body. Once again he uses strong imagery to describe her charms: her thighs are like the jewelry crafted by an artisan; her navel is intoxicating like mixed wine; her belly resembles wheat encircled with lilies; her breasts are like the twin fawns of the gazelle; her neck is pristine white as ivory. The glistening accents of sunlight and the dense mountain growth characterize the delicate coloring of her body and the shimmering brilliance and thickness of her hair. The mysterious quality of deep tranquil water aptly describes her eyes, and the sharp decline of rock, her stately nose.

In the eyes of this man, the woman he loves possesses the same strong authenticity as found in nature. Her beauty is neither counterfeit nor superficial; it is unfeigned. Her sensuality is as genuine as the mysterious life forces that govern the world. The man expresses no desire to control her or to protect her. He wants only to enjoy her and the love that they share. He may call her by pet's names, but they are in no way belittling.

I Sought Him

The woman in the Song is self-possessed and self-determined. She is able freely to offer herself and she does this to the man whom she herself has chosen rather than to one chosen for her by the men in her family. She enjoys freedom of movement which allows her to go unattended into the unfriendly city, where she endures violence and humiliation (3:2-3; 5:6-7). She speaks assertively to the daughters of Jerusalem (2:7; 3:5; 8:4), unafraid of revealing the extent of her passion.

This woman is unwilling to conform to patriarchal strictures. She seems undeterred by the disapproval of her brothers (1:6; 8:8-9) or of the sentinels in the city (5:7), a disapproval that seems to have less to do with morality than with social convention. Motivated by genuine love, she moves beyond custom, which may guarantee security but which also imposes confinement, to a more independent plane, which offers self-reliance but which also requires personal responsibility. Her autonomy is not the emancipation of disobedience, but that of maturity. She clearly does not fit the stereotype usually associated with the ancient Near Eastern woman.

The Song depicts mutual desire for and respect of the other. There is no gender domination in this relationship. The woman is an active partner in this love, not merely the object of the man's desire and attention. The man is ravished by the woman (4:9), and she is faint with love for him (5:4-6). The initial assertiveness of the man is far from oppressive or self-serving. There is no doubt about his eagerness to appease his yearning for the object of his love. The speed of his advance toward her is evidence of this (2:8-9). Still, he is respectful of her and the control she exercises over her surroundings. He does not force his way in to her. Instead, he invites her out (2:10-14). This is not a one-sided affair where one person dominates the other and the interests of that dominant party are the only ones considered.

There is an ebb and flow in the mutually deferential assertiveness/responsiveness in their encounter. Neither partner is inordinately aggressive nor unduly withdrawn; neither is insensitive to nor minimized or frustrated by the other; neither is a pawn for the exclusive pleasure of the other. At one time, it is the amorous longing of the man that directs the movement; at another, it is the equally forceful desire of the woman. If anything, it seems that in this book the woman wields more influence. Chauvinistic stereotypes of the assertive man and the passive woman are shattered here.

Kissing, embracing and fondling are described in ways that underscore, even exaggerate, their amorous character. Still, there is nothing vulgar in this expression of passionate desire. Nothing suggests that this candid eroticism is unseemly. On the contrary, it appears to be quite natural. The sensuous poetry may be flamboyant, but it is clear that the behavior of the lovers is in fact restrained. Though both are prompted by desire, the man is respectful of the circumstances of the woman's situation, and she in turn is protective of him. There is nothing here that suggests anything shameful or illicit in the attachment of the couple, nor does the poet lead us to question the appropriateness of their infatuation.

Both lovers are depicted as uninhibited in their expressions of passion and in their longing for union. However, the lovers themselves and their desires are seen primarily through the eyes of the woman. The principal perspective is hers; she is the one who decides the course of action; it is primarily her sexual interest and her longing that are featured. Although the man is clearly preoccupied with her beauty, he does not have control of it. He admires it, but he does not possess it. The woman's own assertiveness is evident. She forthrightly orchestrates the duration of his stay when they finally do meet, and she determines the time of his departure (2:17).

This woman is not a victim of some sexual stereotype that claims that women do not experience erotic sensations, or if they do, they do not enjoy them. Nor is she inhibited by a moral code that assigns blame to those who either enjoy such passion or who go in search of it. She possesses a straightforward attitude toward sexuality. Her descriptions of the charms of her lover are both arrestingly poetic and discreetly provocative. She uses imagery that is sensuous but not obscene; her references are earthy but not vulgar; her adulation is explicit but not lewd. It is clear that for her, sexuality is an integral component of her world and of her love, not an artifice with which to manipulate or a weapon to be used against another.

When asked by the daughters of Jerusalem about the uniqueness of her beloved, the woman describes the matchless splendor of her beloved with a *wasf* of her own (5:10–16). She, too, uses a term of endearment, *dod.* Some form of the word is found thirty-three times in the Song and only in reference to the man. An Akkadian equivalent, which means 'beloved' or 'darling' and is also reserved for men, occasionally appears in that literature as part of a royal epithet.[20] This specific connotation might help to explain some of the other references and allusions to royalty that are found in the Song (1:4,12,17; 3:6–11; 7:1,5). The use of the word by the woman is a clear expression of her devotion and the exalted regard in which she holds her beloved.

The characterization itself is compelling. In language that is both graphic and hyperbolic, the woman praises the color, the sweetness, the beauty, and the strength of the man's body proceeding from his head to his legs. She first describes the properties of his head and face, properties that can easily be observed without risking being accused of indecorous scrutiny. She then directs her attention to his belly, legs and feet. In addition to the references to animals and vegetation used by the man in describing her, the woman also appeals to various natural features of gems and precious metals (see Dan 2:31-33). It seems that his imagination was captured by nature, while hers is inspired both by nature and by some familiar statues of the bodies of gods.[21] She uses the first kind of imagery to extol the beauty of his head and facial features, and the second kind to exemplify the splendor of the rest of his body.

His head is gold, like the statue that appeared in the dream of king Nebuchadnezzar (Dan 2:32). His thick, wavy hair, black as the raven must have been an astonishing sight against his golden skin. The same Hebrew word (*'ayin*) means both eyes and spring. The man's eyes possess the calm behavior of doves standing by springs of water (see Joel 3:18 [Heb]), resemble the smooth thickness of milk (see Job 29:6), and are firmly set. The woman next appeals to the intoxicating properties of the man's cheeks, not whiskers as some commentators argue[22], and his lips.

Moving further down his body, the woman applauds the man's jeweled fingers or arms and belly. Praise of the man's body ends with a characterization of his legs and feet as marble columns set on bases of gold. The strength of marble and the costliness of gold complete this picture of extraordinary worth. His head is gold, as are his feet. From head to toe, the man is priceless. There is no base element in this image, no clay feet (see Dan 2:33f). The man is the embodiment of elegance, stature and quality. The majesty of this man, tall and strong and beautiful and sweet smelling, is compared to the magnificent cedars of Lebanon. The *wasf* is complete.

The woman has a robust appreciation for the man's entire body and she celebrates it with unabashed candor. Hers is not some prurient fascination; it is genuine admiration of the form and substance of the man she loves. This poem sketches a reversal of the customary practice of men commenting on women's physical qualities. It belies the misconception held by many that women are not at all interested in the male physique, but are only concerned about how men will care for them and provide for their every need.

In the *wasf*, the man extols the charms of the woman which are revealed as she dances (7:2-6). Although there is neither an explicit identification of the nature of the dance performed nor mention of the motivation that impelled her to perform it, the dance itself was clearly provocative and it reveals the woman's own lack of sexual inhibitions. The character of its movement, or the costume worn during its rendition, or both, revealed parts of her body that were normally concealed from view. Nothing in the poem suggests that she was either embarrassed by her sexuality or intent on flaunting it. The dance appears to be as genuine and unaffected as is the love that the woman and man share.

The portrait sketched in this poem is of a woman who is self-possessed. When called upon to dance, she does not obey blindly but instead asks for reasons for such a performance (6:13b). When she does actually dance, she is in complete control. She appears to be unafraid of her own sensuality or of the sexual interest that it can generate. At the same time, she does not seem to be manipulating others with it. Her sexuality is a facet of her maturity and she does not exploit it.

Of Solomon

The Wisdom books contain instruction for righteous living that is in accord with the order believed to have been set by God at creation. Their teaching is timeless; their instruction cuts across cultural boundaries. Because of the universality of the concerns that they address, they relate situations and describe sentiments with which all people can easily identify. They teach indirectly through poetic imagery and suggestion. They recount how life works; they illustrate the consequences of specific human behavior. They do not command; they cajole. All of this is done to encourage a way of living that will provide happiness, well being, *shalom.*

The Wisdom teachers were humanists, concerned with human beings and attentive to human welfare, values and dignity. They taught that whatever benefited humankind was a good to be pursued and that whatever was harmful should be avoided and condemned. They did not advocate the pursuit of happiness for its own sake. Happiness or success was believed to be a byproduct of an upright life. Since the sages regarded well being and happiness as evidence that one's life and behavior were in accord with the order of creation, success was considered concrete evidence of the wisdom or righteousness of the person who succeeded. There were usually very definite lessons that the sages wanted to teach, lessons about cosmic, familial, or civic order. Their teachings frequently contained an oblique 'the moral of the story is...'

Although the wise women and men believed that there was a proper way of behaving, they did not insist on a rigid standard that would fit every circumstance They acknowledged that varying circumstances made each case unique. In fact, only those who were able to evaluate the situation and decide on the best course of action were considered wise. The truly sagacious person was the one who could draw on a store of wisdom gained from life experience, and who knew which course of action fit which situation.

The Song of Songs has much in common with books within the Wisdom tradition. Like them, it addresses a profound reality, a reality that is integral to every human life. Just as Proverbs offers direction for living a successful life, and Job struggles with the mystery of unexplained suffering, so the Song addresses the magnificence of the love between a woman and a man. Accorded Solomonic legitimation, the teaching of its passionate poems is considered wisdom instruction. For believers, it is even more. It is religious literature; it is Sacred Scripture; it is the word of God.

The woman in the Song of Songs may not have played any significant role in the history of Israel, as did the four Israelite heroines mentioned at the beginning of this study, but interpretation of her has greatly influenced believers down through the centuries to our own day. Placing the Song of Songs within the Wisdom tradition suggests that it contains lessons beneficial for right living, insights that will enhance human life. Like Susanna, she is a model of innocence; like Judith, she demonstrates courage; like Esther, she assumes leadership; like Ruth, she devotes herself to the welfare of others. Like all of these women, she does indeed break gender stereotypes, and so she is as subversive a figure as are they. Perhaps she is even more subversive, and that is why the acceptance of the book that contains her characterization required Solomonic legitimation.

The portrait that is sketched is remarkable in many ways. The explicitness of the sensuality that is drawn, the extravagance of the imagery that is chosen, the diversity of the metaphors that are employed all contribute to a characterization that is unique in its representation. The woman's femininity is undeniable, and so is her assertiveness. She is undaunted, risking misunderstanding and censure as she pursues her love. She is independent, making decisions for herself. She is responsible, being accountable for her actions. These are characteristics that traditionally have not been ascribed to women.

These virtuous characteristics add depth and color to the portrait of the woman that is sketched in the Song. It is her passion for the man and her desire to protect and nurture the love that they share that have called forth these admirable qualities. Unlike the other depictions of women found in Israel's wisdom literature, this woman does not serve the agendas of men. This uniqueness has led some commentators to wonder about the identity of the poets who shaped the original poems or the editor who brought them together. Might one or the other of them have been a woman, who wished to offer an image of women that was different from the conventional one? This question of authorship cannot be answered with certainty.

The depiction of this woman challenges the prejudiced stereotype out of which contemporary women and men are emerging. It applauds the dignity of women who, though very different from men, have been similarly graced with integrity and strength of character. It places before us, a model of commitment and self-possession that can inspire women and men alike. As we learn the lessons taught by this wisdom book, we may be better enabled to fashion a society wherein such a woman is no longer considered unconventional.

Endnotes

1 This study is part of an upcoming work to be published by New City Press.

2 André LaCocque, *The Feminine Unconventional: Four Subversive Figures in Israel's Tradition* (Minneapolis: Fortress, 1990), 7-20.

3 See J. Cheryl Exum, "Literary and Structural Analysis of the Song of Songs," *Zeitschrift für die alttestamentliche Wissenschaft* 85 (1973): 47-79; Robert Gordis, *The Song of Songs and Lamentations*, revised and augmented edition (New York: KTAV, 1974), 1, 9; Marvin H. Pope, *The Song of Songs,* The Anchor Bible (Garden City, NY: Doubleday, 1977), 19; Roland E. Murphy, *The Song of Songs,* Hermeneia. (Minneapolis: Fortress Press, 1990), 13.

4 Guillaume Pouget and Jean Guitton, *The Canticle of Canticles,* trans. Joseph L. Lilly (New York: Declan X. McMullen, 1934)

5 Andre Robert, Raymond Tournay and Andre Feuillet, *Le Cantique des Cantiques* (Paris: Etudes Bibliques, 1963).

6 Pope.

7 Murphy.

8 See Pope, 89-229; Murphy, 11-41.

9 See Pope, 93-96; on the writings of the great Rashi and his grandson Rashbam, see Pope, 102-3.

10 Luis Stadelmann, *Love and Politics: A New Commentary on the Song of Songs* (New York: Paulist, 1992).

11 See E. Ann Matter, *The Voice of My Beloved: The Song of Songs in Western Medieval Christianity* (Philadelphia: University of Pennsylvania, 1990).

12 Hans-Georg Gadamer, *Truth and Method* (New York: Seabury Press, 1975), 254-264.

13 Ibid., 341-374.

14 Paul Ricoeur, *Interpretation Theory: Discourse and the Surplus of Meaning,* (Forth Worth: Texas Christian University Press, 1976), 45-46.

15 Paul Ricoeur, *Freud and Philosophy: An Essay on Interpretation,* trans. Denis Savage (New Haven: Yale University Press, 1970).

16 Robert Alter, *The Art of Biblical Poetry* (New York: Basic Books, 1985), 189-194.

[17] See Richard N. Soulen, "The *wasf* of the Song of Songs and Hermeneutic," *Journal of Biblical Literature* 86:183-90; Michael V. Fox, 1985. *The Song of Songs and the Ancient Egyptian Love Songs* (Madison, WI: University of Wisconsin Press, 1985), 269-77; Marcia Falk, *The Song of Songs: A New Translation and Interpretation.* (San Francisco: HarperCollins), 127-35.

[18] Soulen, 220,222-4; critiqued by Fox, 275; Falk, 130.

[19] Murphy, 158.

[20] G. Johannes Botterweck and Helmer Ringgren, eds., *Theological Dictionary of the Old Testament* (Grand Rapids: Eerdmans, 1978), 3:148f.

[21] Othmar Keel, *The Song of Songs: A Continental Commentary*, trans. Frederick J. Gaiser (Minneapolis: Fortress, 1994), 202-4.

[22] Michael D. Goulder, *The Song of Fourteen Songs* (Sheffield: JSOT Press, 1986), 45; Murphy, 166, 172; Keel, 201.

Chapter 2

Culture and Religion in Hellenistic Judaism

John J. Collins

The Jews are unique among the various ethnic groups that lived in Egypt in the Hellenistic age, in having left us a substantial body of literature.[1] The survival of this literature is due in large part to the interest of Christians in their spiritual forebears, but its existence testifies not only to the size and prominence of the Jewish community in Egypt but also to the determination of that community to maintain a distinct identity. The Jews, as Balaam already recognized, were "a people that lives apart." The Jewish tendency towards separatism goes far to explain both the remarkable success of the Jewish community in preserving its identity, and the hostility which it eventually encountered. When Hecataeus of Abdera observes that Moses had prescribed for the Jews a way of life that was "somewhat anti-social and hostile to strangers" (*apanthropon tina kai misoxenon bion*)[2] he should not be suspected of anti-Judaism. He was simply reporting how Judaism appeared to a dispassionate observer. Not all the gentile authors who noted this phenomenon in the subsequent centuries were equally dispassionate.[3] But the Jews in Hellenistic Egypt were not defined only by their separatism. In fact, what most strikes one in perusing their literature is their enthusiasm for Hellenistic culture. Their separatism manifests itself primarily in their incessant attacks on idolatry and their criticisms of some gentile practices on moral grounds—broadly speaking, what we would distinguish as issues of religion. From a gentile point of view, these practices and the worship of the gods were integral parts of Hellenistic culture. The question of Apion, "why, if they are citizens, do they not worship the same gods as the Alexandrians?"[4] applies not only to the controversial matter of the right of Alexandrian Jews to citizenship, but goes to the heart of the problematic relationship of Hellenistic Jews to the culture that surrounded them.

Beginning in the nineteenth century, modern scholarship classified the literature of Egyptian Jewry as "apologetic" and propagandistic, on the assumption that it was intended to defend Judaism from attack and win converts from the gentile world. That view of the literature was overturned by a famous article by Victor Tcherikover in 1956, in which he argued that the literature was addressed to the Jewish community itself.[5] Subsequent scholarship has discredited the view that there was any sustained or systematic Jewish proselytism in the Hellenistic period, or the first century of Roman rule.[6] Nonetheless, much of this literature has an apologetic quality, insofar as it attempts to defend, justify and explain Judaism in the categories of Hellenistic culture. These explanations would not have interested many gentiles, but they were necessary for Jews who wanted to maintain their Jewish tradition and still feel that their claim to Hellenistic culture was not compromised. That culture was not optional for the Jews in Egypt. It was the air they breathed, and was just as much part of their identity as was their Judaism. But they were, so to speak, hyphenated Alexandrians, who drew their identity not from one culture but from two. In many areas of life, this duality was not problematic. Anyone could speak Greek, or try his or her hand at writing an epic or a tragedy, if they had the necessary education. While some Jews might balk at attending the theater or the gymnasium, it is clear that many did not.[7] In certain areas of cult and ethics, however, Judaism had distinctive requirements that were incompatible with the dominant customs of the Hellenistic world, and in these areas dissonance arose between the different components in Jewish identity. Much of the Greco-Jewish literature that has come down to us attempts to reduce that dissonance or resolve the conflict, even if the literature also served other purposes, such as entertainment.

Within the last few years, the question of Jewish identity in this corpus of literature has been brought to the forefront of scholarly discussion by two very substantial books, one by John Barclay, published in 1996 [8] and the other by Erich Gruen, in 1998. [9] These books, different in many ways, have in common a tendency to emphasize the particularist, non-assimilative, aspect of the Jewish literature. This, of course, is in accordance with the spirit of the times. Anthropologists, philosophers and students of religion have all grown wary of universal claims and tend to underline the particularity of all forms of cultural expression. The most striking aspect of Barclay's book is his distinction between literature that is "culturally convergent" and that which is "culturally antagonistic." He does not, of course, claim that either type exists in a pure form, but nonetheless the antithesis is, in my view, misleading, and misconceives the peculiar balancing act that is most characteristic of this literature. Gruen is more subtle, and emphasizes the self-confidence and ingenuity of Jews who found a wealth of new ways to express their identity. I do not dispute these features of the literature, but I want to focus more on the apologetic aspects and the selectivity exercised by the authors with respect to both cultural traditions. No two authors do this in quite the same way, but there is enough consistency in the literature to allow us to speak of a typical strategy.

The Letter of Aristeas

Let us begin with the Letter of Aristeas, as a representative example of the literature often dubbed apologetic in the Ptolemaic era. The Letter purports to tell how the Jewish scriptures were translated into Greek by order of Ptolemy II Philadelphus. The entire account is presented as the report of one gentile courtier to another. Aristeas was not the name of an especially famous person. It was sufficient that he was a Greek, and could supposedly report how Judaism and the Law of Moses were perceived at the Ptolemaic court. The twin poles of the narrative are the generosity of the king and the impressive character of everything associated with Judaism. We are given lengthy accounts of how the king liberated Jewish slaves, of the splendor of his gifts to the temple, and of his generosity to the Jewish translators. We are also given eulogistic descriptions of Judea and the temple. The appearance of the High Priest's garments "makes one awe-struck and dumbfounded. A man would think he had come out of this world into another one" (99). A lengthy banquet scene provides opportunities for the Jewish delegates to display their wisdom, and for the king to express his admiration. Gruen finds it humorous that they contrive to drag God into every response,[10] but I doubt that the ancient Jewish author or his intended readers would have seen the joke. Rather, the scene stamps the (rather banal) wisdom of the Jews with the seal of royal approval, and especially with the approval of the philosophers (131). The translation of the Torah is acclaimed by the priests and by representatives of the *politeuma*, and received joyfully by the king.

Perhaps the most striking affirmation of Judaism that is put on the lips of Greeks in this book is attributed to Aristeas, in the course of a petition for the release of the Jewish slaves: "These people worship God the overseer and creator of all, whom all men worship including ourselves, O King, except that we have a different name. Our name for him is Zeus and Dis" (16).[11] The significance of this statement has been disputed by Barclay and Gruen, because it is spoken by a pagan, not by a Jew.[12] Yet we find an almost identical sentiment expressed by the roughly contemporary Jewish author Aristobulus, who claims that the inherent meaning of the names Dis and Zeus in the Greek poets refers to God.[13] While the two authors need not have identical views, the parallel shows that a Jewish author could identify Zeus and the true God, and should make us wary of attempts to discount the statement in the Letter of Aristeas.

There is, however, a more disjunctive account of the relation between Jewish and Greek religion in a speech of the High Priest Eleazar, that, according to Gruen, "sets matters straight." The High Priest undertakes an explanation of the Jewish law that tackles directly those aspects that were alien, if not offensive, to Hellenistic consciousness, the food laws and the prohibition of idols. He begins "by demonstrating that God is one, that his power is shown in everything, every place being filled with his sovereignty" (132). He proceeds "to show that all the rest of mankind *except ourselves* believe that there are many gods, although they are themselves much more powerful than the gods they vainly worship; they make images of stone and wood, and declare that they are likenesses of those who have made some beneficial discovery for their living, and whom they worship even though their insensibility is readily obvious" (134–5). He goes on to say that "those who have invented these fabrications and myths are usually ranked to be the wisest of the Greeks. There is surely no need to mention the rest of the very foolish people, Egyptians and those like them, who have put their confidence in beasts and most of the serpents and monsters, worship them, and sacrifice to them both while alive and dead." This is why Moses surrounded the Jews with fences "to prevent our mixing with any of the other peoples in any matter, being thus kept pure in body and soul, preserved from false beliefs, and worshiping the only God omnipotent over all creation" (139). "So much for the Greeks," says Gruen. "These are strong words and powerful sentiments, not to be obscured or suppressed in the warm glow of some alleged universalism."[14] Yet this speech is reported by the supposedly Greek Aristeas without any suspicion of offence, and ultimately with admiration. Eleazar, the High Priest, is introduced as a model of *kalokagathia*, "a Greek gentleman" (3). The translators are distinguished in *paideia* (121). They "zealously cultivated the quality of the mean...and eschewing a crude and uncouth disposition they likewise avoided conceit and the assumption of superiority over others" (122). It would seem that Aristeas does not take the derogatory remarks about idolatry personally, and while this admiring Greek is a figment of a Jewish imagination, he represents the kind of Greek to whom Eleazar's speech is addressed. Nothing in the text suggests that this speech is either meant or taken to be offensive. It cannot then be the comprehensive broadside against the Greeks that Gruen takes it to be. Even the despised Egyptians are not comprehensively condemned. Eleazar appeals to the testimony of "the leading priests among the Egyptians," who are respected for their careful research and who refer to the Jews as "men of God" (140). Presumably, these priests are not included among the "very foolish people, Egyptians and those like them," who are dismissed so sweepingly a few lines earlier.

The whole rhetorical situation of the Letter implies that the kind of argument made by Eleazar could be, and in fact was, appreciated by enlightened Greeks such as Ptolemy Philadelphus, Aristeas and Philocrates. In the case of the Ptolemy, this, no doubt, was wishful thinking, but in fact there was a well-established tradition in Greek philosophy that was critical of mythology and of idolatry. Eleazar draws on the euhemeristic explanation of idolatry, that the gods are those who made some discovery beneficial to humanity. Critiques of idolatry can be found from the fifth century onward, and they proliferate in the writings of Stoic and Cynic philosophers. The example of Judaism is sometimes cited positively by pagan authors in this regard. Hecataeus noted Moses' prohibition of images without disapproval. Strabo says that Moses' arguments against idol-worship "persuaded not a few thoughtful men."[15] Varro says that worship of the gods would have been more pure if primitive Roman aniconism had continued, and also referred to the example of the Jews. Plutarch complained that people "give credence to workers in metal, stone, or wax, who make their images of gods in the likeness of human beings, and they have such images fashioned, and dress them up and worship them. But they hold in contempt philosophers and statesmen, who try to prove that the majesty of God is associated with goodness, magnanimity, kindliness and solicitude." While some of these examples are later than Pseudo-Aristeas, the essential lines of the argument had already been established by the early Stoics and Cynics. Plato had severely criticized the mythology of the poets. It remained true that polytheism was nearly universal, and that no other people besides the Jews repudiated it. Poets like Homer were counted to be among the wisest of the Greeks, despite philosophical critiques. But it was also quite possible to envision a Greek like Aristeas, for whom the Jewish critique of idolatry was quite reasonable and inoffensive, and who could accordingly be included in the "us" who were exempted in the general charge of polytheism.

Aristeas and the Ptolemy are part of the implied audience of Eleazar's exposition. The real audience of the text was surely Jewish. The message to this audience was that monotheism and rejection of idols was not un-Hellenic; rather it represented the very best of Hellenistic theology, and was acknowledged as such by eminent gentiles, including the king. Monotheism was not just a matter of revelation or ancestral faith. It was a philosophical tenet, perfectly rational and coherent. Essentially the same critique of idolatry would be repeated in the Wisdom of Solomon and Philo, argued on philosophical grounds.[16] We need not assume that the Jewish community was beset by grave temptations to idolatry. What was at issue was the coherence of the self-understanding of Hellenistic Jews. If some of their neighbors thought that the prohibition of images was odd or un-Hellenic, that was their problem. The best of the Greeks would appreciate the Jewish position on philosophical grounds. There is, then, a genuine universalism at work here. In the words of Moses Hadas: "The theology premised is applicable to all mankind, not to the Jews alone, and God's providence is universal. It is not suggested that God will show special consideration for the Jews simply by virtue of their being Jews, nor is there any hint of proselytization.... The Jews follow their own traditional usage to attain a religious end; the same end may be attained by others by a different path."[17] Not all paths followed by gentiles are approved, of course, and some, such as Egyptian theriolatry, are viewed with contempt, but Aristeas, like Aristobulus, also affirms that gentiles can arrive at the recognition of "the only God omnipotent over all creation," even if they call him Zeus or Dis.

The philosophical reinterpretation of Judaism is also in evidence in the explanation of the food laws in Eleazar's discourse, and here again there are obvious affinities with Aristobulus. Nothing in the law has been set down heedlessly or in the spirit of myth (*mythodos,* 168), and the interpretation is based on the *physike dianoia.* Moses, the lawgiver, is presented as a philosopher, proceeding from principles. The first principle is that God is one and his power is made manifest throughout creation. Hence the attack on idolatry and polytheism. He goes on to offer an allegorical explanation of the laws. Literalism is dismissed with contempt, no less than Egyptian theriolatry: "Do not take the contemptible view that Moses enacted this legislation because of an excessive preoccupation with mice and weasels or suchlike creatures. The fact is that everything has been solemnly set in order for...the sake of righteousness" (144). What the Jews really refuse to mingle with are "vain opinions." The significant distinction is between "men of God, a title applicable to none others but only to him who reveres the true God" and "men of food and drink and raiment" (140). So the particular, concrete commandments are reinterpreted allegorically to apply to universal human virtues. The birds forbidden by the dietary laws symbolize oppression and violence, animals that part the hoof symbolize discrimination, those that chew the cud symbolize memory, and so forth. The law, in short, is one symbolic expression of the truth which can also be approached in other ways. In the words of Aristobulus: "All philosophers agree that it is necessary to hold devout convictions about God, something which our school prescribes particularly well. And the whole structure of our law has been drawn up with concern for piety, justice, self-control, and other qualities that are truly good."

There are two other aspects of Pseudo-Aristeas's presentation of Judaism that I should like to note here. First, the political stance of the book. As Gruen has noted well, "the emphasis again and again is on Ptolemaic patronage, the king bestowing favors that elicit friendship and devotion."[18] This emphasis reflects a basic reality of Diaspora life, that is too often overlooked. Unqualified Jewish nationalism, or hope for outright independence, is extremely rare. Much more typical is the hope for a benevolent patron. This is as true in the tales of the eastern Diaspora, in Esther and Daniel, as in the Hellenistic west. It is reflected in tales of conflict, like 3 Maccabees. Even when the ruler is responsible for the conflict, the resolution invariably depends on his renewal of favor to the Jews. Down to the time of the revolts in the Roman era, the Jews aspired to be good and loyal subjects in the land of their residence and hoped for success through the patronage of their rulers, not through rebellion.

The second point is related to this. One of the most striking aspects of the Letter of Aristeas is the importance of gentile respect. The whole epistle is presented as a Greek appreciation of Judaism. This motif is perhaps most obvious in the table-talk towards the end of the book, when the Jewish sages perform at the royal command and are rewarded with the approval of king, courtiers and philosophers. It would be going too far to say that Judaism derives its self-esteem from the approval of the Greeks, but that approval is obviously wanted and appreciated. It seems to me, then, that the self-confidence of Pseudo-Aristeas must be qualified somewhat. There is a strong sense here that the Judaism is being discovered and evaluated, however positively, by the Greeks. In fact, there is little evidence that the Greeks paid much attention to the translated Torah, but nonetheless they constitute an implied audience against which the Jews felt the need to measure themselves.

The Third Sibyl

Gentile respect is also at issue in my second example of Hellenistic Jewish self-definition, Sibylline Oracles Book 3. The scattered examples of sibylline oracles that have survived from the pagan world are typically very short oracles, dealing with natural and military disasters.[19] (The Roman collection of sibylline oracles was exceptional in including ritual prescriptions for dealing with alarming phenomena such as the birth of an androgyne). A section of Sib Or 3, verses 401–88, which is usually thought to derive from a pagan sibyl (the Erythrean) gives a fair impression of the genre, and is probably included in the Jewish collection for the sake of authenticity. This is a string of predictions of doom for various places, not inherently connected with each other. In contrast to this section, there are several long, continuous oracles in book 3 that are clearly Jewish, in vss. 97–249 and again in 489–829. Despite the objections of Erich Gruen, I don't think there can be any serious doubt that these sections contain a core corpus of Jewish oracles that date to the second century B.C.E. by the fact that a turning point of history is still expected in the reign of "the seventh king of Egypt from the line of the Greeks."[20] The fact that numbers were not part of royal titles in antiquity creates only a small margin of variation (depending on whether or not Alexander is counted as the first king). Jews in the Hellenistic period were not so mathematically challenged that they could not count up to seven without the aid of numbered titles. Neither was the number seven so fraught with mystical associations as to be devoid of numerical significance.[21] One of the oracles that mentions the seventh king predicts that Roman expansion will be halted in his reign: "It [Rome] will cut up everything and fill everything with evils...in many places, but especially in Macedonia. It will stir up hatred. Every kind of deceit will be found among them until the seventh reign when a king of Egypt, who will be of the Greeks by race, will rule" (3:188–93). However surprising it may be to find criticism of Rome in a Jewish document of the second century BCE, the reference to Rome afflicting Macedonia points clearly to the middle of that century. The prediction of the fall of Rome here is mild in comparison with the thundering denunciations that we find in later Sibylline Oracles. Rome has only an incidental role in the core corpus of Jewish oracles in book 3.[22]

The reason why a Jewish author might choose to write in the name of the sibyl is clear enough: to put the praise of Judaism in the mouth of a pagan prophetess of hoary antiquity and respected authority. Even if gentiles viewed such compositions with skepticism, the apparent endorsement of the sibyl was reassuring to Jews and could bolster their pride. The genre lent itself to prophecies of destruction and a tone of denunciation. Consequently, Barclay sees these oracles as a prime example of "cultural antagonism," dominated by "scorn of non-Jews" and Jewish national aspirations.[23] But if the Jewish writers felt only scorn for Greeks and their culture, why would they write in epic hexameters in the name of a pagan prophetess? Sibylline oracles are often vehicles for social and political antagonism, especially in the Roman period, but it is difficult to believe that Jewish authors originally chose this genre to express only cultural antagonism. Besides, as Parke has observed, "the Jewish Sibyllist did not deal solely in gloom."[24] This third book, at least, has a well-developed positive message as well.

The sibyl appeals repeatedly to the Greeks to turn to the worship of the one God and support his temple. They can escape war and slavery by sending their holocausts to the temple of the great God (545-72). Again in vss. 624-34 people are asked to show their conversion by sacrificing bulls and lambs. Finally, the sibyl predicts that after great eschatological upheavals all cities and islands will turn to the great God, send offerings to the Temple, and ponder the Law of the Most High God (710-31). These appeals for conversion do not bespeak alienation or antagonism. Barclay objects that this conversion can only come about when the gentiles abandon idolatry and recognize the unique sanctity of the Jerusalem temple.[25] Indeed. That is how conversion is defined. Even Philo, whom Barclay rightly regards as a model of cultural convergence, says that in an ideal world "each nation would abandon its peculiar ways, and throwing overboard its ancestral customs, turn to honouring our laws alone."[26] The universalism implied is triumphalist and condescending, but it is as generous as believers in an exclusive, revealed religion can ever be.[27] It is far from the hostility to the gentile world that we find later in Sib Or 5. In the words of Erich Gruen: "Insofar as the Third Book contains negative aspersions upon Greeks, it includes them among wayward peoples whose failure to see the truth has led them into arrogance, impiety, and immorality, thus provoking divine vengeance. But Greeks alone are singled out for encouragement to enter the fold of the true believers."[28]

Over against the denunciations of gentile sin stand the eulogies of the Jews—"a race of most righteous men" who avoid all forms of divination and "the astrological predictions of the Chaldeans," and are characterized by "righteousness and virtue and not love of money," helping the poor and sharing with them, "fulfilling the word of the great God, the hymn of the law,[29] for the Heavenly One gave the earth in common to all" (218–47). The future ideal is the restoration of "a sacred race of pious men who attend to the counsels and intention of the Most High" and "fully honor the temple of the great God" with all kinds of sacrifices. These, "sharing in the righteousness of the law of the Most High," will be "exalted as prophets by the Immortal and bring great joy to all mortals. For to them alone did the great God give wise counsel and faith and excellent understanding in their hearts. Hence they honor God, their parents and holy wedlock and avoid homosexuality" (573–600). In the final utopian state, "the sons of the great God will all live peacefully around the temple." The nations will be moved with admiration and resolve: "Let us send to the temple, since He alone is sovereign and let us all ponder the law of the Most High God" and avoid idolatry (702–31).

In all of this the Jewish law has a clear and pivotal place. The sibyl refers explicitly to the law given to Moses on Mt. Sinai (255–58). True worship is specifically located at the temple of the great God, presumably at Jerusalem, and only the Jews, in contrast with "Phoenicians, Egyptians and Romans, spacious Greece and many nations of others," observe the law (597–98). Jews do, indeed, fail on occasion, and can be punished like anyone else, as is illustrated by the Babylonian exile. Yet it is not only to the Jews that the law applies. Other nations, too, can be condemned for failing to keep the law (599–600). The sibyl, like Romans 1 and Wisdom of Solomon 13, seems to presume that the essential law is known to everyone by nature. In fact the requirements of the sibyl could be seen to a great extent in terms of natural law. The basic sin is idolatry. Accordingly, the main requirement for the conversion of the Greeks is that they "revere the name of the one who has begotten all" (550) and bring their sacrifices to the temple of the one true God (545–72). Despite the implication of the superiority of Judaism, this demand is not alien to Greek sensibilities. The accusation of idolatry is based on a euhemeristic account of the origin of Greek religion, which was quite intelligible in a Greek context: "it is a thousand years and five hundred more since the overbearing kings of the Greeks reigned, who began the first evils for mortals setting up many idols of dead gods" (551–54). These condemnations of idolatry were standard fare in Hellenistic Judaism, developed not least by Philo.[30]

The sibyl echoes the common Jewish position on sexual abuses. Her warnings against the dangers of arrogance and greed are also commonplace. The assertion that God gave the earth in common to all (247, 261) rings of Stoicism.[31] The same sentiment is reflected in Pseudo-Phocylides (30): "Let all of life be in common." Phocylides takes a more distinctive position in her unequivocal condemnation of augury, divination, and "the astrological predictions of the Chaldeans" (220–28).[32] Divination had philosophical respectability in the Hellenistic age, since it was defended by most Stoics, but there were notable dissenters, and it was rejected by the Epicureans. Many Jewish writings from the period display a positive attitude on this subject, in sharp contrast to the sibyl.[33] Pseudo-Eupolemus, for example, credited Abraham with inventing astrology. Yet, even here, the sibyl's stand could probably be appreciated by some enlightened gentiles. Cicero could cite with approval the statement of Eudoxus, a pupil of Plato, that "no reliance whatever is to be placed in Chaldean astrologers," and he also listed false prophecies made to Pompey, Crassus, and Caesar.[34] Low-level astrology and Chaldaei were often assailed by Roman magistrates and satirists, and, in 139 B.C.E., the Chaldaei were expelled from Rome.[35] The sibyl was focusing attention on an issue of deep interest to the Hellenistic world, where debate was possible on the basis of one's understanding of nature.

So, while the sibyl remains devoted to the law of Moses, she treats it in practice as natural law. There is no reference to the more peculiar dietary laws of Leviticus, or to the laws which separated Jew from gentile. There is no indication that circumcision was required of converts.[36] At the end, God "will put in effect a common law for men throughout the whole earth" (757–58). It is evident that this law is not only concerned with Jewish traditions but with the fulfillment of human nature.

Yet, for all the universalism implied in the reduction of the law to ethical principles of broad human interest, the sibyl remains stubbornly particularistic. Unlike, for example, Pseudo-Aristeas, she does not say that those who worship Zeus are worshipping the same God; unlike Pseudo-Phocylides, she is unequivocal in her rejection of polytheism. Most significantly, she insists on the primacy of the Jerusalem temple.[37] The demand that Greeks send offerings to the temple goes beyond the admiration of the temple and the appreciation of Greek gifts that we have seen in the Letter of Aristeas. There is no attempt here to justify sacrifices by spiritual meanings. All this suggests that the oracles come from circles who had a more concrete attachment to the temple cult than was usual in Egyptian Judaism, although their presentation of Judaism was not exceptional in other respects.

Despite their vision of an eschatological kingdom in vss. 767–95, these oracles can scarcely be read as a manifesto for Jewish independence. Momigliano tries to find an endorsement of the Maccabean revolt in verses 194–5: "and then the people of the great God will again be strong, who will be guides in life for all mortals,"[38] but neither this verse nor anything else in the book requires a reference to the Maccabees. The only explicit historical reference in that passage is to the seventh king of Egypt, in whose reign the Jewish people will thrive. Scholars have strained to avoid the implication of Ptolemaic patronage on the grounds that the reference is only to the time, not the cause. But why should the turning point be repeatedly identified by reference to the seventh king, unless he had something to do with it?

The one passage where the active role of a human king is described explicitly is in vss. 652–6: "and then God will send a king from the sun (*apo helioio*) who will stop the entire earth from evil war." Here again scholars have strained to salvage the Jewish orthodoxy of the work by identifying the king as a Jewish messiah. But nowhere in the extensive corpus of Jewish messianic literature is the messiah said to come from the sun. The phrase is often translated "from the east" on the analogy of Isa 41:25, *apo heliou anatolon*. The two phrases are significantly different, and, in any case, the figure who is said to come from the sunrise in Isaiah is not a Jewish messiah but Cyrus of Persia. No Jewish messiah is ever said to come from the east. Kings from the east are destructive agents in the Testament of Moses and the Book of Revelation. In contrast, a king from the sun has obvious Egyptian connotations, rooted in Pharaonic ideology.[39] The closest parallel to the sibyl is provided by the Potter's Oracle, where the king from the sun is a native Egyptian ruler who would overthrow the Ptolemies. But the Ptolemies also appropriated Pharaonic imagery. In the Rosetta Stone, Ptolemy V Epiphanes is called "son of the sun, to whom the sun has given victory." Since the turning point is repeatedly located in the reign of the seventh king of Egypt and the king who brings it about is described in Egyptian imagery, the conclusion that they are one and the same seems to me inevitable. To suggest that the Egyptian imagery is here uniquely applied to a Jewish messiah, who is never remotely suggested elsewhere in the book, is completely gratuitous.[40]

I suggest then that the only "messiah" expected by the sibyl is the Ptolemaic king, just as Cyrus of Persia was hailed as messiah by the prophet we know as Second Isaiah. In neither case is there any acceptance of pagan religion. Rather both the prophet and the sibyl hoped, however unrealistically, that the gentiles would turn to the worship of the true God. What the sibyl wants is Ptolemaic patronage, just as

Pseudo-Aristeas had, except that the sibyl is more directly concerned with the political realm. At a time when Palestinian Jews were locked in combat with the Seleucids, it was natural for Jews, especially those in Egypt, to look to the Ptolemies to establish a world situation favorable to them. It was not the first time that Jews had looked to Egyptian kings for help. In this case, as in all previous cases, their hopes would be disappointed.

Concluding Reflections

The picture that emerges from our consideration of Pseudo-Aristeas and the sibyl is fairly consistent, despite the obvious differences in specifics. Both documents strive to show that Judaism is admired and praised by highly respected gentile authorities. Both insistently affirm the superiority of Judaism, but they do so in categories that Greeks could appreciate in principle. At the very least, they show their Jewish readers that there is nothing un-Hellenistic about Judaism. Rather Judaism represents the best in Hellenistic culture and, if the great majority of Greeks fail to appreciate this, it is because they fall short of their own ideals. None of this Jewish boasting implies a spirit of rebellion. Rather, the Jewish authors look to Ptolemaic patronage to realize their ideals. The self-confidence of this reconception of Judaism must be qualified by the persistent need for even fictional gentile approval.

It should be clear from the foregoing that it is grossly misleading to describe any of this literature as "culturally antagonistic." Antagonisms of various kinds can certainly be found in Jewish Hellenistic literature. Antagonism to idolatry is ubiquitous. Some accepted gentile behavior, such as homosexuality and infanticide, is repeatedly condemned. But these condemnations stop far short of rejecting Hellenistic culture altogether. It would not even be correct to say that they entail a blanket condemnation of pagan religion, although they undoubtedly criticize the religious practices of most gentiles. Nothing in the Jewish polemics would apply to the kind of philosophical religiosity expressed, for example, in Cleanthes' *Hymn to Zeus*. Philosophical views of religion might be shared by only a tiny minority of gentiles, but they represented the kind of Hellenistic religiosity that Jews could claim to share. The Jewish apologetic, in short, is based on a discrimination that identified with some aspects of Hellenistic culture and rejected others, especially in matters of religion.

In the Roman era, Jews in Egypt were increasingly involved in social and political conflicts. The most violent anti-gentile animosity in any Jewish literature is found in the fifth book of Sibylline Oracles, composed in the early second century C.E. Yet even here the polemic is expressed in Greek hexameters and makes free use of Hellenistic motifs. Around the same time a Jew in Syria or Asia Minor composed the rhetorical exercise that we know as 4 Maccabees, which glorifies the Jewish martyrs who died rather than eat pork or compromise the law in any respect. In 4 Maccabees, there is no equation of God and Zeus and no appeal to the patronage of a gentile king. Rather Antiochus is portrayed (with justification) as the deadly enemy of Judaism. Yet the composition is written in excellent Greek, shows a command of Greek rhetoric, and claims to be a *philosophotatos logos*, extolling virtues that even the Seleucid tyrant has to admire.

Hellenistic culture was not optional for Hellenistic Jews. It was the sea in which they swam. The currents carried some of them away from Jewish religious observance. The corpus of literature that is recognizably Jewish, however, is so precisely because it attempts to retain a distinct Jewish identity. The challenge was to formulate that identity in ways that were coherent with their cultural context. Whether in the end they succeeded is open to debate.[41] Jewish separatism, and refusal to assimilate with Alexandrian society as a whole, was certainly a major factor in the upheavals of the Roman era. But there were other factors too, including Roman policy and the character of the Alexandrian Greeks, which were beyond Jewish control. In any case, the literature of Hellenistic Judaism records a remarkable cultural experiment. It was a tragedy that this experiment could not run its course but ended in the flames of rebellion under the emperor Trajan.

Endnotes

[1] For a fuller discussion of the themes of this essay see my book *Between Athens and Jerusalem: Jewish Identity in the Hellenistic Diaspora*, revised edition (Grand Rapids: Eerdmans, 1999).

[2] Hecataeus, in Diodorus 40.3.4. M. Stern, *Greek and Latin Authors on Jews and Judaism* (Jerusalem: The Israel Academy of Sciences and Humanities, 1976), 1.26-35.

[3] P. Schäfer, *Judeophobia: Attitudes toward the Jews in the Ancient World* (Cambridge, MA: Harvard, 1997).

[4] Josephus, *Against Apion*, 2.65.

[5] V. Tcherikover, "Jewish Apologetic Literature Reconsidered," *Eos* 48 (1956) *Symbolae Raphaeli Taubenschlag Dedicatae*, 3.169-93.

[6] M. Goodman, *Mission and Conversion. Proselytizing in the Religious History of the Roman Empire* (Oxford: Clarendon, 1994); S. McKnight, *A Light among the Gentiles: Jewish Missionary Activity in the Second Temple Period* (Minneapolis: Fortress, 1991). A dissenting view may be found in L. H. Feldman, *Jew and Gentile in the Ancient World* (Princeton: Princeton University Press, 1993), 288-341.

[7] Feldman, *Jew and Gentile*, 59-63.

[8] J. M. G. Barclay, *Jews in the Mediterranean Diaspora* (Edinburgh: Clark, 1996).

[9] E. Gruen, *Heritage and Hellenism: The Reinvention of Jewish Tradition* (Berkeley: University of California Press, 1998).

[10] Ibid., 219.

[11] R. J. H. Shutt, "Letter of Aristeas," in J. H. Charlesworth, ed., *Old Testament Pseudepigrapha* (henceforth *OTP*) (2 vols.; New York: Doubleday, 1983, 1985) 2. 13, mistranslates: "Their name for him…"

[12] Barclay, *Jews in the Mediterranean Diaspora*, 143, claims that "the attribution of this statement to a Greek gives it less significance than if it were from a Jew." See Gruen, *Heritage*, 216.

[13] Aristobulus, Fragment 4; Eusebius *PE* 13.12.7; Holladay, *Fragments*, 3. 173.

[14] Gruen, *Heritage*, 216.

[15] Strabo, 16.2.36; Stern, 1.300.

[16] See J. J. Collins, *Jewish Wisdom in the Hellenistic Age* (Louisville: Westminster/John Knox, 1997), 209-13.

[17] M. Hadas, *Aristeas to Philocrates* (New York: Harper, 1951), 62.

[18] Gruen, 214.

[19] H. W. Parke, *Sibyls and Sibylline Prophecy in Classical Antiquity*, ed. B. McGing (London: Routledge, 1988), 10.

[20] Sib Or 3:192-3, 318, 608-10. J. J. Collins, *The Sibylline Oracles of Egyptian Judaism* (Missoula, MT: Scholars Press, 1974), 21-33; "The Sibylline Oracles," *OTP*, 1.354-61.

[21] Gruen, *Heritage*, 276-7.

[22] *Pace* Gruen, *Heritage*, 286-7.

[23] Barclay, *Jews in the Mediterranean Diaspora*, 216-28.

[24] Parke, *Sibyls*, 13.

[25] Barclay, *Jews in the Mediterranean Diaspora*, 222. He recognizes the vision of repentance only in "the final oracle."

[26] *De Vita Mos.* 2, 44. See A. Mendelson, *Philo's Jewish Identity* (Atlanta: Scholars Press, 1988), 128-32.

[27] Gruen, *Heritage and Hellenism*, 288, calls the gesture of the sibyl "noble and magnanimous." See also M. Simon, "Sur quelques aspects des Oracles Sibyllins juifs," in Hellholm, ed., *Apocalypticism*, 219-33: "Un souffle universaliste anime ces écrits" (p.232).

[28] Gruen, *Heritage*, 287.

[29] *ennomon hymnon*. The adjective is a play on *nomos* as harmony and as law.

[30] *De Decalogo* 52-81; *De Vita Contemplativa* 3-9; *De Spec Leg* 1.13-29; 2.255. See J. Tromp, "The Critique of Idolatry in the Context of Jewish Monotheism," in van der Horst, ed., *Aspects of Religious Contact and Conflict in the Ancient World* (Utrecht: Faculteit der Godgeleerdheid, 1995), 105-20.

[31] Nikiprowetzky, *La Troisième Sibylle*, 81. See Zeno in Plutarch, *De Alexandri Virtute* 1,6 (*SVF* 1,264).

[32] See P. van der Horst, "Jewish Self-Definition by Way of Contrast in Oracula Sibyllina III 218-247," in idem, ed. *Aspects of Religious Contact*, 147-66.

[33] J. H. Charlesworth, "Jewish Interest in Astrology during the Hellenistic and Roman Period," *ANRW* II.20.2 (1987), 926-50.

[34] Cicero, *De Divinatione*, 87-99.

[35] E. Bickermann, "The Altars of the Gentiles," *Studies in Jewish and Christian History* (AGJU 9; Leiden: Brill, 1980) 2:329; A. Baumstark, "Chaldaei," *PWRE* 3 (1899) 2059-60.

[36] J. J. Collins, "A Symbol of Otherness: Circumcision and Salvation in the First Century," in idem, *Seers, Sibyls and Sages* (Leiden: Brill, 1997), 212-14 (originally published in J. Neusner and E. S. Frerichs, ed. "*To See Ourselves as Others See Us": Christians, Jews, "Others" in Late Antiquity* (Chico: Scholars Press, 1985), 163-86.

[37] In this regard, it is noteworthy that Sib Or 3, unlike Pseudo-Phocylides does not attach a spiritual significance to ablutions. The precise meaning of 591-93 ("at dawn they lift up holy arms towards heaven, from their beds, always sanctifying the flesh [or "hands"] with water") is unclear. (See Nikiprowetzky, *La Troisième Sibylle*, 238-40). These practices are said to be typical of Jews but are not required of gentiles. In any case, neither prayer nor ablutions could be unfamiliar to a Hellenistic audience (See E. Pfister, "katharsis," *PWRE* Supp 6 [1935], 146-62).

[38] A. Momigliano, "La Portata Storica dei Vaticini sul Settimo Re nel Terzo Libro degli Oracoli Sibillini," in *Forma Futuri. Studi in Onore del Cardinale Michele Pellegrino* (Torino: Erasmo, 1975), 1081.

[39] Collins, *The Sibylline Oracles*, 41.

[40] Contra Gruen, *Heritage*, 278.

[41] On the coherence of Jewish theology as exemplified by the Wisdom of Solomon, see J. J. Collins, "Natural Theology and Biblical Tradition: The case of Hellenistic Judaism," *CBQ* 60 (1998), 1-15.

Chapter 3

The Life of Study

W. Dow Edgerton

The author of Ecclesiastes writes, "Of the making of books there is no end, and much study is weariness of the flesh" (12.12)." There is indeed a life of study which is weariness to the flesh. There is a life of study which is weariness to the mind, as well, and to the spirit. There is a life of study which is weariness to the community. When is study a weariness? When it is not for the sake of life, not for the sake of wisdom, not for the sake of faith, not for the sake of healing, not for the sake of transformation, not for the sake of community.

But there is another life of study, of a very different kind. It is a life of study which has everything to do with testimony and praise; everything to do with being seen, known, found and found out; everything to do with a journey of transformation; everything to do with humility; everything to do with prayer, hope, and freedom. It is of this life of study I write in these pages, because it is to such a life of study that André LaCocque opened new doors for me decades ago.

A memory: As a student many years ago, I heard André pronounce the phrase, "the *Book*" with such intensity and wonder that it was as if I was hearing it said for the first time. The shock was that he held in his hand nothing more than what I held in mine: a Bible, which was moments before a particularly excellent and important book, but for all that a book among books. Yet on that morning, in that room (it is not far from here, I pass it most days, and sit in it now as a teacher myself), it began to become strange to me.

Say it this way: the book began to become the Book. But even after so many years I struggle to explain what it means to say "the Book". It is the same difficulty as giving an account of what is meant by mystery, and the two have everything to do with each other. But to speak of the Book points to special aspects of mystery. It has to do, in part, with a sense of the center, the rock. It bespeaks fixity, a stability, something that stays, endures. Anchor, cornerstone, mountain, still point, north star, a place to stand. No matter that within it there may be storm, ruin, avalanche, vertigo, thick cloud, quicksand. Such dangers are held by the Book. They are contained, safe, permanent in their impermanence; they have a place, a house not made with hands. No matter that what is within the Book takes my balance away, decenters me, drives me out, away from any Eden called "here" into the land of wandering. Am I not "there", too? Are not all my days inscribed, even if I cannot read them?

What kind of study is appropriate to what can be called the Book? Perhaps our experiences have some points of contact. The Book is open upon the desk. The movements by which it has come to be there are automatic; stop and try to remember them and you may not be able to, you have been this way so many times before. Your body knows this book. The weight, the texture of the cover, the feel of the binding cupped in the curve of your hand, the feel of the paper beneath your finger. But also the smell of it, and the sounds of opening, closing, the lisp of the page turning. You have shaped yourself to this book. In order to read you have composed yourself, and hour upon hour your body has revolved around it. Leaning forward, pushing back, a rocking motion, a cradling in your lap, a peering, a shaking of your head, a cramp, the muscles around your eyes which tighten in a frown, the same muscles which stretch to smile, the chin resting upon the hand, the elbow resting upon the desk. Your body knows about the Book, this silent partner who promises nothing, asks nothing, and responds to nothing. And, of course, which promises, asks, and responds to everything. If you were to see yourself reading, what would you see? Something like a walk, perhaps, an embrace, a wrestle, a dance, the movements of a liturgy?

This is an intimate knowledge, and like every intimate knowledge it is marked by ceremony and ritual. And as with every authentic ceremony and ritual, the heart of it lies in what we enact beneath our awareness; not where we perform the rite, but where the rite performs us; not the meaning we bring to it, but the meaning which the rite gives to us who enact it.

It is an irony that the more we recognize and understand what we do and why, the deeper the heart of our actions withdraws. The more it withdraws the deeper one is drawn after. By understanding I come to the edge of my understanding of these things that I do, only to find that I must reach out from there now. Authentic ritual and ceremony begin past the last grasp of our reach, but only just past, maybe even close enough to be touched by the ends of our fingers, but not held. Authentic ritual and ceremony lie in what we do not yet recognize we are doing, because we are actually doing it, knowing it in our bodies, not explaining. The proper goal of a liturgy is to be transformed into the most immediate acts of a day, so that we know them no longer as liturgy, but as the way we live.

So it is with the ceremony and ritual of study. Learn to read, and everything you learn signals ever more clearly that reading really will begin the next time you open the Book, for which all the reading until now has prepared you. The Book also continually withdraws in the same way that our liturgies do. Drawing you forward toward the Book which is inscribed everywhere and which you read in the same way you breathe.

The mystery of the Book also has to do with the sense of fount, headwaters, the darkness from which we come. In the Book one can read, "In the beginning..." and therefore have a place to begin again. In the Book one can read, "And God said..." and therefore have something to hear. In the Book one can read "Let us make humankind in our own image, according to our likeness..." and therefore have something to say. To speak of the Book, then, testifies to a sense of "from", a claim that there is a past which reaches this far, a history. There is a Story, not just time. And even if we can only tell stories, just as the Book tells stories, those stories are themselves held and held together by the Book. In all their improbability (indeed, impossibility), partiality, incompleteness, distortion, untruth, mistakenness, evil, godlessness, they are nevertheless held. They are remembered and taken up (how else, but by grace?). Not erased, but granted to be the past for us, even for our sake. And am I not also one who is included in this "for-our-sakeness"? Not one who is forsaken, but exactly the opposite: for-our-sakened.

To speak of the Book also means to speak of a sense of "toward." In the Book we read of an Omega, a holy city, promise transformed into fulfilment—not just *a* promise, but promise itself fulfilled. The beginning is necessary if there is to be an end, but it is the end which draws the beginning forward. It is the end that defines the beginning as the "beginning of the good news," the beginning of what still lies ahead. The end is where the stories meet in all their improbability, incompleteness, and the rest, to be redeemed together with us—and how could it be redemption if the Book were not redeemed, too? How could it be the wiping away of all tears if it did not include the tears shed with, because of, and by the Book?

"The book is as old as water and fire," wrote Edmond Jabés. As old as water: the waters above and below are older than creation. They are not made, but gathered into place, divided. They are there, waiting to be filled with light, earth, life, humankind. The book old as water is the Book waiting to be written. The Book waits to become what it will be, and the spirit broods over the face of the Book.

As old as fire: take a match and put it to paper. How old is the fire burning inches from your hand? Moments ago it wasn't there, not this fire. Yet this fire *is* the same fire which has burned and will burn. Whether it flickers or roars, whether it burns as the lights in firmament above or curls around the corner of the paper it is both ancient and newly born.

If the Book is fixity (and this is not an historical claim, but an ontological one), and if Jabés' Reb Rafan is right, then it is the strange fixity of water and fire. The Book is the fixity of movement, wave surge and combustion, from beginning to end, constantly consuming and consumed, constantly flowing down, out, dispersing, rising, gathering, falling.

Another memory: As a senior seminarian I sat for an oral examination of what was called a position paper. In it we presented the core of our theological position and its warrants. I had written a paper which seemed to me theologically and biblically very strong. It was a bit too fastidious I recognized, and the language was often dense and intellectually self-conscious; it was also rather confident (reflecting the confidence of its author) of its systematic "grammar." After the examination had gone forward for almost an hour, André said, "What troubles me about your paper, Dow, is that it is merely correct. You have not suffered what is written here."

I was taken aback. What did this mean, "merely correct?" Correct was good, wasn't it? And rather a lot, not "merely". André explained: the paper was indeed theologically "correct" but the words written there showed no sign of why they might make all the difference, the difference between life and death. I had not *suffered* them, he suggested, in the older sense of the word; that is, I had not borne them and been changed by them. They were only well constructed theological grammar, merely "correct."

An experience of judgment can be an experience of grace, which may be how we discern whether or not it is God's judgment. I am happy to have been called to account on that day more than twenty years ago, and to have glimpsed the direction in which freedom and responsibility pointed a life of study with the Book. What follows, therefore, is a reflection upon Psalm 19, read as an invitation to such a life.

I.

The heavens are telling the glory of God;
  And the firmament proclaims God's handiwork.
Day to day pours forth speech,
  And night to night declares knowledge.
There is no speech, nor are there words;
  Their voice is not heard;
Yet their voice goes out through all the earth,
  And their words to the end of the world.

The life of study is a life attending to testimony and praise in the inexhaustible profusion of voices speaking in every moment. The Psalmist insists that the heavens themselves testify, the earth is flooded in praise (Psalm 104). Day calls to day, and night to night, now in a shout, now in a whisper, now in a clamor, now in a murmur, ceaselessly and everywhere God's glory is spoken. In the deepest stuff of the universe there is a song of affirmation, of praise, a *yes.*

Who has eyes and ears for it? To study means to turn and attend. To lift your eyes, to clear your head, to see, to hear what is speaking all around you. To see, to hear, to taste, to smell, to feel, to think: the life of study is as basic as this. (There are after all, those with eyes who do not see and so on.) What is most basic is usually what is most difficult. Hence the temptation to move on to more "important" matters. (Perhaps this is why Calvin insisted that the clearest statement of the gospel is not to be found in preaching, but at the Lord's table, because there the gospel is received not only by the ear, but by all of one's senses.)

"Outside the open window," writes poet Richard Wilbur, in a poem entitled "Love Calls Us to the Things of This World", "Outside the open window, the morning air is all awash with angels." What has he seen? A clothesline full of clothes billowing in a bright spring breeze. The clothesline is telling the glory of God! The laundry proclaims God's handiwork! But this is not disclosed to those who look and look away.

It is disclosed to those who look and see and ponder and wonder over what they see.

When my older child was learning to talk, he would awaken at night sometimes and want to be taken from his crib and walked. I'd pick him up, and immediately he'd lean (lurch!) and point toward the window that overlooked the yard and the street. I'd stand there holding him up above the sill, and he'd peer out wide-eyed to see what was there and call out the names for things, the wonderful *names*! Each name was worth a shout, it was so wonderful that there were things and names, and we could *say* them. Tree! Light! Street! Car! Grass! Rain! It was as if he was discovering in elemental wonder that there was a *world* and it had voices and names, and they could call and we could hear and answer! And we could hear marvelous sounds that are the true names of things, and maybe even be called by name ourselves! Wide-eyed at the window he'd call out to the wonder. This is the life of study attending to testimony and praise.

There is another kind of testimony and praise which can be heard, however, and it tells glory in a different way. Call it the testimony of longing and the praise of hope. The voice of testimony sometimes is the voice that longs for freedom, for peace, for love, for bread (for what is most basic, and, again, most difficult). The voice of praise is sometimes the voice of hope in the promise of God. Thus says the Lord: "For I am about to create new heavens and a new earth." (Isa. 65.17). In how many places does the cry rise up, Amen! Come Lord! Let your time come, your day, your way. Let it be among us according to your word! This cry is also being called night to night, day to day; this cry also floods the earth, and each of us can name a place where the cry just now is especially loud. Lima, Capetown, Kosovo, Taipei, Manila, Calcutta, Mexico City, Washington, Chicago, in schools, kitchens, shelters, farms, bedrooms. Wherever the cry for God goes up, there we must study. There we must study hard to learn the truth about the vast powers seen and unseen that work such unholy destruction upon mind, body, soul, community. A life of study means attending to this testimony of longing and hope for the bread of life which is bread indeed, and the life which is the only life we know.

II.

In the heavens God has set a tent for the sun,
Which comes out like a bridegroom from his wedding
canopy,
And like an athelete runs its course with joy.
Its rising is from the end of the heavens,
And its circuit to the end of them;
And nothing is hid from its heat.

The life of study is a life of being seen, sifted, known, found and found out. It is a life of being discovered, just as one standing in an open place is discovered by the sun moving across the face of the earth. "Lord, you have searched me and known me" (Ps. 139). To study means to come to know oneself. But this is *not* the knowledge which comes, first of all, from introspection, from looking in the mirror. A mirror is only as trustworthy as the one who looks into it. I have looked too many times and seen only what I want to see to have much confidence in mirrors—at least in one held by my own hand. The life of study means coming to know oneself—not from the inside out—but from the outside in. Not simply in the partial truth and vanity of my own imagination, but in the encounter with difference.

We need to encounter a word that comes from outside of us, from beyond us. Sometimes it is the word of the Book, sometimes the word of the neighbor, sometimes the word of the stranger, sometimes the word of the enemy. We need the word of people whose lives are different from our own. We need the word of the forbears who have lived, thought and written. We need the word of disagreement. The poet Adrienne Rich writes, "How can I know what you know unless you tell me? There are gashes in our understandings of this world." Such an image—gashes in our understanding! Of the world, yes, but also of ourselves.

It is a terrible thing to be abandoned to yourself. It is a terrible thing to be left alone without a word from outside. It's like being locked in a hall of mirrors, with only your own endlessly repeating reflection.

Years ago, during the Vietnam time, I was a conscientious objector working at a state mental hospital in Iowa. It was a violent place—physically, emotionally, spiritually. Some of the violence was necessary, I suppose, or at least inevitable, things and people being the way they are. But when violence and violation are daily bread, you become dulled by it. One day a new social worker came to work on our ward. He had transferred over from the state penitentiary some thirty miles away, and knew something of violence. After a few weeks on the ward he asked me over for supper. As we sat at the table he said—very gently, and very clearly—"Are you aware that you have become a violent man?" And he proceeded, very gently and very clearly, to tell me what violence he saw in me and the people around me, in what we were doing, and in how we were doing it. There was no accusation, no condemnation, just the simple statement of what he saw, so it was clear that *he* was not confronting me, the confrontation was with my own life which he put in front of me. Part of my soul was saved that night. I know in my own flesh that this salvation, which we work out in fear and trembling, includes being found and found out in just such a way.

If study includes being seen, then it means coming out of hiding. Presenting oneself to be examined. It is not tests we're talking about here, it is examination by which others judge what we know on the basis of who we are, and how we live. It is the examination beyond what we know by head, into what we know by heart; beyond what we have memorized, into what we remember in our own members, what we gather together in our bodies.

A life of study, therefore, is not fundamentally solitary, but face to face, life to life, public, seen, known, found and found out.

III.

The law of the Lord is perfect, reviving the soul;
The decrees of God are sure, making wise the simple;
The precepts of God are right, rejoicing the heart;
The commandment of God is clear, enlightening the eyes;
The reverence of God is pure, enduring forever;
The ordinances of God are true and righteous altogether.
More to be desired are they than gold, even much fine gold.
Sweeter also than honey, and drippings of the honeycomb.

The life of study is a journey of transformation. It is a journey of revival, wisdom, rejoicing, enlightenment, a journey toward what lasts, toward what is trustworthy and true. Transformation is what the life of study is all about. What matters most is new creation, and the language of the faith is forever straining at boundaries, breaking words apart and putting them back together, flashing from horizon to horizon to express some *part* of it all. Creation itself groans in anticipation of transformation, and the emblems of astonishment, the emblems of wonder around which our lives in Christ are shaped—cross, table, book, bread, wine, font—are all pointing to this transformation journey. Call us stewards of the mystery of God, as Paul does. The life of study is lived in stewardship of mystery, returning again and again to those mysteries which refuse to be contained in mere explanation. It is lived in stewardship of that mystery, which is both the road and the goal. How shall we exhaust the meaning of such words as resurrection, reconciliation, renewal? When will we have heard all there is to hear in such words as faith, hope, and love? What accounting is adequate to words such as eternal life, freedom, forgiveness of sin? Who can explain the bread and cup and water? To these we must turn again and again and again, to meet again what they offer again in the most ordinary moments of a day. That is, we must *study* them. Even knowing that they will always elude our grasp the life of study reaches forward toward these mysteries again and again—because that is the road of transformation.

Rainer Maria Rilke writes,

> My eyes already touch the sunny hill,
> going far ahead of the road I have begun.
> So we are grasped by what we cannot grasp; it has its inner
>   light, even from a distance-
> and changes us, even if we do not reach it,
> into something else, which, hardly sensing it, we already are;
> a gesture waves us on, answering our own wave...
> but what we feel is the wind in our faces.[1]

IV.

> *Moreover by them is your servant warned;*
> *In keeping them there is great reward.*
> *But who can detect their errors?*
> *Clear me from hidden faults.*
> *Keep back your servant also from the insolent;*
> *Do not let them have dominion over me.*
> *Then I shall be blameless,*
> *And innocent of great transgression.*

The life of study is a life of humility. It is a life lived in the sure knowledge that we do not have sure knowledge within ourselves. We have puzzling reflections, glimpses, guesses, questions, faith, not sight. It is a prayer to be saved from one's own vanity, one's own cruel certainty. A prayer for the gift of understanding. And it is a prayer also to be freed from the domination of the insolent, of the proud; that is—to be saved from those who are full of themselves, sure of themselves, those who are folded in upon themselves. Truth is not finally being right or wrong in a given opinion. It has to do, rather, with a walk, a heart, an attentiveness, a humility. Great transgression is not making a mistake. It is, rather, being closed in upon and within oneself.

Once the great rabbinic houses of Hillel and Shammai were locked in argument over the interpretation of a point of conduct, halachah. Neither could convince the other, and neither would yield, so at last they they called to God to decide between them. A great voice came from heaven saying, "the ruling is according to Hillel!" At this the house of Hillel rejoiced, of course, but the voice continued, "The ruling is according to Hillel, but *both* opinions are the word of the living God!"

Both are the words of the living God? How can that be? Because the word of the living God cannot be held as a possession by this person or that. It is met where we meet. It takes shape between us. Great transgression is not making a mistake; great transgression is turning away from the word of the living God, which can only take shape between us, the word which pierces beyond what is correct to discover the heart. "All deeds are right in the sight of the doer," says Proverbs, "but the Lord weighs the heart" (21.2).

Augustine once put forward this radical claim: If you have interpreted the scripture in such a way that it builds up the love of God and the love of the neighbor then you have interpreted it correctly—even if it can be shown that in that particular place that is not what the passage means! How can he say this? Because, he insists, this is what the word of God *is*. The word of love that builds love. This is the meaning which is in, under, around, and through, the *words*. It is from love they come, and toward love they go.

Study is patient and kind. Study is not envious or boastful or arrogant or rude. It does not insist on its own way; it is not irritable or resentful. It does not rejoice in wrongdoing, but rejoices in the truth, bearing, believing, hoping, enduring.

So the life of study is indeed, a life of humility.

V.

Let the words of my mouth and the meditation of my heart,
  Be acceptable to you,
  O God, my rock, and my redeemer.

Finally, the life of study is a life of prayer upon the rock, the foundation, and prayer toward the horizon, the freedom.

I remember a student named Tom who once described an experience he had. He was studying in his dorm room, up late reading theology at his desk. Only the desk lamp was on in the room, so the desk, the book, and his hands rested in a circle of light, while everything else was in shadow. As he read he heard an indistinct music coming through the wall from the next room where a young man named Mazi Africa lived. Mazi was also up late, sitting at his desk, apparently; as Tom listened he realized that the music was Mazi singing hymns alone on the other side of the wall. Tom struggled to find words to describe the mixture of thoughts and feelings which came over him as he sat there. It was as if Mazi's voice supplied something that was missing there in Tom's small circle of light.

It was not so much a feeling of guilt that he should have been singing or praying instead of studying. It was more like this: he realized that he had not yet learned to make his study into prayer. He had not yet learned how to make study a sacrifice, a living sacrifice, a fragrant offering, a drink offering, a grain offering, an offering of incense. He had not yet learned how to make reading into prayer, how to make thinking into prayer, how to make writing into prayer. He had not yet learned how study could be praise, and how study could be thanksgiving, how study could be confession of sin, petition, intercession for the neighbor and stranger. Through the wall Mazi sang to God. "To whom," Tom wondered "do I sing what I am doing here at this desk?" It was a gift, that voice through the wall, and the question that it put. Karl Barth, in his odd and particularly German way of saying things, wrote "Human thought and speech cannot be *about* God, but must be directed *toward* God...True and proper language concerning God will always be a response to God, which overtly or covertly, explicitly or implicitly, thinks and speaks of God exclusively in the second person [as *you*]. And this means that theological work must really and truly take place in the form of a liturgical act, as invocation of God, and as prayer."[2]

The life of study is a life of prayer, which means it is a life in search of the rock, in which you discover again and again that the rock is already beneath your feet—and like Jacob dreaming you awake to discover that you were already on holy ground. Study is because of the rock and for the sake of the rock, and such a life begins over and over again at the beginning, the foundation.

But if study is prayer upon the rock, then it is also prayer turned toward the horizon. The most urgent prayer of the faith is "Come!" God of the poor, Come! God of justice and peace, Come! God of forgiveness and mercy, Come! God of freedom, God of joy, Come! God of the cross and the tomb and the empty tomb, Come! God of the Beginning and the End, Come! God of all that is past, passing, and to come, Come! God of the holy mountain, God of the holy city, God of the redeemed gathered in peace to feast, past mourning, tears, and the tyranny of death, Come! Come!

To join this most urgent prayer, to turn toward the horizon and lift your eyes and look, this too is the life of study. William Butler Yeats wrote,

> I balanced all, brought all to mind.
> The years to come seemed waste of breath,
> A waste of breath the years behind,
> In balance with this life, this death.[3]

Endnotes

[1] *Selected Poems of Rainer Maria Rilke,* Robert Bly, trans. (New York: Harper & Row, 1981), 177.

[2] Karl Barth, *Evangelical Theology: An Introduction* (Edinburgh: Clark, 1963), 164.

[3] William Butler Yeats. "An Irish Airman Forsees His Death," *Selected Poems and Two Plays of William Butler Yeats.* M.L. Rosenthal, ed. (New York: Collier Books, 1966), 55.

Chapter 4

My Dinner with André

Robert M. Grossman

Many of the essays about André LaCocque in this tribute will deal with his accomplishments as a distinguished scholar and teacher, as they should. My words about him, though, will center more on how I—as one who is rooted in a tribe to whom he has devoted his life—sees him, responds to him.

Jews tend to be apprehensive about Christians, even in America. Our experience as a people makes this apprehension understandable. Some worrisome gesture, some expression, some reference, some vulgarity, whether willful or unintended, is not unexpected. At the same time, no matter how far apart one Jew is from another—in personality, in background, in position—no matter how unlike they may act or appear, when one meets another, whether for the first time or the hundredth, an unspoken bond from their past pervades their coming together in whatever setting. Once having met, they may never wish to see each other again, but initially there is an open door between them which for others must be unlocked with a key. Though hidden bonds and understood nuances exist among all peoples of common heritage and background, the bond among Jews has been there ever since 70 C. E., and for more than a thousand years before then, and like others who have suffered through the centuries, the link that binds one to the other is forged of the iron that emerges from the furnace of persecution.

While the comfort of Jews with Christians is slowly growing, there is still a long road ahead. Most Jews of my generation remember being taught how their brethren in Germany perceived themselves prior to 1933 and in the early years thereafter. They were Germans first whose religion was Jewish; they were accepted; they thought they belonged to the land. They learned.

The sense of belonging of Jews in America mirrors theirs, though it instead arises from this country's deep and abiding ideal, not often enough achieved, "to do unto others as you would have them do unto you," while still being tempered by the memory of the Holocaust and the hidden fear of its revival. Though this fear is always there, it affects the lives of American Jews in varying degrees, often depending on that element of the Jewish community to which one is attached, by birth or choice. To protect themselves and their ways, the ultra-Orthodox have very little contact with the outside world and dismiss the legitimacy of Conservative and Reform Jews. The modern Orthodox and Conservatives, who are largely involved in the broad urban life of America, look upon the Reform much as the Catholics look upon the Protestants. But whatever aspect their Judaism reflects, most would question why a Jew such as myself, who does not carry a rabbinic shield, would pass behind what they perceive to be the iron curtain of a Christian seminary.

The answer is André. I have made many dear friends at Chicago Theological Seminary during my years as a trustee, but "my dinner with André" is the essence of it. He knows more about my tribe than I do, and while he doesn't keep kosher (nor do I), he and I have spent countless hours in the last decade sharing meals together as I learned from him about my past and present and as we searched for ways to build on his creation of The Center for Jewish-Christian Studies.

As with so many enduring aspects of one's life, André's arose out of a searing experience in his youth. He was born and grew up in Belgium, and during the Second World War his family sheltered Jews who were being hunted and ravaged by the Nazis. His exposure to this had a lasting impact on his future. He and Claire, as newlyweds, went to Israel in 1950, two years after it became a country of its own, and he was one of the first non-Jews to study at Hebrew University in Jerusalem. After returning to Europe and completing his graduate studies in France, he was invited to Chicago Theological Seminary in 1966.

André's presence assured me that I was among good people of open minds and truthful intentions. His statements about the roots of Christianity, so often ignored in the larger Christian community, were unequivocal.

> [Our] vocation is to lead in the direction of rerooting Christian thinking into its Jewish seedbed. Christian studies are also by definition Jewish studies, for Christianity is a branch of Judaism and its Messiah is the 'Central Jew' saluted as such by the best of modern Jewish thinkers.

André's determination to look back with openness and reach out to others fortified me in one of the first encounters I experienced as a trustee. I was attending a board meeting in the early 90's at which various changes in the Seminary's mission statement were being discussed. These changes had been approved by the Academic Affairs Committee and were presented to the full board for the first time. In reading through the entire statement I came upon a provision which apparently had been altered some but still essentially stated that unless you were a Christian you could not teach at the Seminary. I waited for one of my fellow trustees to question that language but no one spoke up. Since rabbis had served as adjunct professors, the restriction certainly seemed inconsistent with what André had introduced through The Center for Jewish-Christian Studies, which was an integral part of the Seminary. As the only Jewish trustee present, I hesitated to be the one to raise the issue, but there were no other voices. Finally, I said, "If it were determined to teach a course on the Koran, would a Muslim professor be precluded from consideration?" That broke the ice and the restriction was eliminated.

What this incident demonstrated to me was that fine people of good will coming largely from the same background can casually pass over accepted language which others might find distressing. Faculty members had raised the issue internally but not in the presence of the board. It reinforced the significance of having people of different perspectives sitting together at the same table; what one good person is blind to, another sees quite clearly. In more than 30 years of teaching a multitude of students, many of whom sought to study in whatever courses he taught during their time at the Seminary, André brought to them that other perspective that helped them see more clearly.

I have known André in many roles, as friend, mentor and colleague, and each role has further cemented the bond between us. One evening while we were having dinner at his home, he suggested that we teach a course together. His idea was to combine a study of biblical law and the U. S. Constitution. He would teach the first and I, the second, and we would spar with each other over our perceptions. I was excited at the prospect of learning and teaching with André, and after talking through the elements of the course we decided to call it "Moses, Jesus and Madison." The assumption in western civilization has always been that American law is derived from the English common law. While there is much truth to this, the ethical roots and many of the basic concepts of that law derive from the bibilical, scriptural and rabbinic heritage. As the course developed, André cited and expanded on the source of such accepted notions as majority rule, political asylum and refuge, the rights of the accused and the place of judges in society. My job was to show how these and other biblical teachings worked their way into Supreme Court cases on such issues as freedom of religion, due process of law, the death penalty and racial discrimination, and to expose the students to the general development of American law through judicial decisions.

In conceiving the course, one of André's aims was to teach seminarians the role of law in relation to the other courses they were taking at the Seminary and to prepare them for the larger and harsher world they would soon be entering and influencing. Since our Constitution contains no references to the Bible and the First Amendment keeps religion out of the hands of government, the impression exists that religion played little or no part in the life of the American colonies or the formation of the United States. In fact, though, it is because religion was such a dominant factor in the lives of the early Americans that the writers of the Constitution, and particularly James Madison, determined not to permit the new federal government to impose any religious preferences or involvement as it governed. Even though André is now emeritus, this is the one course he expects to continue teaching at the Seminary, and for me this is a special honor.

Formal retirement can bring with it the fear of no longer being needed, a concern of all those who reach that stage of life, no matter how distinguished their careers may have been. André need never have had any such fear. As I write this, he and Claire are somewhere in Asia where he has been invited to lecture in Korea, Japan and China. Indeed, he had hardly been able to break himself free to accept these invitations because of his efforts to complete books on which he is working on and to embark on new ones that his publishers want him to write. And on his return he will find requests for lectures throughout this country and in other parts of the world.

In the face of these continuing demands on his talent and wisdom, my hope is that I will often be able to have "my dinner with André," for there is still much to talk about. His legacy as founder of The Center for Jewish-Christian Studies, the first of its kind at a free-standing theological seminary in America, must be enhanced through the creation of a Chair in Jewish Studies as a reflection of his pioneering achievements. And, because of those achievements, it will happen.

Chapter 5

The Question of Idolatry: A Formal or Material Principle?

Theodore W. Jennings, Jr.

Modern theology has made use of a critical distinction between the finite and the infinite, the conditioned and the unconditioned or absolute, in order to provide a critique of religious-political systems as idolatrous. This principle has been derived from biblical critiques of idolatry. In this paper I want to suggest that the critique of idolatry as typically formulated in this modern theology has concentrated on a merely formal principle of critique of such systems but that the Bible in fact may offer a more compelling and useful material criticism of idolatry that has important implications for our evaluation of political as well as theological systems.

I will first review the way in which the critique of idolatry has functioned in modern theology and the texts upon which it has apparently been based. I will then propose, on the basis of Psalm 82, what I will call a material critique of idolatry and show how this critique relates to a range of Old Testament concerns. Finally, I will suggest some of the ways the adoption of such a material principle would affect our ways of understanding political and theological systems.

Biblical Foundations

The texts that have most often served to fund a theological critique of idolatry come from the prophets. One of the earliest texts of importance in this regard is from Jeremiah.

> Thus says the Lord: Do not learn the way of the nations, or be dismayed at the signs of the heavens; for the nations are dismayed at them.
>
> For the customs of the peoples are false: a tree from the forest is cut down, and worked with an ax by the hands of an artisan; people deck it with silver and gold; they fasten it with hammer and nails so that it cannot move.
>
> Their idols are like scarecrows in a cucumber field, and they cannot speak; they have to be carried for they cannot walk. Do not be afraid of them for they can neither do evil nor is it in them to do good.
>
> There is none like you, O Lord; you are great, and your name is great in might.
>
> Who would not fear you, O King of the nations? For that is your due; among all the wise ones of the nations and in all their kingdoms there is no one like you.
>
> They are both stupid and foolish; the instruction given by idols is no better than wood!
>
> Beaten silver is brought from Tarshish, and gold from Uphaz. They are the work of the artisan and of the hands of the goldsmith; their clothing is blue and purple; they are the product of skilled workers. But the Lord is the true God and the everlasting King. At his wrath the earth quakes, and the nations cannot endure his indignation (10:2-10).

The essential contrast here seems to be between that which is confined to one place and constructed of human hands as opposed to the one who judges nations and the whole earth. The prophet Isaiah, in the time of exile, wrote:

> All who make idols are nothing, and the things they delight in do not profit; their witnesses neither see nor know. And so they will be put to shame. Who would fashion a god or cast an image that can do no good? Look all its devotees shall be put to shame; the artisans too are merely human.

The ironsmith fashions it and works it over the coals, shaping it with hammers, and forging it with his strong arm; he becomes hungry and his strength fails, he drinks no water and is faint. The carpenter stretches a line, marks it with a stylus, fashions it with planes, and marks it with a compass; he makes it in human form, with human beauty, to be set up in a shrine,

He cuts down cedars or chooses a holy tree or an oak and lets it grow among the trees of the forest. He plants a cedar and the rain nourishes it. Then it can be used as fuel.

Part of it he takes and warms himself; he kindles a fire and bakes bread. Then he makes a god and worships it, makes a carved image and bows down before it. Half of it he burns in the fire; over this half he roasts meat, eats it and is satisfied. He also warms himself and says " Ah I am warm, I can feel the fire!" The rest of it he makes into a god, his idol, bows down to it and worships it; he prays and says, "Save me, for you are my god." (44:9-17)

The prophet here castigates those who engage in the fashioning of idols for being stupid and deluded. It is similar to the point Paul will make in Romans 1:18ff where he supposes that turning from God to the creature produces a kind of social and cultural insanity.

The Psalmist too holds up idolatry to ridicule. After recalling the acts of God in delivering the people from bondage in Egypt, the Psalmist continues:

The idols of the nations are silver and gold, the work of human hands. They have mouths, but they do not speak; they have eyes, but they do not see; they have ears but they do not hear, and there is no breath in their mouths. Those who make them and all who trust in them shall become like them. (Psalm 135:15-18)

But here the critical contrast is with the God who "will vindicate his people, and have compassion on his servants" (v. 14). Here is a hope grounded in the mighty acts of deliverance in the past (vv. 8-12; see also Psalm 115 vv. 3-8). The God of Israel, of the prophets, of the Psalmist, of Paul is no idol made of wood or metal who cannot hear our cry but a living God who saves.

The Formal Principle

One of the most common proposals of mid-twentieth century theology is the appropriation of a prophetic denunciation of idolatry for purposes of a systematic critical principle over-against all attempts to absolutize particular movements, values and so on. The emergence of this principle to become a commonplace of theological reflection must be seen against the background of the emergence in Europe of powerful social movements which claimed the absolute loyalty of their adherents.

Until this period of political crisis, the biblical critique of idolatry had most commonly been appropriated to critique religious practices other than Christianity. Thus the critique of idolatry had been synonymous with a critique of superstition, pagan religious rites or the manufacture of religious objects, especially by other religions or by other religious traditions within Christianity.

In the early centuries of Christianity the critique of religious practices of other traditions became a commonplace of Christian apologetic rhetoric. The way to this critique had already been supplied by the work of Hellenistic Judaism in making an alliance between the prophetic voices to which we have just attended and elements of popular Greco-Roman philosophy that were critical of the religious "superstitions" of the empire. Thus Philo could detect a common cause between prestigious forms of philosophical skepticism and the prophetic denunciation of religious practices. This could be understood as enhancing the prestige of the "scriptures" and so of the traditions of Judaism. To this Christian apologists added a critique of certain practices of Judaism itself thereby laying claim to the mantle of the philosophical and prophetic traditions. As Christianity developed its own distinctive religious practices this critical principle was directed not against religious rites as such but against those who worshipped "other gods". This became the common sense of the matter so that all other religions could be understood as idolatrous whatever their practices, including even an iconoclastic Islam.

In the early modern period—as Christianity came into contact with the religious traditions and practices of other peoples in Asia, Africa and the Americas—the prophetic critique of the idolatry of the mighty empires in Israel's immediate world was transformed into a critique of the religious practices of relatively powerless peoples thus undergirding the practices of colonial domination and, in some cases, enslavement or extermination. One of the great ironies with which the history of Christianity is replete is that the prophetic rhetoric deployed in the sixth century to enable Israel to resist the ideological prestige of the imperial powers comes to be used as a license for the worst excesses of the imperial policies of an aggressive Christendom.

At the same time the critique of idolatry could be used to incite inter-religious suspicion and hostility within Christendom itself. This had already happened in the "icon wars" of eighth and ninth century Byzantine Christianity, but it also became a weapon in the struggles between Protestants and Catholics over the cult of the saints or of the virgin and within protestantism itself over the relative presence or absence of "images". This has gone to such an extreme that many Protestant churches in Latin America refuse even to have crosses in their sanctuaries.

Until the twentieth century, then, the primary use of the critique of idolatry was in exacerbating inter- and intra-religious conflict.

But the emergence of deadly nationalism in the first world war and the emergence of even more powerful movements of national reconstruction following the devastation of that war led a number of theologians to appropriate the principle of a critique of idolatry not as a weapon against any and all other religious traditions and practices but as a critique of social political movements whether or not they were tinged with religious or even with Christian elements.

Thus Reinhold Niebuhr, writing in the *Nature and Destiny of Man* identified the "sin of idolatry" as "the error of defining God in finite and contingent terms."[1] His brother, H. Richard

Niebuhr agreed that "the great source of evil in life is the abolutizing of the relative" and could see this as occurring in Christianity itself when there is a substitution "of religion, revelation, church or Christian morality for God."[2]

Similarly, Paul Tillich who had made use of this notion in his social political writings in Germany developed it in general terms in his *Systematic Theology*.

> Idolatry is the elevation of a preliminary concern to ultimacy. Something essentially conditioned is taken as unconditional, something essentially partial is boosted into universality, and something essentially finite is given infinite significance (the best example is the contemporary idolatry of religious nationalism).[3]

Tillich makes use of a similarly formulated principle as his "protestant principle" even in relation to conceptions of the divine which are too heavily loaded with concrete symbolic or even personalistic meaning.[4]

In contemporary theology, it is Gordon Kaufman who has most clearly exhibited the use of this critique of idolatry as a systematic principle. In *God the Problem*,[5] Kaufman suggested using God as a limit category capable of relativizing all human experience and projects. In his *Theology for a Nuclear Age*, he proposed that the conception of God must have a relativizing function: "The proper criterion for our talk about God, we decided therefore, is not the postulation of some being or reality beyond the world but rather concern with the relativising and humanizing activity going on within the world."[6] But it is in his *In Face of Mystery*,[7] that Kaufman spells out in greatest detail his own concern:

> What are needed are criteria for distinguishing God from all idols.[8]

> Monotheistic frames of orientation are thus especially susceptible to developing into fanaticisms.[9]

> The only possible check against the monumental deceits which human religiosity works on our gullibility—and on our desire for certainty in a terrifying world—is the constant reminding of

ourselves that it is indeed mystery with which we humans ultimately have to do.[10]

In the case of Kaufman, we have a particularly advanced example of the way in which the critique of idolatry is redeployed from a critique of self-absolutizing religio-political movements to become a general principle of humility with respect to the adequacy of any symbolic or theological formulation of the being or nature of God.

Thus the theological principle of the critique of idolatry has moved from functioning as a critique of other religions and their practices to a critique of religio-political movements demanding sacrifice and loyalty in the crisis time of the twentieth century to becoming a systematic principle which seeks to guard the idea of God from a too-specific content which might compromise the transcendent function of the category of God. I say transcendent *function*, since for Kaufman, God is not transcendent in the ordinary way of being external to the world of finite things but is rather the coherence of these things as an immanent principle which aims at evolutionary humanization. The critique of idolatry here keeps us face to face with the limits of our understanding of this process, face to face with mystery and so with a critique of all our attempts to absolutize even our conceptions of God.

Toward a Material Principle

While there is no doubt that the development of the critique of idolatry from the incitement of religious arrogance and conflict to become a principle of critique of worldly systems and religious arrogance itself is a most important feature of our contemporary theological landscape, I want to suggest that it does not provide us with an adequate way of distinguishing the divine who is the subject of the biblical witness from the ways of articulating the divine which betray that witness. It is indeed a good thing that we no longer use the issue of idolatry as a way of insisting on the correctness of our religion against all others; that it has instead become a formal principle for distinguishing the absolutizing of the relative from a passion within the relative for the absolute. But this alone may leave us with a way of speaking of God that has little critical force over against truly demonic forces in our religious and political life. In Kaufman's terms it may help us to *relativize* and moderate our language but it will not by itself help us to know whether our conception of God helps to *humanize* ourselves or our world.

In order to do this we need, I believe, not only a formal but also a material principle to help us distinguish between idolatrous and faithful conceptions of the divine. And I believe this is precisely also the concern of the biblical traditions from which the critique of idolatry has been taken. Let us begin with a look at one of the most remarkable passages of the Bible, the 82nd Psalm:

> God sits in the divine council; in the midst of the gods God holds judgment:
> "How long will you judge unjustly and show partiality to the wicked?
> Give justice to the weak and the orphan; maintain the right of the lowly and destitute.
> Rescue the weak and the needy; deliver them from the hand of the wicked."
> They have neither knowledge nor understanding, they walk about in the gloom of night;
> all the foundations of the earth are shaken.
> I say, "You are gods, children of the most High, all of you; nevertheless, you shall die like mortals, and fall as a single person."
> Rise up. O God, judge the earth; for all the nations belong to you.   (Inclusive NT and Psalms)

It is a most astonishing scene. YHWH arrives at a council meeting of all the gods. It is a scene we might imagine on Mount Olympus. The deities of all the nations are present. It is a scene, moreover, that reminds us of the first story of creation in Genesis. "Let us make the earthling in our image" (1:26). Or, a similar scene in which the divine council takes note of the building of the tower of Babel "Come let us go down" (11:7). In the divine council the gods have acceded to the creation of the earthling in the divine image. In the divine council the gods have acted to prevent the earthling's assault upon heaven. In these scenes all that is divine seems to be of one mind, following the lead of YHWH Elohim.

But, in the psalm, the God of Israel stands over against all the other gods and calls them to account. The God known to Israel holds judgment over all the other gods and thus steps out from this "divinity in general" of the divine council to be the voice of judgment, the claim of justice. In this, the God known to Israel stands over against the gods in general.

The One we encounter in this extraordinary scene then is not "divinity as such" or "divinity in general" nor some specialized aspect of divinity but one who stands over against the divine in general or as such—and does so precisely to call for justice for the weak and defenseless, the violated and humiliated. And in this call and claim of justice for those who are vulnerable, this One stands over against all those divine principles that in one way or another, directly or indirectly, through approval or acquiescence, collaborate with the violent of the earth in their rapacious and voracious rule of the earth.

That these gods do not heed this claim is that which makes it clear that they are not true gods after all. Their lack of understanding, their living in bewilderment and gloom is precisely what makes them in biblical terms, mere idols. Not because they are made of human hands but because they do not come to the aid of the violated and humiliated. Faced with the claim of justice for the vulnerable these gods stumble into darkness and thus the foundations of the earth tremble and totter. What the New Testament would later term the pillars of the cosmos (Colossians 2:8) become weak and beggarly elemental powers (Galatians 4:9). The principalities and powers stagger under the weight of the claim of justice for the violated and humiliated.

In the 82nd Psalm, the gods come under the sentence of death: those who seemed to be immortal are recognized as mortal, those who seemed to rule over the nations fall as a single individual.

The Psalmist glimpses here God becoming God, the crumbling of the powerful but false gods of the earth. The Psalmist calls out to God to do that which the vision has anticipated: become the God of all the earth, the God of all the nations. And how is it that God may and must do this? Precisely in making this claim of justice for the violated and humiliated. In this and in this alone consists the deity of this God whereby ersatz deity is exposed and expelled.

The Deity then of the God, who speaks through the Psalmist and is called upon by the Psalmist, is precisely the deity of this unwavering call and claim:

> Give justice to the weak and the orphan; maintain the right of the
> lowly and destitute.
> Rescue the weak and the needy; deliver them from the hand of
> the wicked.

Attending to this Psalm in connection with the critique of idolatry, we discern a material principle for the distinction between a biblical view of God and the many divinities that are paid homage within and without Christendom. Here the principle is not whether or not there are images or whether or not these images are taken seriously but whether the divinity thereby indicated has a morally serious character. For the difficulty of reducing the critique of idolatry to a formal principle is that the moral or ethical gravity of the biblical conceptions of God comes thereby to be lost or weakened. But it is precisely this concern for justice that is at the heart of the prophetic traditions from which the critique of idolatry has been drawn. Whether in the law or the prophets or the Psalms, God is hailed as the one who is concerned with this justice, so much so that God can even turn against the people God has chosen when they abandon the most vulnerable members of their communities, when they ignore the plight of the widow, the orphan, the immigrant alien, the poor.

The problem with religious practices and theological theories is that they too often promote or permit a forgetfulness of the poor, of the violated and the humiliated, of the vulnerable and the wretched. It is this forgetfulness of the poor which makes clear that they foster the worship of that which is not the God of Abraham, Isaac and Jacob, not the God of the Exodus or of Sinai, not the God of the covenant or the prophets. Not in greater or lesser degrees of abstraction, not in greater or lesser degrees of symbolic representation, but precisely in this concern for justice that brings into question the pretensions of religious and ideological systems lies the critical distinction between true and false representations of divinity.

In order to see how this bears upon our problematic it is necessary to remind ourselves that the name of God is often related in the western tradition to the constitution of a totality out of the multiplicity of what is. This is a regular theme of the discourse of philosophical theology.

The preponderate tendency is to think God as that by virtue of which the multiplicity becomes a totality, and thus to think of God as the organizing center, principle, ground or goal that fosters such a totality.

Although with the enlightenment this totality no longer has a concrete reference to Christendom, at least among the illuminati, it is nonetheless invested with the attributes of divinity; a totality that providentially and sovereignly guides humanity to its apotheosis.

But what is not thought in this enlightenment project is the way in which this totality is what Anselm Min has called a concrete totality.[11] Thus the totalizing project of the enlightenment is not thought about in relation to the invention of chattel slavery (which accompanies its birth), or of colonial conquest and genocide, or of capital exploitation, still less of total (world) war or totalitarian politics, or what is now thought to be the end of history in the triumph of consumer capitalism legitimated by formal democracy.

Yet, these are the specific concrete historical mechanisms for the construction of totality as a global system and thus for the plausibility of the goal of the unification of global consciousness.

What are we to say of the relation of the name of God to this concrete predatory totalization of consciousness, of culture and of world? Is the name of God the name of this totalizing process for whose sake bloody sacrifice is offered on a stupefying scale? Is the name of God the name of a bare transcendence that merely relativizes this world historical project in the same way and to the same degree that it relativizes the prophets of protest and liberation *vis-a-vis* this world historical project? Or is the name of God to be understood as the protest precisely against the totalitarian project of consciousness, culture, history and world?

Does "God" identify that in the name of which the tower of Babel is constructed? Or is the name of God that by virtue of which this tower is dismantled and humanity not consolidated but dispersed and disseminated; made other to one another through the otherness of language, culture and consciousness? And moreover summoned to turn toward one another in the quest for justice and mercy?

Now if the transcendent is that which destabilizes or reconstructs the babelian synthesis and if this synthesis is not only theoretical but also constituted as a web of practices that absorb the other into the hegemony of the same,[12] then it is clear that the transcendent is attended precisely in attending to the other: the colonized, the marginalized, the impoverished, the violated and humiliated.

Any avoidance of this reality is an avoidance of the transcendent and thus an avoidance of God under the concrete conditions of our history. But such an avoidance is an avoidance of the God who speaks and is spoken of in the Bible.

Thus it must be clear that the test of our talk of God must be whether and how that talk of God directs us to the violated and humiliated of the earth: to the cry of indigenous peoples who are being culturally and socially and bodily subjected to genocide, to the cry of peasants driven from subsistence on the land into surplus labor in the cities, to the cry of the urban underclass, to the cry of battered and violated women and children, to the cry of exploited and scapegoated immigrants, to the cry of child slave laborers, to the cry of the earth itself.

Any so-called doctrine of God which enables us to avoid or postpone the claim, call, and cry of the impoverished is the doctrine of a false god. Any doctrine of God that enables us to avert the gaze from the plight of those who cry out for justice and mercy cannot be a doctrine of the biblical God of YHWH or ABBA.

Now it must be clear that an abstract conception of God which relativizes any and all representations of the divinity is by no means an adequate defense against idolatry in the sense in which we are now developing the term. For an abstract or exalted sense of God as the God beyond God or as unfathomable mystery may still leave us complacent with respect to the issue of justice in general or with respect to the plight of the violated and humiliated in particular.

Deity in general is precisely what falls under the critique of the gods in the Psalm we have cited and in the biblical tradition which it represents. For it is precisely deity in general that may serve to deflect attention away from the plight of the impoverished or to suggest that this is not at its core a theological problem, indeed *the* theological problem by which it is decided whether we have to do with God or with an idol. In order then to be able to distinguish the One who is attested in these traditions from the gods we fabricate for ourselves we need not only a formal principle (the difference between the unconditional and the conditioned) but also a material principle: the doctrine of God as critique of all forms of injustice.

Conclusion

What is idolatry and why is it a problem? Some Jews and Christians and most Moslems believe that the problem with idolatry is the material representation of the divine in pictures, statues, or other objects. Such objects, they believe, violate the second commandment and the holy transcendence of God. But most Christians suppose that the problem is not with material representations of the divine for these, as icons or sacramental signs, have the power of pointing beyond themselves toward the holy God and so may be helpful in relating God to the world in which we live.

What then is the difficulty with idolatry? We know that neither the ancient Babylonians nor the contemporary villagers of Africa or the Andes thought that the divine was simply the material object you can make or break. Rather these are representations, symbols, windows onto the divine. The problem really is whether these objects represent true divine power or demonic power, the power of life or of death.

An idol then is something that represents demonic power, the power of death. The idol is the product of our anxiety about ourselves, our society, our place in the world. The idol represents the power that assures us of security and prosperity and privilege in the face of our anxiety. But the God of the Bible is the power that beckons us toward justice (not security), toward generosity (not prosperity), toward service (not privilege). The irony is that the idols that answer to our anxieties only fuel our anxiety and make us more anxious, more enslaved to the power of death.

The most common idols in human religious life are the "idols of the hearths," the domestic idols of familial fertility and prosperity. Today these idols are found in the way we extol certain "family values". Instead of pointing us to cross generational care and enduring loyalty these "values" become a club to condemn the life situations and styles of people different from ourselves and a veil of secrecy and silence to cover over domestic violence and violation. They become demonic and death dealing.

Another common set of idols are those of the market place. Here the values of economic life become distorted and demonic. Instead of pointing us to the diversity of gifts and to the mutual interdependence of persons, societies and the whole earth, these values become the legitimation for over voracious plundering of wealth from the earth, the exclusion of millions of our neighbors from the bare essentials of life, and the condemnation of myriads to death by impoverishment.

Promising prosperity these idols instead demand unending human sacrifice.

The Holy One of the Bible calls us to a new way of being in which the protection of the most vulnerable is the only mark of true security, in which the satiety of the impoverished is the only mark of true prosperity. The way of this God in the world is truly a scandal to the religious and folly to the wise, but it is the power and wisdom of God. For it is only justice and mercy that can produce peace and joy and life, life abundant and everlasting.

Endnotes

[1] Reinhold Niebuhr, *Nature and Destiny of Man* (New York: Scribners, 1941), 166.

[2] H. Richard Niebuhr, *The Meaning of Revelation* (New York: MacMillan, 1941), viii-ix.

[3] Paul Tillich, *Systematic Theology*, Vol. 1 (Chicago: University of Chicago Press, 1951), 13.

[4] See his *Courage to Be* (New Haven: Yale University Press, 1952).

[5] Gordon Kaufman, *God the Problem* (Cambridge: Harvard University Press, 1972).

[6] Gordon Kaufman, *Theology for a Nuclear Age* (Philadelphia: Westminster Press, 1985), 37.

[7] Gordon Kaufman, *In the Face of Mystery* (Cambridge: Harvard University Press, 1993).

[8] Ibid., 10.

[9] Ibid., 77.

[10] Ibid., 63.

[11] Anselm Kyongsuk Min, *Dialectic of Salvation* (Albany: State University of New York Press, 1989).

[12] Enrique Dussel, *Philosophy of Liberation* (Maryknoll: Orbis, 1985).

Chapter 6

Debate Concerning a Heritage

Bernard Keller

The present study, which is dedicated to Professor André LaCocque, is intended as a testimony to friendship.[1] It is also the affirmation that fifty years of shared commitments have traced, for both of us, paths of faithfulness. Faithfulness to an unceasing combat for recognition: recognition on the part of Christians of the Jewish roots that nourish their existence, and recognition on the part of Jews of the specificity of their Christian counterparts. Our paths have now become long. After a common point of departure, they have continued in parallel, on opposite sides of the Atlantic. For this reason our face-to-face encounters since the moment when André and Claire LaCocque settled in the U.S. can be counted on the fingers of one hand. And yet, I never cease to be amazed at the rare proximity that we have experienced, each on his own, at the university, in Israel and at the various forums at which we have attempted to share our convictions.

There is one point on which I would like to insist: that is, the full meaning which would be understood concerning our privileged tool, the word. In referring to the Hebrew term *davar*, it denotes discourse which is indissociable from acts and experience. That is why, in rendering hommage to the pedagogical competence of A. LaCocque, I offer here an unusual presentation of a text on the relation between the Jewish Passover and Christian liturgy. The text itself, for which we offer a reading in the first part, will be followed by a description of the circumstances surrounding its composition and its reception, in manuscript form, by the members of the Jewish community. This will provide the setting for a reflection on the perspectives of contemporary university pedagogy and on current relations between Jews and Christians of good will.

The Text :
A Christian Perspective on
Pessa'h (Passover)

Judaism is not a mystery religion. Its holy books are accessible to whomever wishes to read them, and the distinctive marks of Jewish life are public ones. An illustration: during the *Seder*[2] a door is left open towards the exterior. Therefore it is not surprising that throughout history various perceptions have been recorded regarding the Hebrew Bible and diverse aspects of Jewish existence. This has resulted in interpretations exterior to the Jewish tradition which have gone so far as to constitute other parallel traditions, which are distinct from, but unquestionably linked to, Judaism itself. Do we not speak of "Jewish–Christian culture" to describe a considerable portion of Western civilization? The hyphen between "Jewish" and "Christian" is the symbol of this relation. Regarding *Pessa'h*, the spellings in the French language also attest to this close link: Jews celebrate *la Pâque* (Passover) and Christians celebrate *les Pâques* (Easter). It is instructive to go beyond the resemblance and the difference in these names and to make the effort to investigate the interpretation which Christians gave to *Pessa'h* when they were first constituted as a people of believers, rooted in Judaism from which it descended, but beginning to develop independently.

From the outset, *Pessa'h* was cited to explain the central and founding event of the Christian Church. In the middle of the second century C.E., independent Christian communities had been in existence for only a matter of years. The community in Corinth was experiencing a crisis severe enough that the apostle Paul addressed to it a number of long letters, several of which have been preserved in the New Testament. For him, what mattered was to return to the essential, that is, to the person and work of Jesus. In a paragraph of his First Epistle to the Corinthians (5:7–8) he says the following:

> For Christ, our Passover lamb, has been sacrificed. Therefore let us keep the Festival, not with the old yeast, the yeast of malice and wickedness, but with bread without yeast, the bread of sincerity and truth.

This passage is obviously incomprehensible if one has no prior knowledge of the text of the Torah and of Jewish ritual. To reach his readers Paul uses a sort of slogan: "Christ is our Passover lamb"; he sought a striking expression, a weighty summary which would contain in one word all the richness of this "gospel" ("good news") which is the foundation of the Christian faith. The first Christians, those of Corinth and elsewhere, are people who know what *Pessa'h* is; they have taken their distance with respect to Jewish tradition, but their eyes return unceasingly to the verses of the book of Exodus. Whether of Jewish or pagan origin, they all consider themselves to be the beneficiaries of the message of *Pessa'h*, for they all recognize as their God the One who acted to bring about the departure from Egypt.

What are the essential significations which Christians distinguish in the account of the Exodus and in the *Pessa'h* ritual, and on which Christian existence is founded?

- *the passage from death to life*: the intervention of God, who commanded that animal blood be used to mark the doorposts, preserves the life of believers;

they should have died, but they find themselves alive.

- *liberation*: the first Passover was that of an exodus, that is, the departure from a universe in which one is a slave, in order to attain the vast open spaces of liberty.

- *communion*: *Pessa'h* instituted a meal, shared elbow to elbow. The conviviality of this feast creates a bond of community between the participants. Historically, it symbolizes the fact that a slave population has become a people.

- *purification*: it is in this regard that the symbolic function of the unleavened bread comes into play. Leavening, the agent of fermentation, and thus corruption, is absent during the days of *Pessa'h*. The participants are new beings, called to live in the future, which begins that night.

- *rupture*: within the logic of purification, represented by abstaining from leavening and by the historical reality of the departure from Egypt, *Pessa'h* constitutes a rupture, a separation, which operates at all levels of existence, in both time and space, the latter being both geographic and social.

- *movement*: "with your cloak tucked into your belt, your sandals on your feet and your staff in your hand, you will eat it in haste." *Pessa'h* is a point of departure, a launch pad. The believer knows that an itinerary stretches itself before him, in which each stage will bring him closer to the Promised Land.

- *service*: if we are not satisfied with a superficial reading, we will give full weight to the verse which says, "the LORD brought you out of the land of

Egypt with a mighty hand... *so that the law of the LORD might be on your lips.*" There is a time of preparation, a departure, and a precise destination, and the itinerary is not left to the fancy of those who have just been liberated. *Avodah* is the key word of the caravan in the desert.

• *already and not yet*: they are already living and free, but 40 years will be necessary in order for them to become a people, purified by the trials of the desert, consecrated to the service of God. For each generation, the joyous experience of the "already" introduces the hope of the "not yet." This situation, often experienced as an uncomfortable one, is in reality the only durable dynamic possible in the existence of individuals, families and communities. *Pessa'h* teaches us to take into account the past, the present and the future, as responsible adults and as grateful believers.

These are the perspectives which must have been present in the minds of the Christians of Corinth when they read the passage of the letter sent to them by Paul. In listening to the Gospel, they had come to consider themselves, as well, as a people living in the present the experience of the Exodus:

having passed from death to life, liberated and purified, constituting a community which was in rupture with their former life and with the surrounding society, they felt themselves to be in movement towards a life of passage, consecrated to the service of God, in tension between what had already been given and what was not yet a tangible reality: the kingdom of God.

This Christian reading of *Pessa'h* was not an isolated event, limited to a letter of Paul to the Corinthians. Several years later, the oral tradition of the first communities began to be put in writing and, one after another, the different Gospels which are today compiled in the New Testament made their appearance: Mark, Matthew and Luke, and John.

A reading of the Gospels shows that all four recorded the conviction of the Christians of the first generations that the interpretation of the person and the work of Jesus depends upon what is signified by *Pessa'h*.

The first three Gospels, Mark, Matthew and Luke (the "synoptics") are in accord in describing an element of greatest importance that will mark the entire history of Christianity to the present time: the Lord's Supper, celebrated by all Churches as the high point of their worship and closely related to the *Seder*. The different Christian confessions use different names for the Lord's Supper: "eucharist" for Roman Catholics, "the Lord's Supper" for Protestants, "Holy Communion" for Anglicans and "Divine Liturgy" for the Eastern churches. Despite the difference in name, the reality is the same in all cases; it consists of a symbolic meal during which bread and wine are shared by the faithful. The narrations in the synoptic gospels describe the circumstances in which this meal was instituted. Following is how Mark reports the events:

> On the first day of the Feast of Unleavened Bread, when it was customary to sacrifice the Passover lamb, Jesus' disciples asked him, "Where do you want us to go and make preparations for you to eat the Passover?" So he sent two of his disciples, telling them, "Go into the city, and a man carrying a jar of water will meet you. Follow him. Say to the owner of the house he enters, 'The Teacher asks: Where is my guest room, where I may eat the Passover with my disciples?' He will show you a large upper room, furnished and ready. Make preparations for us there." The disciples left, went into the city and found things just as Jesus had told them. So they prepared the Passover.
>
> While they were eating, Jesus took bread, gave thanks and broke it, and gave it to his disciples, saying, "Take it; this is my body." Then he took the cup, gave thanks and offered it to them, and they all drank from it. "This is my blood of the covenant, which is poured out for many," he said to them; "I tell you the truth, I will not drink again of the fruit of the vine until that day when I drink it anew in the kingdom of God" (14:12-16, 22-25).

Historians today are not agreed upon the exact sequence of the events that constitute what it is customary to call "holy week," in the middle of which this narration is situated. The Gospel of John gives a different account. But what is clear is *the intention* of the synoptic Gospels in placing these crucial days within the paschal perspective: the allusion to the blood of the victim, to cups which circulate, to the singing of psalms. It is clearly a transformed *Seder*, whose multiple significations are preserved and to which believers of all origins are now invited, on the basis of a universalist vision which designates all of humanity as the direct beneficiary of the revelation given to Israel.

The Gospels simply reflect and record the beliefs and practices of the Christian communities of their time. This means that, around the Mediterranean basin, communities are beginning to constitute a people that considers itself the people of the Exodus (not in order to substitute themselves for the Jewish people, as has been pretended, but in order to form around the latter a universal circle of believers, in which the Jewish people retains its central position). In these conditions, one should not be surprised to find throughout the New Testament affirmations which correspond, point by point, to the set of significations of *Pessa'h* enumerated above:

- *the passage from death to life:* "Here is the bread that comes down from heaven, which a man may eat and not die" (John 6:50).

- *liberation:* "The creation waits in eager expectation for the children of God to be revealed. For the creation was subjected to frustration, not by its own choice but by the will of the one who subjected it, in hope that the creation itself will be liberated from its bondage to decay and brought into the glorious freedom of the children of God" (Romans 8:19–21).

- *communion:* Following is how Jesus expressed himself in a prayer recorded in the Gospel of John, during his last conversation with his disciples: "My prayer is not for them alone. I pray also for those who will believe in me through their message, that all of them may be one, Father, just as you are in me and I am in you" (John 17:20-21).

- *purification:* Jesus also said to his disciples: "You are already clean because of the word I have spoken to you" (John 15:3).

- *rupture:* "You do not belong to the world, for I have chosen you out of the world" (John 15:19).

- *movement:* "For whenever you eat this bread and drink this cup, you proclaim the Lord's death until he comes" (I Corinthians 11:26).

- *service:* "Do not offer the parts of your body to sin, as instruments of wickedness, but rather offer yourselves to God, as those who have been brought from death to life" (Romans 6 :13).

- *already and not yet:* "And you also were included in Christ when you heard the word of truth... having believed, you were marked in him with a seal, the promised Holy Spirit, who is a deposit guaranteeing our inheritance until the redemption of those who are God's possession" (Ephesians 1:13).

In the quotations above, the Gospel of John is well represented. One of the original features of this Gospel is that in it concerning relation between *Pessa'h* and the person and work of Jesus is not underscored in the course of a *Seder* meal but by another, equivalent yet different, means: the death of Jesus is situated within "holy week" during the afternoon when the paschal animal victims were sacrificed at the Temple. This coincidence is easy to interpret. In the same fashion as the lamb or deer dies as a symbol of life and liberation, Jesus dies so that men of all origins might live fully and gain access to liberty.

We have seen that a Christian tradition was rapidly formed on the basis of this particular perspective on *Pessa'h*. It is essential to the life of believers, for it bears the message of life and of the liberty of the Gospel. Its ritual format, that of a symbolic meal, permits it to descend from one generation to the next, bearing its load of meaning. It is easy to distinguish the parallelism with the *Seder*, itself borne by the tide of time, from past millenia, in the unfolding of Jewish life.

The peaceful tone of this summary of research carried out on texts and rites does not convey the conflicts which have marked past centuries. These two tables, each a memorial of an act of life and liberation, these places of communion, have been the scenes of battle. The early church experienced its well-known "Easter controversy." In the Middle Ages the accusation of ritual murder that was made against Jews found its pretext in the preparation of the *Seder*. At the time of the Reformation, the Lord's Supper was one of the subjects of hottest debate, opposing not only Roman Catholics and Reformers, but also the Reformers among themselves. The debate is not yet closed, although the accusations and anathema have lost some of their violence.

Is there not a challenge in this sorry state of affairs? When I look upon another and discover at the same time similarities and differences between him and me, do I look on him with jealousy or mistrust, with a feeling of superiority or of condescension? Or, on the contrary, with fraternal interest, with wonder and amazement at finding my own values, interpreted and lived in another, complementary fashion?

Being a Christian, I am reminded of a saying of Jesus: "In my father's house are many dwellings." It is probable that the table is not set in quite the same way in each of these dwellings.

Prehistory of the Text :
A Collective Research Project

The Department of Protestant Theology of the University of Strasbourg (France) includes a department of continuing education, which caters to students already engaged in professional activities. Some of these students come seeking answers to the problems raised by their commitment to the Church; others, dissatisfied with the contemporary secular cultural context, particulary that of French society, find in this department an environment in which to come into contact with theology.

It was in this context that several different groups worked on the biblical texts relating to the Jewish Passover and the echo which it finds in the New Testament. In the first phase, chapters 12 and 13 of the book of Exodus were examined under the guidance of an instructor. In addition to guiding the study's progress, the role of the instructor was to provide historical information, namely the literary history and the history of institutions in ancient Israel. The study continued with the collation and examination of the different appearances of the Passover in the rest of the Hebrew Bible, in particular the memorable Passover feasts whose memory was conserved by the biblical writers, and the allusions to this feast in the prophetic books. Additional information was given to the participants concerning the *Seder*, from the end of the Biblical period to the present.

After this preparation, the participants sought to express in existential terms the different meanings of this founding event whose feast is composed of a memorial. At the end of the study, seven aspects of the Passover feast were identified. It is these aspects which are enumerated in the text following the introduction.

As a natural prolongation of the study, the question of the reception of this heritage by the New Testament arose. At this stage the role of the instructor was once again to provide information. He exposed the inherent problems in the reading of the New Testament texts, particularly in passages in the synoptic gospels that describe the institution of the eucharist, or the date of Passover in the year of Christ's passion, and the metaphorical treatment of the Passover in the Gospel of John. After this necessary introduction, the participants distributed among themselves the task of exploring the entire New Testament in order to identify the different aspects of the Jewish Passover which were taken into account by the first generations of Christians. This investigation took the form of individual or small-group research, and took place between the plenary sessions. The findings were shared and examined at each plenary meeting.

The fruit of this effort was a catalogue similar to the one which had been established for the Hebrew Bible. The following conclusion became evident: the heritage was received. The transposition, in terms of universality, of the particular features of Judaism was able to take place by finding its center in the person and work of Jesus. This is illustrated in the next part of the text, which is condensed from the research results.

This bald summary of the reseach carried out by the different groups does not render adequately either the sheer mass of information that was recorded by the participants or the skills acquired during the exchanges between the groups. One can only summarize by saying that, behind these few preceding descriptive pages lie two years of work and meetings. We might add that a third year of study was devoted to the symbolism of the Passover throughout the history and practice of the Churches. The seven aspects identified at the outset were used as a framework for reading the texts of the Church Fathers. We were able to determine that, in this period as well, the heritage was transmitted, in spite of the reticence exhibited with regard to Judaism. Lastly, we put to use the diversity of ecclesiastical backgrounds of the participants by asking each to examine the liturgical texts of his or her denomination and to share his or her discoveries with the rest of the group. By this means it was possible to appreciate the differing sensitivities expressed on this subject by Lutheran, Reformed, Roman Catholic, Coptic, Mennonite, and Pentacostal communities.

The Perception
of the Text by Jews

This method, proposed to groups of Christian background, served mainly to bring to light the relation between the Biblical world and historic Judaism, while analysing at the same time the aspects of the Jewish heritage which were retained in the Christian tradition. This attitude is a necessary corollary to the battle against the "teaching of contempt." [3] It is necessary theologically, in order to evacuate anything that might resemble marcionism. It is also necessary humanly speaking, in order that the necessary repentance of Christians not be limited to the fostering of a sterile sentiment of guilt.

There remains another aspect of the question : How do Jews perceive the appropriation of their references by the theological systems of Christians? We have been able to observe that, in most cases, it is indifference that dominates. The present age is no longer interested in the medieval *disputationes*. The fact that the latter often constituted for them a snare, as well as many other historical circumstances, explains, at least partially, the fact that this indifference on the part of Jews can be interpreted as an attitude of defensive withdrawal. We might thus add to the research findings the attitudes expressed on the part of Jews with regard to the above text, by quoting in the following section several of the reactions it provoked.

The author has occasionally contributed to various Jewish publications and has regularly participated as an invited guest at the annual meetings of the Intellectuels Juifs de Langue Française. In 1987 he was twice solicited for an article and sent on each occasion the manuscript entitled "A Christian Perspective on Passover." Each time the text was refused.   Following are excerpts of the reasons given for these refusals:

> In the first case, the regional Chief Rabbi, a friend of long standing, telephoned to explain that the text was not appropriate for a community bulletin, as it was too "difficult" for the average reader. In the second case the publication in question was a volume of tribute presented to this same Chief Rabbi on the occasion of his departure for Jerusalem. The notification of refusal was sent in the name of a delegation of leaders, of which two members had participated for more than ten years in an interconfessional Bible study group which met monthly, and thus were also long-standing friends. It is of interest to report, word for word, the motive given for this refusal: "Les lecteurs juifs seraient choqués" ("Jewish readers would be shocked"). In ensuing conversations it was impossible to move beyond this expression of an emotional reaction.[4]

It thus became apparent that the reasons behind those expressed for this repeated refusal would have to be sought elswhere.   The author thus turned to André Neher—*'alav hashalom*—who was one of his masters.[5] Following are excerpts of the correspondence exchanged on this subject ⋮

> *From Bernard Keller to André Neher*
> Strasbourg, March 27, 1987
> ...I would like to submit to you a question which has greatly intrigued me these past several months. At the issue of a Biblical reseach project to which I associated a group of students, I drafted the text which you will find enclosed herein. It happens that, in the aftermath, this reflection on *Pessa'h* and Easter was returned to me with a *non possumus*, on two occasions, by members of the community of Strasbourg who had solicited from me an article.... In both cases, I had the impression of a polite refusal whose true motive remained obscure.
>
> I am not able to discern the reasons for this reaction, and it is in this context that I felt that by addressing myself to you, there is a chance that I might be able to see more clearly. I would appreciate your willingness to share with me your reaction. I am convinced that I need not worry that the latter would be masked by a veil of obligatory politeness! Let me express in advance my gratitude to you.

From André Neher to Bernard Keller
Jerusalem, May 3, 1987
By means of the incident in which your text was repeatedly refused by Jews who are your friends and who, we know well, feel nothing but respect and gratitude for you, we have an example of one of the areas which illustrates the fact that *Jewish-Christian relations do not involve reciprocity.* I think that you can attend a *Seder* meal during the Jewish Passover (or any other Jewish liturgy) and construct for it a "Christian perspective" without being obliged to renounce any part of your Christian faith, without questioning or putting in doubt this Christian faith. On the contrary, for the Jewish liturgy contributes to the nourishment of the roots of your Christian faith. The same is not true for the Jew. One cannot speak of a Jewish religious reading of the Gospels or of the eucharist. In the eucharist there are certain moments in which a will is expressed by various words and gestures to make the auditor enter into a *communion* to which the Jew, if he wishes to remain a Jew, does not have the right to adhere. It is one of the very meanings of his Judaism which causes him to refuse this call on the part of Christianity and to respond "this far, but no farther."

Now your text, dear Bernard, is not an *historical* document which could have been written by an unbeliever. It is a *religious* text, almost a liturgical one. It is very beautiful, very attractive. It invites me, by the attraction of its power, which springs from the depths of your faith, to penetrate with you in an eucharist with many facets which are so eloquently enumerated, but in which there is no room for me if I wish to remain a Jew as authentically as you are a Christian, as expressed in this text which your Christian faithfulness would not allow you to compose in any other way.

I have addressed you, as you can see, with the complete frankness which you asked of me, dear Bernard. I have done so with profound friendship and respect for the ties which bind us, for the only thing that separates us is the difference created by your faith and mine, and our committment to friendship requires that this difference be respected by both sides. [emphasis mine]

Reflections

Officially, the Churches' outlook on Judaism has undergone a spectacular conversion since the last world war. The teaching of mistrust has given way to simultaneous expressions of repentance and mutual interest. Religious instruction tends to focus on Christianity's roots in Judaism. Officially, at least, as attested by numerous texts and recommendations from the leadership and councils of the principal denominations. In practice, we find that a large number of Christians show sincere interest in Judaism and a willingness to form closer ties with the Jewish community. Naturally, this occurs in disparate fashion, sporadically, for one could hardly hope that attitudes that have extended over centuries of history might evolve in an identical way in all individuals, or even in all faith communities. In any case, the project which is described here illustrates admirably that it is possible to integrate the values of Judaism in Christian teaching, by showing how those values have been decisive in the values of Christianity.

What warning should we draw from the non-acceptance of this project by Jewish leadership or individuals? Let us examine in parallel the intentions of the project and their interpretation as André Neher expresses it. The goal was, first, to analyse the existential contents of the Passover in the Hebrew Bible, without any attempt to shape these contents through Christian typology, and, secondly, to show that the significations of the ritual are present in the New Testament. To put it another way, to demonstrate that Christians recognize themselves to be the inheritors of Jewish values. By so doing, they place themselves in the context of the metaphor of the branch grafted onto the olive tree, as presented in Rom. 11:7. Nowhere is it suggested that this heritage dispossesses Israel of what remains its own, nor does it appear in the text that Christianity be portrayed as superior to Judaism: there is nothing in the text which constitutes an invitation extended to the Jewish reader to abandon his Judaism.

There is therefore a misunderstanding. One might find the explanation for this in "Le juif face au chrétien" (The Jew in face of the Christian), a text by André Neher which dates to 1962.[6] It is that, in spite of close personal relations and in spite of the explicit character of the discourse, the stamp of history puts into place implicit relational dynamics that transcend the individuals. Two sentences by André Neher illustrate this point:

> A history which will soon span two millenia...the history of relations between Christians and Jews, in which I have constantly, uniformly, unilaterally played the role of the victim in the face of the persecutor and the executioner.[7]

> At any level whatsoever, the Jewish-Christian relation carries, for the Christian, a sacramental signification. The Jew is a potential convert. And it is this which continues to impede my approach to Christianity: in Jewish-Christian dialogue, the two persons speaking to each other do not possess the same scale of values by which to appreciate each other.[8]

From this affirmation the following warning may be deduced: today Jews and Christians are drawing together. A movement has begun, and there is no indication that suggests it will cease. However, the weight of the past illustrates that considerable time will be necessary in order to accomplish what we can glimpse at present for the future. The acceleration of history which we are experiencing at the approach of the 21st century will undoubtedly mark this evolution, but the present era represents the "already" and the "not yet." Does not André Neher conclude by saying,

> I hold dearly the invincible conviction that the two expressions of faithfulness (the Jewish and the Christian), however different they may be, are complementary and fruitful in their divergences ...as are two brothers who know each other well...?

Endnotes

[1] The present article was drafted in French. I would like to express my gratitude to Dr. Wendy A. Pradels for her willingness to prepare the English translation.

[2] *Seder*: the Passover celebration.

[3] "The teaching of contempt" is a term used by Jules Isaac to describe the dogmatic, catechistical or liturgic contents of texts formulated and distributed by the Churches in their presentation of Judaism. See Jules Isaac, *L'enseignement du mépris* (Paris: Fasquelle, 1962).

[4] Another contribution by the author, submitted in place of the refused one, was published in *Zar Zahav* (Strasbourg, 1987).

[5] André Neher is one of the most representative of Jewish thinkers after the Second World War. Among his works which have been translated into English, the following merit mention : *The Prophetic Existence* (New York and London: A.S. Barnes, 1969); *Moses and the Vocation of the Jewish People* (New York and London: Harper Torchbooks, 1959); *The Exile of the Word: From the Silence of the Bible to the Silence of Auschwitz* (Philadelphia: Jewish Publication Society of America, 1981);   and *Jewish Thought and the Scientific Revolution of the Sixteenth Century: David Gans* (Oxford: Oxford University Press, 1984). When André Neher began teaching at the University of Strasbourg in 1953, André LaCocque and Bernard Keller were among his first students.

[6] André Neher, *L'existence juive. Solitude et affrontements* (Paris: Seuil, 1962).

[7] Ibid., 232.

[8] Ibid., 234.

Chapter 7

Three Biblical Portraits
of the Divine-Human Encounter

Vernon Kurtz

The Biblical record has stood the test of time in that it remains a work most relevant to people during all generations of human history. The stories recounted for us in the Hebrew Bible continue to instruct us concerning theology, moral issues and patterns of conduct. I wish to examine the stories told of three major Biblical characters who are all tested by God. In turn God too is tested and the lessons that are learned from each of these encounters remain instructive for us in our modern age.

We will examine specific life-changing episodes in the lives of Abraham, Jacob and Moses. Each of the tests administered is different, each reaction is individual and the results are all dissimilar. One character passes his test with flying colors, another passes but is injured during the trial, and the third fails the test miserably. Each of the episodes will be examined in light of the Biblical record and with the aid of the medieval Jewish Biblical commentators. These commentators examine the text through the looking glass of Jewish tradition, very often basing their comments and understanding on past Jewish exegesis of Biblical stories and verses.

It was the task of these commentators to make the text understandable to the people of their generation. On the one hand, they attempted to simply comprehend the plain meaning of the text. On the other, they very often sensed the responsibility of making the text relevant for the people of their time in the hope that they might gain further insight into this record of the Divine-human encounter. These commentators do not approach the text in a vacuum. Their comments often reflect the earlier comments of the Talmud and the Midrash in which other Rabbis had already attempted to make the text comprehensible and relevant. At the same time, each of the commentators interprets the text in the light of his own point of view and through the milieu of his individual culture.

The first Biblical character to be examined is Abraham, the patriarch of the Israelite nation. It is Abraham who follows the dictate of an unknown God showing faith and loyalty to this Deity. "And God said to Abram, go out of your land, and from your kindred, and from your father's house, unto the land that I will show you" (Genesis 12:1). Thus, begins Abram's journey, which will end with his name being changed to Abraham and his example serving as the prototype of a man of faith. According to Jewish tradition Abraham is tested ten times during the course of his lifetime,[1] but the tenth and final test is by far the most severe and complex. In the twenty-second chapter of the Book of Genesis we are told that God decides to test Abraham in an extraordinary fashion. "And it came to pass after these things that God did test Abraham, and said unto him, 'Abraham!' And he said, 'Behold, here I am.' He said, 'Take now your son, your only son Isaac, whom you love, and go to the land of Moriah, and offer him there as a burnt offering on one of the mountains that I shall show you'" (Genesis 22:1-2).

The medieval Jewish commentators were most puzzled by this turn of events. Why must God test Abraham? Did not Abraham always follow God's path? Had Abraham ever shown a lack of faith? Even if God had wished to see whether Abraham would live up to these new challenges, surely God knew the answer even before the test was administered.

Thus, they must, in their own way, devise reasons for this most challenging and difficult test.

The Biblical text itself is concise, elliptical and complex. There are no reasons given whatsoever as to the rationale of the test, the purpose of its being retold or even the proper desired outcome. Thus commentators throughout the ages have attempted to understand the role of God, Abraham and even Isaac in the drama. The medieval Jewish Biblical commentators were no different. In fact, for them the answers to these questions were even more critical than they might be, for example, for modern Biblical scholarship. For them, the Hebrew Bible was a book of faith and direction. It emphasized the Divine-human encounter and its commanding voice throughout the centuries. Thus, solutions and interpretations must be found so as to give meaning and significance to the story and its outcome.

Rabbi Solomon ben Isaac, known as Rashi, (1040-1105) comments on the words "after these things": "Some of the Rabbis say that it means after the words of Satan who denounced Abraham saying, 'Of all the banquets which Abraham prepared not a single bullock nor a single ram did he bring as a sacrifice to You.' God replied to him, 'Does he do anything at all except for his son's sake? Yet if I were to bid him sacrifice him to Me, he would not refuse.'" According to Rashi, a drama is occurring in the heavenly precincts between God and Satan, one of the members of God's heavenly court. The test, thus, is really a trial proposed by God to demonstrate the loyalty and fealty of Abraham. This particular proposal offers the suggestion that God only instituted the trial to demonstrate the total faith of Abraham to others.

Other commentators recognize that this proposal creates its own set of theological problems. If God is omniscient, then surely He must know the outcome of the trial. What is to be proved by Abraham undergoing this ordeal? Rabbi Moses ben Nahman, known as Ramban, (1194-1270) suggests that "the test is issued since man has the freedom of choice granted to him. It is called a test by he who is tested for he has the capacity to perform or not perform the action. The one who administers the test commands him to put his actions into reality." Rabbi Abraham ibn Ezra, known simply as Ibn Ezra, (1084-1164) suggests that indeed God did know the outcome of the trial but gave Abraham the challenge of fulfilling the command "so that he could gain reward for his deeds." According to these two commentators God already knew the outcome of the trial. The reason for the issuance of the command was to be able to follow the actions of Abraham as he carried out the Divine imperative.

Rabbi David Kimhi, known as Radak, (1160-1235) suggests a fascinating interpretation which must be seen in the light of society in which he lived. "And the real reason the test was administered was to show the peoples of the earth the total love of Abraham to his God. The purpose of the story was not for the generation of Abraham's time but for succeeding generations who believe in Moses' Torah." He continues his commentary by suggesting that Abraham's activities serve as a model for all. "And after the Torah became known to all there were believers and non-believers. Today after idol worship is no longer prevalent most of the world believes in Moses' Torah and its stories. They only disagree as to whether the commandments are binding, for some say they were given as parables. But since most of the world believes in this story it serves as an outstanding witness to the total love and devotion of Abraham to his God." Radak is most assuredly offering his comments as a reaction to other faith systems around him which accept the Biblical record but disagree as to its normative nature. In portraying the love and devotion of Abraham to God, he is attempting to show the special relationship between Abraham, the patriarch of the Jewish people representing the entire nation, and God. It is a remarkable comment in that Radak sees the text as having eternal purpose in the ongoing history of world religions and not just a one-time event in the life a Biblical character.

All of these comments attempt to construct possible rationales for the perplexing problems created by the Divine command to Abraham to offer up as a sacrifice what is most precious to him, his son, Isaac. None of these commentators have any doubt that Abraham would carry out the imperative. While they may not have understood the genesis of the command, they trusted that Abraham's complete faith in the God of Israel would lead him to fulfill the request.

The modern mind, however, is not so sanguine in comprehending Abraham's behavior in this episode. After all, didn't Abraham protest God's proposed destruction of the cities of Sodom and Gomorrah in Genesis 18? If Abraham protested the slaughter of innocents in that case, when his only next of kin present was his nephew, Lot, surely he should have done the same when God proposed that he slaughter Isaac upon the altar? Perhaps, Abraham was actually being tested to see whether he would protest this command emanating from God. Indeed, a modern Biblical scholar, Nahum Sarna, in his commentary on the Book of Genesis, asks that very question. He states that "it is strange that Abraham does not protest the inhumanity of the divine request that he sacrifice his son on the altar."[2] Sarna responds that God has desginated Abraham progenitor of a new nation, one, which is to be endowed with a unique destiny among the family of nations. "He must therefore unequivocally prove his worthiness to be God's elect. The totally disinterested nature of his devotion to God must be established beyond any doubt." Thus, according to Sarna, the trial was put in place to see whether Abraham was worthy of being the father of the Israelite nation. When he passes the test with flying colors, Abraham receives God's covenant.

Lippman Bodoff, in a recent article, suggests another interesting point of view.[3] He writes that the episode described in Genesis 22 is a dual test. "I believe," he writes, "that God was testing Abraham to see if he would remain loyal to God's moral law, but Abraham, who could not know this, was simultaneously testing God to see what kind of covenant and religion he, Abraham, was being asked to join." Bodoff suggests that Abraham accepted his mission because he wanted to see if God would stop him. While he proceeds to follow God's command, he never states that he is going to fulfill its dictates. Thus, according to Bodoff, "at each step Abraham is waiting for God to evidence a change of mind, to withdraw His command." Abraham, therefore, "had to have an enduring, unshakable faith in God's justice and righteousness, a faith that allowed him to proceed with the test, not with the steadfast, zealous intent to kill Isaac, but with the steadfast, serene faith that God, without the need for human pleading, would ultimately pronounce for all, and for all time, the prohibition against murder." Bodoff, thus, concludes that, "In his determination and his willingness to go forward with God's command until ordered to stop, Abraham passed the twin tests of the strongest moral courage and the purest religion."

However we may wish to see the story, it is clear that Abraham passes the trial. He is rewarded, God is vindicated in the heavenly court in relation to Abraham's steadfastness, and the story remains as a classic tale of faith and loyalty to the Divine command.

The second character to be examined is Jacob, a most troubling and troubled individual in ancient Biblical history. Jacob, the second born son of Isaac and Rebecca, uses trickery and ruses to wrest the birthright away from his older brother, Esau. After the second episode in Genesis 27, when Isaac bestows the blessing of the older child upon Jacob, the latter recognizes, because of the warning given to him by his mother Rebecca, that he must flee. He sets out for Haran and works for over twenty years for Rebecca's brother, Laban. After this lengthy absence from the land of Canaan, Jacob recognizes that it is time to go home. But in order to do so he must be prepared to meet his brother Esau, who has sworn to slay him.

As he prepares for this fateful meeting the Bible tells us that he has a most extraordinary experience:

> And he rose up that night, and took his two wives and his two handmaids, and his eleven children, and passed over the ford of Yabbok. And he took them and sent them over the stream and sent over that which he had. And Jacob was left alone; and there wrestled a man with him until the breaking of the day. And when he saw that he was not able to prevail against him, he touched the hollow of his thigh; and the hollow of Jacob's thigh

was strained, as he wrestled with him. And he said, 'Send me away, for the day breaks.' And he said, 'I will not send you away, except that you bless me.' And he said unto him, 'What is your name?' And he said, 'Jacob.' And he said, 'Your name shall be called no more Jacob, but Israel, for you have striven with God and with men and have prevailed.' And Jacob asked him, 'Tell me, I pray you, your name.' And he said, 'Why do you wish to know my name?' And he blessed him there. And Jacob called the name of the place Peniel: 'for I have seen God face to face and my life is preserved.' And the sun rose upon him as he passed over Peniel, and he limped upon his thigh (32:23-31).

This enigmatic story has raised many questions about Jacob's mental, emotional and spiritual state as he attempts to come to grips with his own inner nature and prepares for his meeting with Esau. While there is no direct contact between Jacob and God, it is clear from the context that the 'man' is a messenger from God or, at least, represents the divine will in the story. This episode serves as a turning point in the life of Jacob. Not only is his name changed, but he is now prepared to reenter the land of Canaan and assume his role as the leader of his family and his people as well. He left the land as Jacob, "the one who takes by the heel," (Genesis 25:26) and returns as Israel, "the one who strives with God and with men and prevails" (Genesis 32:27).

The medieval Jewish biblical commentators were most puzzled by this turn of events. This story in the life of Jacob was an integral part of their faith system and theology. In it Jacob becomes Israel and forevermore his descendants assume this appellation. Thus, this episode in the life of this patriarch needed to be examined and explicated. What concerned them first of all was the identity of the 'man' with whom Jacob had striven. Many of them, led by Rashi, suggest that it was "Esau's guardian angel." This view was rather prevalent among earlier Rabbis of the Midrash and then the medieval Jewish commentators. Even modern Biblical scholarship has often subscribed to this explanation. Nahum Sarna[4] suggests that the identity of this 'man' "must stand for Esau in some manner." He writes, "The mysterious creature who assails Jacob as he is about to cross the future border of Israel is none other than the celestial patron of Esau-Edom, who is the inveterate enemy of the people of Israel. The entire episode foreshadows the impending confrontation with Esau."

Other commentators instead of attempting to identify the 'man' are more interested in interpreting the word in verse 25, "Va-Yeavek" ("wrestled"). Ibn Ezra explicates the word as "they wrestled until dust was raised by them." This interpretation is based on the Hebrew word "avak" ("dust"). Rashi suggests that the word could be derived from "Va-Yeachabek" ("they embraced, they joined"). In each of these cases it is very difficult to discern whether the commentator contemplates an actual struggle with a person, an apparition, or an internal struggle within Jacob's psyche. However they understand it, there is no doubt that they see this as a turning point in the life of the patriarch.

Radak seems to harmonize both possibilities. He suggests that "the entire episode could be in Jacob's subconscious but that leaves the difficult problem of the physical injury to Jacob's thigh." Therefore, he explains that at that moment in a miraculous fashion the 'man' "assumed physicality and actually touched Jacob in the thigh." While this interpretation is forced, one may, at least, comprehend the difficulties that the commentator is trying to explain.

What occurs during the struggle itself is most informative and transforming. Jacob seems to be winning the battle and refuses to allow the 'man' to take leave of him. It is only when he blesses Jacob that he is allowed to leave. In the change of Jacob's name to Israel the blessing seems to be given public affirmation.

This episode, I believe, describes Jacob's ultimate test. Before he meets Esau, he must show himself to be worthy of the mantle of leadership. In this encounter he undergoes a challenge. He must struggle with a Divine apparition, or with a celestial patron of his brother Esau, or undergo an internal wrestling match in order to prove himself either to God or to remove his own doubts. Even after he prevails, he must be satisfied with the fact that he will never know all that he wishes to ascertain. He asks for the name of the 'man' but is not granted that privilege. Instead, he must be satisfied with the blessing affirmed through his change of name.

In this great struggle Jacob is injured. He is forced to limp upon his thigh. If, as the text states, "You have contended with God and men and prevailed," then it only stands to reason that God too was involved in this struggle. Does the verse suggest that God was a loser in the wrestling match, if Jacob was the victor? I would like to suggest that a simple reading of the Biblical text leads to the conclusion that neither Jacob nor God is totally victorious in this match. Jacob does undergo some life-changing events. His name is changed, he gains new confidence in his leadership abilities, and he is ready to undergo the major challenge of his early life, meet his brother Esau. But he is wounded physically in the encounter and his descendants will always recall this episode in the patriarch's life for:

> The children of Israel eat not the sinew of the thigh vein which is upon the hollow of the thigh, unto this day; because he touched the hollow of Jacob's thigh, even in the sinew of the thigh vein (32:33).

Perhaps the text is suggesting that Jacob's descendants are to see the patriarch's actions as a prototype for their own struggles and challenges throughout history.

But Jacob, alone, is not the only one challenged. God too seems to be involved in this struggle. What does it mean that Jacob struggled with God and prevailed? According to the text, the 'man' wished to take leave of Jacob but was prevented from doing so by the patriarch. Was it the original intent of the 'man' to bless Jacob or did he have no choice if he wished to return to his place of origin? The text is inconclusive and it is only later interpretations that offer the possibility of seeing the story as portraying the willing intent of God to change the name of the patriarch. It seems to me that the text suggests that neither Jacob nor God is totally victorious in this wrestling match. Each is somehow wounded, Jacob in his physical body, and God in a most mysterious manner. This test is not only one which Jacob must undertake but God as well. When Jacob left Canaan he brazenly offered a vow:

> If God will be with me, and keep me in this way that I go, and will give me bread to eat, and raiment to put on, so that I come back to my father's house in peace, then shall the Lord be my God. (Genesis 28:20-21)

He seems to put God on trial. It is only after this episode in chapter 32 that Jacob understands that he has been protected (verse 31) and must show his gratitude to God. In relationship with the patriarch Jacob, God must continually act with faithfulness and although God passes the test it is clear that the divine will requires Jacob's participation.

The third episode to be examined is the sin of Moses. The life of Moses occupies most of the final four books of the Pentateuch. He is the Prophet, par excellence, the leader of the Israelite people and the one to whom God reveals the Torah. Yet, Moses always seems to undergo one crisis of leadership after another. The people of Israel are never satisfied with his leadership qualities and complain against him—and by extension against God. Moses must have constantly wondered whether he wanted to continue in this most difficult mission. The situation comes to a head in the story told to us in Numbers chapter 20.

The people complain to Moses over and over again and are never satisfied with the gifts that God has granted them. At every juncture Moses fulfills the word of the Lord. In this case, however, when the people ask for water, he does not follow God's dictates.

> And God spoke to Moses, saying: "Take the rod, and assemble the congregation together, you and Aaron your brother, and speak unto the rock before their eyes; and it shall bring forth to them water out of the rock; so you shall give the congregation and their beasts drink." And Moses took the rod from before God, as He commanded him. And Moses and Aaron assembled the congregation before the rock, and he said to them: "Hear now, you rebels, are we to bring you forth water out of this rock?" And Moses lifted up his hand and smote the rock with his

rod twice; and water come forth abundantly, and the congregation drank and their beasts also. And God spoke unto Moses and Aaron: "Because you believed not in Me, to sanctify Me in the eyes of the children of Israel, therefore, you shall not bring this assembly into the land which I have given them." These are the waters of Meribah, where the children of Israel quarreled with God and He was sanctified in them (20:7-13).

The medieval Jewish commentators were bothered by this turn of events in the Biblical record. Moses had given so much of his life to the Israelite people. He had faithfully followed God's dictates, had led them out of Egypt, rescued them at the Reed Sea, brought them to Mount Sinai where they received the Torah, and had endured many trials and tribulations in order to carry out his mission. He had but one request of God, that he be allowed to enter the Promised Land, the land of Canaan. Did Moses' failure to follow God's exact directives at Meribah merit such a terrible punishment? Did not God once before direct Moses to strike the rock so that water might flow forth from it? Why did Moses take the staff with him if there was no possibility of his hitting the rock in order to bring forth water? Did the 'sin' merit Moses being banished from the Promised Land?

In order to comprehend this difficult passage and attempt to respond to its many challenges the commentators confront the behavior of Moses and his transgression. Rashi suggests that the real sin of Moses was not only that he struck the rock but his attitude before and during the episode. Moses refers to the people as "you rebels." He did so, according to Rashi, because he lost patience with the people, "He could not distinguish the rock, for the rock had vanished and taken a place among the other rocks when the well disappeared after Miriam's death. Israel, then, said to them, 'What difference is it to you from which rock you bring forth water for us? It was for this reason that he said 'you rebels.' ' From this rock about which we have received no Divine command can we bring forth water for you,' he said." Rashi continues his interpretation of the events by elaborating on God's explanation to Moses of his transgression:

> For had you spoken to the rock and it had brought forth water I
> would have been sanctified before the whole congregation for
> they would have said, "What is the case with this rock which
> cannot speak and cannot hear and needs maintenance, since it
> fulfills the bidding of God, how much more so should we do so?"

Rashi, thus, suggests two possible alternative explanations. One is that the sin of Moses was his impatience with the people of Israel. The other is that he had an opportunity to hallow God's name in front of the entire congregation of Israel and failed to do so.

Ramban, in a very comprehensive survey of opinions on this subject, attempts to outline and describe Moses' great transgression. In addition, to the commentary of Rashi, he considers other comments that have come to his attention. Maimonides (1135–1204) interprets Moses' great sin as that of anger expressed against the people of Israel. When Moses called the people "you rebels" he lost his cool and showed the ugly attribute of anger against them. Ramban also quotes Rabbi Hananel ben Hushiel of Kairouwan, (ca. 980–1056) who states that Moses transgressed when he said, "Must we bring you forth water out of this rock?" He should have said, "Must God bring you forth water out of this rock?" Perhaps that is the reason that God felt that Moses had missed an opportunity to hallow His Name in public. In arrogating to himself the miracle, Moses had gone beyond the bounds of his ministry. Ramban then offers another explanation: In the previous case (Exodus 17:6) Moses and Aaron had been told to strike the rock twice. In this case, both Moses and Aaron had already decided to strike the rock twice even before they approached it. "Because you believed Me not," God said to them, the punishment would be severe.

After he rejects each of these interpretations Ramben suggests that there is a difference between the episode in Numbers 20 and that in Exodus 17. In the latter case, the people issued their complaints against Moses but in Numbers 20 the object of their complaints was God. The failure of Moses and Aaron is a failure of leadership. The people blame God rather then sanctify God. Moses and Aaron are responsible for the people's fatihlessness and and thus were punished.

Needless to say, since the Bible itself only hints at the seriousness of Moses' transgression, and that of Aaron as well, each of the commentators must stretch the meaning of the verses to answer the many dilemmas caused by this event and its outcome. Not only did they see it as a difficult passage, but it also presented serious questions of faith. If Moses, the most faithful servant of God, could transgress but one command and be punished so severely, what could be expected of anyone else? Thus, they needed to see Moses' transgression as an especially serious error that necessitated God's severe decree.

In a modern Biblical commentary, Jacob Milgrom[5] notes that modern critics claim that the sin of Moses has been lost or deliberately obscured so as not to detract from the glory of Israel's founder. He discounts these theories because the Biblical text is not afraid to single out the weaknesses of its major characters. Like Ramban before him, he refutes many other interpretations of the severity of Moses' transgression. Milgrom relies upon the singular contribution of Joseph ben Isaac of Orleans, known as Bekhor Shor (12th century).[6] He suggests that the two episodes in Exodus and Numbers are really two versions of the same story and he brings as evidence a number of Biblical verses that suggest a close relationship between Massah and Meribah where these incidents were described as taking place. Deuteronomy 33:8 reads: "Whom you tested at Massah, Challenged at Meribah." In the Book of Psalms the names are either interchanged (Psalm 95:8–9) or reviewed together (Psalm 78: 15–31). Indeed in our section in Numbers it is recorded, "This is the water of Meribah, because the children of Israel quarreled with God." Milgrom suggests that this language indicates that the place had been mentioned beforehand. And indeed it has, in Exodus 17:7: "The place was named Massah and Meribah because the Israelites quarreled and because they tried God."

Milgrom then suggests that the real sin of Moses was that he attributed the miracle to himself, "Must we bring you forth water out of this rock." In not attributing the miracle to God, Moses had performed no ordinary transgression. "In defying God," Milgrom writes, "Moses did not merely countermand His order; indeed, his behavior could be interpreted as a denial of God's essence."[7]

This explanation opens up a very interesting way to understand the episode as part of an on-going relationship between Moses and God. If this episode is related to "Massah," does it also perhaps raise for us the possibility that it was a test administered by God to Moses? Is there a relationship between what occurred at Massah and the test administered by God to Abraham in Genesis 22? It seems to me that Moses is constantly tested both by his people and also by God. Will he always be able to live up to his responsibilities as a leader? Does he continue to have the patience, the strength, the faith and the will to continue to lead his people? Does he possess the strength of character to recognize that the Divine command must be performed scrupulously at all times?

Moses does not succeed in this particular test. For whatever reason, he fails this trial and is severely punished. Moses in his conduct "revealed that he was not a leader who could address the concerns and crises of a new generation, one which would enter the Land of Canaan. Moses was still tied to methods and perspectives of leadership which, though proper for the needs and concerns of the generation that left Egypt, were ineffective and inappropriate in the new situation."[8] Moses was continuously tested. Unfortunately for him and his nation, he didn't pass every test.

It seems to me that in this episode the limits of God's ability to effect a specific outcome is also at issue. The relationship between Moses and God is like no other in the Biblical record. God forgives both the people of Israel and Moses a number of times throughout the Biblical story. He may even have wished to forgive Moses for this transgression. But that was not possible. The die had been cast. I do not believe that it is accidental that the deaths of both Aaron and Miriam also appear in Numbers 20. Moses' two older siblings serve with him as a triumvirate of leadership. Perhaps since Aaron and Miriam will not enter the Promised Land, neither will Moses. Their tasks were accomplished; new leadership must be found. Moses was an excellent leader for the desert experience but a warrior and a conqueror are now necessary. Even God recognizes this and, I believe, is saddened by the outcome.

Three Biblical portraits and three tests: Abraham passes his trial and is granted a full set of blessings; Jacob holds on until a blessing is forthcoming but is wounded physically in the encounter with the 'man' in the midst of the night; Moses fails his test and the die is cast concerning the end of his leadership role within the Israelite nation. In each of these three cases, God is also tested and the results mirror those mentioned previously. On mount Meribah, God is vindicated and solidifies the covenantal relationship with Abraham and his descendents. At Peniel, Jacob wrestles with God and is preserved. But he is also partially wounded. So, too, is God who cannot totally dictate the situation. In Moses' failure at Meribah, God fails as well and must issue a severe irrevocable decree.

The medieval Jewish commentators attempt to understand these Biblical episodes as they explicate the simple meaning of the text and also portray important lessons of meaning and faith to the people of their generation. Each of these Biblical figures is a most intriguing personality with strengths and weaknesses and each has successes and failures throughout a lifetime of activity. Such is the lot of all human beings. Perhaps that is the reason that the Bible remains the most popular of books. We continue to add our interpretations hoping to discover the meaning of the text in its milieu and in ours. The Divine-human encounter continues throughout all generations. The trials of Abraham, Jacob and Moses will remain paradigmatic for us of the dynamic relationship between God and all humanity.

Endnotes

[1] Mishnah Avot 5:3.

[2] Nahum Sarna, *Genesis: The Traditional Hebrew Text with the new JPS tranlation* (Philidelphia: Jewish Publication Society, 1989), Excursus 17, 392.

[3] Lippman Bodoff, *Bible Review*, October 1993, 53-56; 62.

[4] Sarna, *Genesis*, Excursus 24, 403-404.

[5] Jacob Milgrom, *Numbers: The Traditional Hebrew Text with the new JPS translation* (Philidelphia: Jewish Publication Society, 1989), Excursus 50, 448.

[6] Ibid., 449.

[7] Ibid., 451.

[8] Nathaniel Helfgot, "And Moses Struck the Rock: Numbers 20 and the Leadership of Moses," *Tradition* 27:3, 1993, page 55.

Chapter 8

A Preacher's Teacher: Lessons on Ministry from One Who Proclaims the Word

Craig Mousin

I call heaven and earth to witness against you today that I have set before you life and death, blessings and curses. Choose life so that you and your descendants may live (Deuteronomy 30:19).

You had prepared us well, André, but at that moment of truth, I failed. You had prepared us to proclaim the truth of the Gospel. Yet the site of the question threw me; I knew the answer, but the location told me I should be careful. Careful, yes, careful I was, and, careful, I failed.

Early in 1987, I represented A.J., a young Salvadoran in deportation hearings, before an United States Immigration Judge. The young man had been a catechist in his hometown. He had seen the military sweep his schoolyard and take young boys, some still in their early teens, conscript them, and order them to fight a tragic and cruel war against the people of El Salvador. He had heard stories of how soldiers in the Salvadoran Army had tortured civilians, raped women, and killed innocent civilians. He had also heard that those boys of conscience who refused orders to kill were themselves killed by their superiors, with no benefit of trial or court martial. As a much younger boy, he had often sat with his parents to listen to the weekly radio homilies of Archbishop Oscar Arnulfo Romero. Although A.J. could not actually remember Romero's last homily where he urged all young men of Salvador to put down their rifles and refuse to kill, he did remember his parents discussing the teachings of the Archbishop who was killed by a death squad bullet on the day after that homily.[1] At his parents urging, A.J. fled to the United States and sought the assistance of the agency where I had begun an internship. Having entered the Chicago Theological Seminary after practicing law for a number of years, my public ministry internship called me to represent refugees like A.J. who sought political and religious asylum in our nation. A.J.'s trial transcript included the following dialogue begun with a question I, as his legal counsel, posed regarding A.J.'s conversation with a friend who had been a sergeant in the Salvadoran Army:

Q: (By Counsel) And what did he tell you?

A.J.: He told me that he was a sergeant and that he ... they ordered people ... or soldiers that had just come into the army to kill or to abuse sexually women.

Q: And why did you not want to kill people or abuse women sexually?

A.J.: According to my religion it prohibits me from doing these things, killing people, abusing ... sexually abusing women or torturing people.

Q: What is your religion?

A.J.: Catholic....

Q: (By Counsel) And what parts of your religion tell you not to kill or abuse women sexually or to torture?

A.J.: According to the command ... God's commandments.

Q: And what are those commandments?

> Q: (By Judge) Are your referring to the ten commandments handed down to Moses on Mount Sinai? Is that what you're referring to?
>
> A.J.: Yes.
>
> Q: (By Judge) All right. Thou shall not kill, is that the commandment you're referring to?
>
> A.J.: Yes
>
> Q: All right.
>
> Q: (By Judge) And Counsel, is it not the translation of the Jewish word which means murder?
>
> A: (By Counsel) I'm not sure I have the … expertise to … answer that your Honor.[2]

You had prepared us well, André, for I knew that sixth word of the Ten Words, one of the Ten Commandments, indeed translated best as thou shall not murder (Ex. 20:13; Deut. 5:17),[3] yet I confessed in my stuttering words that I was not expert enough to testify in court to God's word. The lawyer in me feared a trap by the Judge. Caught up in dualisms of law and theology, attorney and minister, citizen and refugee, I conceded that I was not expert enough to name the word of God in that courtroom.

You had prepared us well, André, to see and name all the dualisms with which the world confronts us with to quiet the word of God. From your personal integrity, your scholarship and your passion for the truth, you prepared us to proclaim the Gospel. Few teachers, in my experience have ever matched your authenticity, scholarship and passion for the Word of God.   You taught, as you lived, that the prophets who proclaimed God's Word, *dabar*, spoke from the very core of their being. For in Israel, "[t]here was no dissociation between the thought and its expression, between the people and their words. *Dabar* (word) in Hebrew expresses a vital flux coming from the innermost heart of the speaker. When

God or his mandatory (priest or prophet) speaks, he draws from his 'back,' from his innermost, the exposition of his identity. The priestly word is therefore not an opinion but an incursion, an interpretation, an invocation: it forces into dialogue."[4]

You invited your students into that dialogue and welcomed that interpretive act. You opened your inner self to us while inviting each of us to be prophets and priests, to hear the Word, interpret the Word, and yes, with temerity and confidence, utter our own word in response to God's call. In a time of spin doctors and dissemblers, you taught us that ministers of the Gospel have neither the time nor the luxury for such dualisms. We could be tempted by our culture to seek the material manifestations of success, but we could never ignore the call to dialogue with God and God's people.[5]

You demonstrated that the choice to minister as a call belongs not just to the few named Abraham and Sarah, Moses or Ruth, Judith or David,[6] Susanna or Daniel,[7] Jonah or Esther. Rather, God gives that choice to each of us in our own life context, as "each individual has a word to utter, each is gifted with a logos that is indispensable for the integrity of human discourse."[8] Regardless of who sat in your classroom, regardless of our life experiences, you urged each of us to accept Deuteronomy's invitation to choose life. In your invitation, we knew the authenticity of your witness to the truth of the Word. You spoke with your whole person to proclaim the living Word, always encouraging us all to participate in God's salvation history in our own midst. You invited us to hear *dabar* and to integrate it into our lives.

And you revealed through your passion and scholarship that you, too, would be with us if we accepted that invitation. For many of us, your classes and publications were foundational to all of our ministries. Your challenge to explore through exegesis and dialogue the complex meanings of the text and story opened our eyes to the biblical roots of our many different ministries. Through our ministry and research, you persuaded us to enrich the meaning of the text with new understandings of the poet's word.[9] Your classes rarely ended when the formal class concluded, but often groups of us would interpret and discuss the class of the day for hours later on the Seminary's steps or in the Reynolds Club. When one of us was unprepared or failed to take a class seriously, your pain showed through your whole person. Not, it was clear, because a particular rule was broken or an assignment missed, but rather, because a relationship had been threatened and weakened. We had not felt the immediacy of the choice or the imperative of the call.

That call came to us as individuals, but also as participants in a more universal response. You defined the Israel of the Bible as a people in dialogue with God,[10] "for Israel is hardly an ethnic label; it is the *name* of a movement, a process, a becoming."[11] Similarly, "Israel therefore is not a race, but a function, a style of life, a "doing," a choice, an experience."[12] You invited us to make that choice to become "Israel" ourselves, to become an interpretive community in covenant with the God of Abraham and Sarah.[13] You invited us to proclaim the Word so that it was so integrated within our lives that, as ministers of the Gospel, we could invite others into that process.

In your proclamation, moreover, you helped us refine the call of our vocations, while you simultaneously prepared us with the tools of interpretation and the passion necessary for our ministries. You inspired me to seek the internship representing refugees. You pointed me to resources to understand that the biblical call to welcome the stranger, to offer hospitality to the sojourner, was not so much a biblical command, but a gift that God offers to all of us in welcoming the other. You explained the stranger's presence in the land as "a reminder and a sacrament of the pilgrim character of the covenant people (Gen. 17:12 and 27; Ex. 22:43; Lev. 22:25; Ezek. 44:7-9; Ps. 18:46; Isa. 60:10, etc)."[14] But you reminded us that the Bible does not simply call us to charity, to just help the other. Instead, "it stands to reason, therefore, that the Israelites should love the 'Gerim' (the stranger) as themselves (Lev. 19:34; Deut. 10:19) for it really *is* a matter of themselves. The strangers are a mirror of the Israelites' own soul. Like the Jews themselves, they are under God's compassionate and jealous protection (Deut.

10:18; Mal. 3:5; Ps. 146:9).... This is the perspective in which life here and now must be lived." [15]

Your proclamation grounded our work in that long biblical tradition. Too often biblical exegesis, theological discourse, or preaching remains divorced from the reality we face in our parishes and ministries. One never felt that disconnection in your classroom. You taught and still speak with such authenticity. Born twelve years prior to the German invasions of Bohemia, Moravia, and Poland, you, too were forced to flee from Belgium with your family, thus becoming a refugee yourself. [16] Returning to Belgium, your family sheltered Jews. After the war, you and your wife Claire ministered to refugees in France and Germany, helping them to make new lives after the carnage of World War II. When you taught about the stranger in our midst, you spoke with a personal knowledge few of us could comprehend. When you taught that we were the stranger, you spoke with a personal intensity and truth that was grounded in the experience of those war years. Critically, you never boasted or told tales of that ministry that drew attention to yourself. We knew you had been involved, but in a striking example of teaching simulating life, your personal history of witnessing and responding to evil of World War II integrated itself so thoroughly with the core of your being that your proclamation revealed the truth of the message. Thus, when you invited us to be priests and prophets, to name the Word as our innermost self, Deuteronomy's teachings took hold of lives: "...the word is very near to you; it is in your mouth and in your heart..." (Deut. 30:14).

You urged us, however, to go beyond the classroom and know God's truth in the world outside of those walls. By encouraging my ministry to the refugee and the immigrant, you demonstrated how God's love for the stranger and sojourner teaches us about ourselves. Listening to the testimonies of refugees, I discovered that this biblical command to love the foreign born as the native transformed into another gift of God's grace. As you wrote, the stranger to our land finds biblical meaning in the context of citizens and natives with whom we minister:

> with Abraham, leaving rich Chaldea behind him and journeying in the desert, with the Hebrews, tearing themselves away from the heights of the civilization, culture, and wealth of Egypt (the very image of our western society), the stranger's contribution acquires its true significance namely of transition from 'having' to 'being.' For God, the Living God, the true God, the God of Abraham, Isaac and Jacob, the God of Job, the God of the Suffering Servant, the God of Jesus, is none other than He who is still the Poor, the Oppressed, the Injured, the Stranger.[17]

But many of our ministries today take place in the context of a prosperous republic premised on democratic principles that, nonetheless, divides the foreign-born stranger from the native. We have laws that establish national boundaries and terms of membership called citizenship. We have laws that name who can enter and who must be deported and forcibly removed. We even sanction procedures that call humans illegal aliens, stripping them by such language of human dignity. Our nation developed from thirteen colonies that protested restrictive immigration laws as one of the many reasons we sought independence from England[18] to a nation that enacts increasingly restrictive immigration laws. Historically, we have enacted these laws to exclude Chinese, southern Europeans, Japanese, Hispanics and Haitians. Even when the laws did not exclude, the administration of those laws has often denied otherwise eligible persons safe haven. The United States failed to admit thousands of eligible Jews and other refugees before and during the early years of World War II, ranging from deliberate bureaucratic delay that precluded immigration by eligible visa applicants to the forced return of the steamship *St. Louis* to Europe in 1939, condemning its passengers to the concentration camps. We, thus, know how our immigration laws can influence or determine the fate of not only refugees, but ourselves.[19]

How can persons of faith welcome the stranger in this land of law? Looming large behind the question will forever be the shadow posed by the Holocaust. You frequently reminded us:

> After Auschwitz, nothing can be as before, in more than one way, the time since Auschwitz resembles the time after Golgotha; we live in a new era and we *must*, as Paul did in his day, draw the necessary conclusion of the newness of our time: a new world is in place; the old one is gone, and a new order has begun (2 Cor.5: 17).[20]

We cannot delete Auschwitz from our collective memory, nor should we, but how do we choose to do ministry at this time and place? One cannot delete Auschwitz, nor, ignore the killing fields that have swept our globe since Shoah. World refugee numbers continue to grow as hate and greed force ever new faces of displaced persons.[21] Although we celebrate globalization in our seminary communities, another more desperate consequence of a shrinking globe has developed. Since the end of World War II, Hungarians, Cubans, Central Americans, Haitians, Somalians, Rwandans, Liberians, Cambodians, and Vietnamese, to name just a few, have found themselves knocking at the doors of western democracies to seek safe haven.[22] Boats are still turned around and hundreds die crossing the Rio Grande River.[23] We live in a nation of laws that defines membership by citizenship and immigration status and enforces these laws with its military might at its borders, rather than by accepting the stranger as God's grace. We minister to a prosperous people who refuse to share the bounty they have received, who cannot count the costs to others. How do we minister in this land?

You taught us to remember God's call to hope, notwithstanding the tragedies, never ignoring the reality of the horror that surrounds us, and that the choice to engage in God's new order remains ours. God calls us to be witnesses to the world of a better way. Our response to God's gift of the sojourner is one way we respond to that call.

The legal and practical problems of immigrants inform my own ministry. Such problems involve choice. Why did a person decide to become involved in activities in their native lands that placed her or him in danger? Why did A.J. refuse to be conscripted into the Salvadoran Army despite all the authority of the State weighing in against him? Why did Virginia Stoica, once safe in this nation, return to Romania with Bibles smuggled within her suitcases, thus risking her freedom both in this nation and in Romania? [24] Why did a young Muslim, born into a family of wealth, risk everything to engage the leaders of his clan in theological debates over whether Muslim understandings of the Koran called for pacificism and a refusal to shoulder arms in the Somalia violence? Why did E's conversion to Christianity cause him to fear for his life in Liberia? Why did the Vargas family give up all that was familiar to flee El Salvador before their sons could be conscripted into the Army? Why did C. try to organize workers in Guatemala despite his knowledge of the violence the Army and the powers that lashed out against trade union organizers with impunity?

In each case, and in so many others around the world, individuals and families like these decided to act. Some knew the risks, or perhaps more critically, they thought they knew the risks. They still acted. Their actions, intentional or not, often challenged the status quo. The difficulty their legal cases posed is why, then, did they flee? If they accepted the risks when they chose to act, what happened to force them finally to flee? Of course, in each case, the reasons were different.

But some points are often shared. Each, in their own way, like Jonah, is like each of us; each responded to God's commandment to respond to their human vocation.[25] As you taught us, God does not call us to be something more than our circumstances permit. But God does call us to be fully what we are.[26] Few of these refugees made an initial choice to oppose the state or the powers that restricted their liberty. Worship at a Baptist Church in communist Romania led Virginia Stoica to realize that the censorship of Bibles denied friends the word of God. Virginia Stoica knew the choice she must make if she could bring that gift of a Bible to friends otherwise denied. She knew, in her heart, better than I ever knew sitting in a church pew or a classroom chair the wisdom of your teaching that the Bible without a reader or a reader without a Bible makes no sense. Only the encounter between the Bible and the reader permits the Bible to reveal God's world. And each member of the community must participate in that transmission of knowledge that permits each generation to engage the biblical Word.[27] The Romanian State knew what it did in banning the Bible. Virginia Stocia, however, knew what she was doing in smuggling those Bibles to her Baptist friends. Yet her choice placed her in physical jeopardy that remained unmitigated until she received asylum in the United States.

That Somalian pacifist simply tried to reconcile the teachings of the Koran with the ethnic clan violence that he began to see as a manipulation of political leaders rather than a holy call to war. When his questions could neither be rebutted nor answered, he refused to join the militia and kill others Muslims, forfeiting the protection of his clan while marking him as an enemy of all other clans in Somalia. The trade union organizer simply asked why Guatemalan workers earned so little and sought the solidarity of numbers to change the system. He did not leave Guatemala until a roadside ambush by the military left him nearly dead. His friends flew him to the United States for medical treatment.

Each, in the course of his or her life realized what Immanuel Levinas said, "morality begins when I become more concerned about not committing murder than about avoiding death." [28] Each perceived a vocation like "Jonah's vocation...[that] is strictly personal.... [b]ut, paradoxically, the particularism of the vocation does not exclude its universalism; to the contrary, it grounds it." [29] Like Jonah, these refugees responded to God's call and opposed the powers that caused murder, that confiscated the Bible, that denied children medical supplies, not as "a divorce from society but, on the contrary, the true contribution to society, for a person's wholeness in the world consists not in protecting the status quo but in the choice to go further in the quest for truth." [30] Few, if any, of these persons sought to be heroic. They made choices to help friends, to seek medical supplies for poor neighborhoods, to teach children, to rebuild houses, to proclaim the Gospel. Their efforts led them into conflict with the powers of the state.

Virginia Stoica simply sought to share the Word of God with friends in her Baptist community. She could not understand how any Christian could do otherwise. For her, if one had the opportunity to bring these Bibles then one did so, regardless of the consequences. Virginia possessed and revealed *dabar.* She exhibited no distinction between God's call and her response. Virginia, to the best of my knowledge, neither planned nor participated in any conspiracy to subvert the state. But her simple message of faith in transmitting the Word gave others the opportunity to hear the liberating Word of God. Her deep faith in the power of God's Word reverberated through her faith community. Unbeknownst, I am sure, even to her, others have witnessed how the power of biblical language inspired Christians in Romania, much like other oppressed peoples, to seek liberation. Christopher Hill writes that biblical literacy permits persons living under oppression to share powerful messages with friends without the risk of state intervention. Romanians, like those of earlier times, "who knew their Bibles very well...could convey messages through allusions lost on a godless age."[31] Specifically, Hill pointed out that, "the Romanian priest Laszlo Tolkes was able under Ceausescu to get political messages across to his congregation by preaching on Nebuchandnezzar and other wicked rulers. Since most Bibles had been pulped in Romania, it is likely that informers in the congregation might miss some of his subtler points."[32] Virginia knew only that her friends needed the gift of the Bible and she exercised that choice. Virginia Stoica confirmed your teaching that we all have the option of seeing God first, of doing God's work.[33]

Each of these refugees further underscore your claim that each of us is called personally to go further in the quest for truth.[34] A.J., trained as a catechist to lead Services of the Word grounded in Archbishop Romero's call to peace, simply sought to follow God's call in his village without being ordered to refuse God's command. The Somalian could not let political strife stifle God's call of peace. The Vargas family, likewise, merely desired to be good stewards of God's gift of children and protect them from conscription by the Salvadoran Army. Unable to keep their children safe, they risked the long trip to the United States and eventually found sanctuary in Wellington Avenue United Church of Christ.

These strangers to our shores, these refugees from persecution, confirm a common question of ministry for us all. For as you taught us, André, God calls every person who is in dialogue with God to choose life. To not choose, indeed, is the same as choosing to avoid life. Yet we all struggle with the temptations of the world to avoid being that priest or prophet. Or, even when we think we choose, we fail. A. J. told the Immigration Judge that the Bible said, do not kill. I told the Judge that I was not an expert to translate the Hebrew. Yet, given that opportunity again, I pray I would not lose the opportunity to proclaim the truth. Yes, God told us not to murder and that is exactly what my young client tried to tell us. He would risk his life, leave his family and seek safe haven in our nation before he would commit murder. God does not condone murder and that is why that young man spoke the truth that day. [35] A.J.'s life preached that truth, while I was still reconciling the dualisms of law and theology, courtroom decorum and trial strategies.

Yet, André, you also told us in your own pastoral way that we may fail as often as we succeed. Simply acknowledging our agency to act, however, does not guarantee success or achievement of all that we try. To accept a call, whether to participate in that dialogical relationship or to formalize it through the church's ordination only begins the process. By accepting our call to action, we, too, face the all too human side of failure. But the God who calls us also promises that we are not alone. Indeed the gift of the stranger, the other, reminds us time and time again that God's grace sustains us, not the wealth or possessions we somehow manage to eke out of life, notwithstanding tragedy or displacement from the comforts of our native land. You, André proclaimed that promise with a passion empowered by the love of God and tempered with a knowledge of the brokenness of humanity.

But your discussion of the many biblical failures of peoples engaged in dialogue with God did not turn us into victims. Rather, it called us to choose to use those struggles of those who have gone before us to recognize our own humanity, and our own responsibility to continuously respond notwithstanding our failures.

A.J. lost his case in court that day. The Immigration Judge held that "conscription does not equate to persecution" as the "generalized accusations that the military have raped and killed persons in El Salvador has not been persuasive here." [36] A.J. was not alone. In the late 1980s the vast majority of Salvadorans and Guatemalans who fled the persecution in their native lands were denied asylum. Initially, most Immigration Judges found such stories incredible, implausible, and therefore, not worthy of legal relief. Yet, the state with its ideology of control and order will always fall prey to the temptation to categorize and compartmentalize persons, degrade dignity, and exclude by rules and custom.[37] Perhaps, even if I had proclaimed A.J.'s story more effectively, A.J. still would have lost.

You had predicted that those of us engaged in the call would frequently "fail to accomplish the Torah because [we] fail to accomplish [our] liberty. But, on the other hand, one cannot fail without being involved in the movement towards fulfillment. All of us go from defeat to defeat until the ultimate defeat—death; but in the process something eternal is made true in this life." [38] With that knowledge, you also encouraged us that it is never too late for interpretation.[39] God remains in covenantal relationship with us, preparing us for defeats, and strengthening us to keep making the choice to be more fully human. A.J.'s loss in that courtroom, like thousands of other Salvadorans, propelled synagogues and churches throughout this land to become public sanctuaries, housing families and young women and men who fled Guatemala and El Salvador rather than commit murder. Thousands of people of faith said no, we would rather stop murder than consider our own safety.

Those people of faith and good will who sheltered refugees slowly began to prevail in asylum cases.

Eventually, even federal judges could not ignore that the Salvadoran Army "routinely rounds up youths at gun point. Those who refuse to join the armed forces for reasons of conscience are tortured or killed." [40] In 1990, the federal government, in the midst of litigation challenging the fairness of Salvadoran and Guatemalan asylum hearings, agreed to settle the lawsuit by reopening for a new hearing for every denied asylum claim since 1980. [41] Subsequent federal legislation offers further hope for those class members whose cases will be retried in the future. A.J. still awaits his day of legal judgment.

But even as A.J. waits, he lives a life of exile. Like the Hebrews in a foreign land of Babylon, choices still must be made for survival. [42] Although his legal status remains uncertain, for the first time, A.J. contemplates buying a house in Chicago. Virginia lost her own battle with breast cancer and died a few short years after receiving asylum, still burdened with the grief that she could not reunite all of her family in her new land. The Vargas family have seen children married, grandchildren born while some of their sons still wait for lawful immigrant status. E. still waits for word from his orphaned younger siblings in refugee camps near the Liberian border, but remains stymied by technicalities of law from reuniting with them in this country. Many still face sleepless nights punctured by nightmares of torture and separation from loved ones. Exile, despite lawful status, does not diminish the daily problems of living in a strange land. Yet, refugees continue to teach us that we are all exiles in this land, and as such, we must make choices for life. They all give "meaning to history that in the midst of despair, there is hope, in the midst of death, life." [43]

A large black and white photograph hangs in a Holocaust Museum in Budapest, Hungary. I stood transfixed by it several years ago. It shows a train station near or in Budapest. Men and women stand, apparently waiting for a train, milling about. No sign of fear or anxiety creases any of their faces. But for its context, it could be a train station in Chicago or one of its suburbs fifty years ago. The caption below, however, tells us all that shortly after this picture was taken, all of the persons in this picture were boarded on to a train and taken to a concentration camp. I stared at each of those faces, wondering if they had any inkling of the horror they were to face. I wonder what my face looks like as I wait for my daily train.

That picture constantly reminds me that the choice for or against life remains mine each day. Dualisms of security and freedom, order and chaos, energy and fatigue, action and prayer paralyze my actions on many days. But I give thanks for the teaching and preaching of André LaCocque who has helped guide and teach me to choose life. The Seminary course guide informed me that you taught Prime Testament. Indeed, you taught exegesis, history and interpretation. Your scholarship grounds your students' ministries. No course description, however, listed proclamation by your name. But for me, your life and scholarship, your friendship and mentoring all proclaimed a message that taught me to preach each day the good news that God's covenant with humanity still promises life. Thanks be to God for your life and witness, André LaCocque. Amen.

Endnotes

[1] In his weekly homily on March 23, 1980 Archbishop Romero followed his practice of listing the names, ages, and sex of the peasant victims of the Salvadoran military throughout El Salvador. He concluded this particular homily, however, with a new plea:

> I would like to make a special appeal to the members of the army, and specifically to the ranks of the National Guard, the police, and the military. Brothers, each one of you is one of us. We are the same people. The peasants you kill are your own brothers and sisters. When you hear the voice of a man commanding you to kill, remember instead the voice of God: "Thou Shalt Not Kill!" God's law must prevail. No soldier is obliged to obey an order contrary to the law of God. There is still time for you to obey your own conscience, even in the face of a sinful commandment to kill.

Ana Carrigan, *Salvador Witness, The Life and Calling of Jean Donavan* (New York: Simon and Schuster, 1984), 157. Archbishop Romero was assassinated celebrating a memorial mass on March 24, 1980. A.J. was 13 years old at the time of his murder. See also, Archbishop Oscar Romero, "A Pastor's Last Homily," *Sojourners* (May, 1980): 12, 16.

[2] The official transcript of the proceedings is available from the author.

[3] My class notes of a lecture by André LaCocque, People and Faith of Israel I, November 3, 1983, (hereinafter, references to lectures by Professor LaCocque that I attended will be designated by "Class notes..." with the date and name of the course).

[4] André LaCocque, *But As For Me: The Question of Election for God's People* (Atlanta: John Knox Press, 1979), 75.

[5] Class Notes, People and Faith of Israel I, October 20, 1983.

[6] André LaCocque, *The Feminine Unconventional* (Minneapolis: Fortress Press, 1990), 35.

[7] Ibid., 27-28.

[8] André LaCocque and Pierre-Emmanuel LaCocque, *Jonah: A Psycho-Religious Approach to the Prophet* (Columbia, South Carolina: University of South Carolina Press, 1990), 177.

[9] André LaCocque, *Romance She Wrote, A Hermeneutical Essay on Songs of Songs* (Harrisburg, Pennsylvania: Trinity Press International, 1998), 209.

[10] LaCocque, *But As For Me*, 14, 21.

[11] Ibid., 14.

[12] Ibid., p. 31.

[13] Class Notes, People and Faith I, October 4, 1983.

[14] André LaCocque, "For Local Communities: The Stranger in the Old Testament," *Migration Today* 15 (1970): 54, 58.

[15] Ibid., 59.

[16] The following biographical information was obtained from "André LaCocque: A Man Between," by Donald Scott, Ph.D., presented at a Chicago Theological Seminary dinner honoring Professor André LaCocque, June 1996.

[17] LaCocque, "For Local Communities," 60.

[18] The Declaration of Independence includes the claim, "The history of the present King of Great Britain is a history of repeated injuries and usurpations.... He has endeavored to prevent the population of these States; for that purpose obstructing the Laws of Naturalization of Foreigners; refusing to pass others to encourage their migration hither...."

[19] See David S. Wyman, *The Abandonment of the Jews: Americans and the Holocaust 1941-45* (New York: Pantheon Books, 1984), 100, 124-142. See also, Paul Johnson, *A History of the Jews* (New York: Harper & Row, 1987), 503, which states that the United States only admitted 21,000 Jewish refugees during the war years, only 10% of the number actually permitted by law.

[20] LaCocque, *But As For Me*, 163.

[21] The U.S. Committee for Refugees estimates that 14,482,000 persons were either refugees or asylum seekers in 1996. It further estimates that another 19,000,000 persons are internally displaced, that is while remaining in their native lands, unable to return to their homes. *World Refugee Survey, 1997* (Washington, DC: U.S. Committee for Refugees, 1977), 5-6.

[22] The *World Refugee Survey* for 1997 lists 44 countries that have "produced" 10,000 or more refugees fleeing their native lands in 1997. Ibid., 6.

[23] A University of Houston research report by Nestor Rodriguez found that over 1,185 people died of exposure or dehydration or had been hit by automobiles while trying to cross our boundary with Mexico over the last four years. The report suggests that many deaths continue to be unreported. Sam Howe Verhovek, "'Silent Deaths' Climbing Steadily as Migrants Cross Mexico Border," *New York Times*, 24 August 1997, Sec. 1, 1.

[24] Virginia Stoica's case was completed and I have permission to use her real name. I have used fictional names for the others that I have mentioned as their cases remain open.

[25] LaCocque and LaCocque, *Jonah*, 59.

[26] LaCocque, *The Book of Daniel* (Atlanta: John Knox, 1979), 238-39; LaCocque, *But As For Me*, 35.

[27] Class notes, People and Faith of Israel II, January 13, 1987.

[28] Immanuel Levinas, *Totality and Infinity: An Essay on Exteriority*, Trans. Alphonso Lingis (Pittsburgh: Duquesne University Press, 1969) 47, as quoted in Thomas W. Ogletreee, *Hospitality to the Stranger*,

Dimensions of Moral Understanding (Philadelphia: Fortress Press, 1985) 45.

[29] LaCocque and LaCocque, *Jonah*, 173.

[30] Ibid., 69.

[31] Christopher Hill, *The English Bible and the Seventeenth-Century Revolu-tion* (England: Penguin Books, 1993), 49, quoting John Sweeney, *The Life and Evil Times of Ceausescu* (London: Hutchinson, 1991), 196-7.

[32] Ibid.

[33] LaCocque, *Feminine Unconventional*, 61.

[34] LaCocque and LaCocque, *Jonah*, 69; LaCocque, *But As For Me*, 29, 59.

[35] LaCocque and LaCocque, *Jonah*, 190.

[36] Oral Decision of the Immigration Judge at 12. (A copy of the decision is in the author's file.)

[37] See LaCocque, *Feminine Unconventional*, 9; LaCocque, *Romance*, 58.

[38] LaCocque, *But As For Me*, 64.

[39] Class Notes, People and Faith of Israel II, February 16, 1987.

[40] *Canas-Segovia v. Immigration and Nationality Service*, 902 F.2d 717, 721, 729 (9th. Cir. 1989), rev'd. other grounds, but see *Canas-Segovia v. Immigration and Nationality Service*, 970 F.2d 599 (9th Cir. 1992).

[41] *American Baptist Church v. Thornburgh*, 760 F. Supp. 796 (N.D. Cal. 1991). It has been estimated that approximately 250,0000 Salvadorans and Guatemalans constitute the class membership eligible for relief.

[42] LaCocque, *Feminine Unconventional*, 71.

[43] LaCocque, *Daniel*, 238-239.

Chapter 9

Toward A Post-Holocaust Practice Of Biblical Criticism

Daniel Patte

To Be Critical a Biblical Interpretation Must Be Accountable to Jewish Communities

The first point I want to make in this essay is that:

In the aftermath of the Holocaust, to be critical a biblical interpretation must include an assessment of the ways in which it affects Jewish communities or individuals.

It is one thing to say that we, Christians, must assess the ways in which our biblical interpretations affect Jewish communities or individuals. In the aftermath of the Holocaust, this is a minimal gesture of decency required, at least in the European-American context, of all Christian readers of the Bible, including biblical scholars. It is quite another thing to say that this assessment is, in the European-American context, a necessary part of critical interpretation, both as a litmus test which reveals whether or not a biblical study is really critical and as a condition of possibility of an interpretation which makes explicit its procedures and choices—as a critical study is committed to do.

By saying that any interpretation of the Bible must be assessed in terms of its potential effects upon Jewish communities and individuals I repeat what I learned in the context of the Center for Jewish and Christian Studies in 1966 from André LaCocque—the rare Christian biblical scholar who in the early 1960s saw it as a necessary part of his training as a biblical scholar to go and spend a year in a kibbutz. In following the bloody twentieth century during which biblical interpretations fueled anti-Judaism and unspeakable crimes against European Jews, one cannot forego such an assessment. Before being declared "valid" (i.e., having appropriate value), our interpretations of the Bible must be tested in the fire of the Holocaust. We, Christian biblical scholars, must be able to uphold without shame our interpretations in presence of a Jewish community.

Long before one could raise the issue of ethics in biblical interpretation, for LaCocque and a few other biblical scholars the millions of voices silenced in the Holocaust called us to accountability in biblical studies. Yet at a time when there was not yet a word for the Unthinkable ("the term Holocaust seems to have come into common use only in the late 1960s"[1]), I was far from perceiving the radical implications of this call. I did not imagine that it demanded from us to view as a litmus test for the *critical* character of any biblical interpretation questions such as: How would it affect Jewish communities and individuals? Does it include an explicit or implicit anti-Jewish teaching? Does it carry in itself the seeds of the Holocaust? I was even farther from envisioning that it required from us to redefine the task and scope of biblical criticism. And yet, the way in which André LaCocque was practicing biblical studies in the classroom as well as in his publications at that time already manifested that these were the implications of his call to accountability toward Jewish communities. Before understanding it I needed to gain, together with other biblical scholars, a different conception of the relationship of value-laden questions to biblical criticism. This conception changed over time.

Accountability Toward
the Jewish Communities
as Hermeneutical Application

Accountability toward the Jewish communities was at first exclusively a matter of hermeneutical applications. In the 1960s, when critical biblical studies was understood as a description of "what the text meant," [2] one could not even imagine that questions of ethical accountability might be an intrinsic part of the practice of biblical criticism. Accordingly "the conditions necessary for critical understanding" included accepting "that scripture has one simple meaning" [3] which a critical interpretation is expected to describe. From this perspective, there was no room for a choice based on value judgments that appeal to values external to the text, be they doctrinal values or social justice values. Actually, critical inquiry needed to be totally detached from such value questions; it could not tolerate any other authority than the textual evidence itself. [4] Ethical issues belonged to a stage beyond biblical criticism—the stage of hermeneutics conceived as an appropriation of the teaching of the text for today, "what the text means." At this second interpretative stage, one had the choice of living by this teaching of the text or not doing so, of viewing it as authoritative or not, as Word of God or not. Furthermore, one had the choice among various ways of applying this teaching to the specific cultural and social contexts of one's life.

From this perspective in the 1960s many biblical scholars understood the prophetic call of LaCocque and of a few other Christian scholars as exclusively concerning "hermeneutical" appropriations of the biblical text. One could and should be held responsible for the effects upon Jewish communities and individuals of one's hermeneutical appropriations, because one could choose among several actual alternatives. But one could not be held responsible for the effects of one's critical exegesis upon people, since one could not choose among several legitimate critical interpretations. The only ethical issue was a matter of probity in applying critical methods and their "morality of knowledge." [5]

Yet, already in the 1960s this view of critical biblical studies was challenged for not abiding by the very morality of knowledge it claimed to follow, in part because one could not truly hold to a clear distinction between the value-free descriptive task of what the text meant, exegesis, and the investigations of what it means for today, hermeneutics. Thus Van Harvey, along with the proponents of the "new hermeneutic," denounces the lack of integrity of historical critical studies which allowed doctrinal and ideological concerns (e.g., about Jesus' resurrection) to put limitations to rigorous historical investigations. [6]

Such internal critique did not change the practice. Despite the awareness that one cannot escape the hermeneutical circle, and even, following Hans-Georg Gadamer, [7] that pre-understandings have necessary and positive interpretive roles, the hope of escaping the hermeneutical circle and pre-understandings continued to structure the practice of critical biblical studies. Accordingly, biblical criticism as detached *Wissenschaft* remained distinct from hermeneutical applications. Yet such close scrutinies of critical biblical interpretations for their doctrinal and/or ideological biases opened the door to hermeneutics of suspicion vis-a-vis the critical interpretations themselves. Some of these might be anti-Jewish because of a lack of scientific rigor.

With this ambivalence toward the practices of critical biblical studies, the Holocaust is heard not only as a call to be cautious in one's hermeneutical appropriations of the teaching of biblical texts (as earlier), but also as a call to be more rigorous in one's critical work. In the first case, a hermeneutic of suspicion is primarily directed toward the New Testament texts, in the second toward the "critical" interpretations themselves.

Hermeneutics of Suspicion
Toward New Testament Texts

When a hermeneutic of suspicion is primarily directed toward New Testament texts, critical biblical interpretations which show that certain New Testament texts have anti-Jewish teachings are viewed as critically accurate (i.e., as legitimate).   This is "what the texts meant," as Samuel Sandmel concluded, and as many Christian scholars who contributed to the collective books edited by Alan Davies and by Peter Richardson et al. also did.[8] Since, from this perspective, the text "has one simple meaning," biblical criticism has no choice but to present this anti-Judaism as the teaching of these texts.

Of course, in the aftermath of the Holocaust, as moral agents biblical scholars do not remain indifferent to the ways their critical conclusions regarding the teaching of biblical texts affect others, and Jewish people in particular. Yet from this perspective, the best one can do, as Gerd Lüdemann still does, is to deplore the presence of such texts in the Bible and to warn people against a hermeneutic that would involve appropriating these texts and their teaching as authoritative Scripture for their lives.

The question is: Which texts should one hold as "holy," as Word of God? At the very least one needs to have a canon within the canon, constituted by setting aside anti-Jewish texts. Yet, if anti-Judaism is rooted in the christologies of the New Testament texts,[10] all New Testament texts should be suspected of anti-Judaism.   From this perspective, Lüdemann proposes to replace the *unholy* Gospels of the canon by a new non-christological "Gospel" focused on the historical Jesus—a reconstruction of Christian origins, especially in its Jewish Christian form.[11]

This hermeneutic of suspicion toward the biblical text is not limited to scholars who use historical methods. Sophisticated post-modern scholars also adopt it. Thus, as he wrestles with Christian anti-Judaism in Matthew (dangerous wild boars!), Fred Burnett ends up proposing a "detached" critical study that presents "what the text meant"—that is, the norms according to which the text is to be read "correctly," namely the "implied author" as a narrative textual dimension. He argues that "the basic norm which guides one's reading of Matthew is the characterization of God as Jesus' father" and that this norm encourages readers in every age to read this Gospel in an anti-Jewish way.[12] "The Jews" are portrayed as being denied access to God and thus to election and salvation, since God is Jesus' father and his followers' father, but no longer the father of Jews. Consequently, it is not merely Matthew's christology which is anti-Jewish; the ground of this christology, Christian theology is itself anti-Jewish.[13] Then, raising in his own way the hermeneutical question regarding "what the text means," Burnett offers a post-modern way of addressing the problem. One should expose the implied author in Matthew for what it is—a construct which manipulates readers into accepting an anti-Jewish ideology—with the hope that this will help contemporary readers to resist this manipulation.

The above examples show that anti-Judaism is not merely inscribed in a few specific passages of the New Testament texts (such as 1 Thessalonians 2:15-16). It pervades these texts, since it is linked with their central religious teachings, christology and theology. A post-Holocaust biblical criticism must therefore include a close examination of the religious dimensions of the New Testament texts, and also take into account that as religious texts they have power for believers—for Christians, they are "holy" Scriptures, Word of God. Unfortunately these are issues that biblical criticism finds difficult to handle, because the "holy" or the "unholy" (Lüdemann) cannot be directly described and the "ideology" cannot be contained into a text—despite a phrase such as "the ideology of Matthew" (Burnett). Meditating before the Holocaust will help us ponder how biblical criticism can account for the "religious" manifested through these texts.

The above examples raise another issue that can be more directly addressed. They show that a hermeneutic of suspicion toward biblical texts developed as a response to the Holocaust surreptitiously introduces ideological choices at the core of biblical criticism, as feminist and other hermeneutics of suspicion also do. By the very fact that these critical biblical scholars are *concerned* about the potential anti-Jewish teachings of New Testament texts (a concern which is the basis for the *value judgments* involved in the following choices), they end up focusing their interpretations upon certain themes and upon certain textual dimensions (or features). They have *chosen* to focus their interpretations upon *certain themes of the teaching* of the text rather than upon other of its themes—a choice made on the basis of *epistemological judgments* which verify that it is appropriate to *make sense* of the teaching of this text in terms of these themes. Similarly, in order to elucidate legitimate evidence for the teaching of the text about these themes, they have *chosen* through a *judgment of legitimacy* to focus their critical tools—be they historical or literary methods—upon certain textual dimensions which include particularly significant features related to the chosen themes.[14]

This observation should not be misunderstood. I do not mean to say that the role of these interpretations are inappropriate, because they involve choices based upon ideological concerns, value judgments, and epistemological categories related to a post-Holocaust cultural context. These do not compromise the critical character of these interpretations. This is what happens quite explicitly in all critical thematic studies, whatever might be the theme taken as a subject matter—and nobody would dispute the possibility of conducting several thematic studies of the same text. Whatever might be the themes upon which they are focused, such thematic interpretations are equally legitimate and plausible despite quite different conclusions about the teaching of the text. This point can be generalized; similar choices implicitly happen in all critical interpretations. In sum, as concerns for sexism, racism, colonialism, and other forms of oppression also do,[15] concerns for anti-Judaism cannot but bring to light interpretive processes that usually remain hidden even from the interpreters—namely, their interpretive choices governed by their judments about legitimacy, epistemology, and value.[16]

Then, if any interpretation includes a series of interpretive choices (however these choices might be conceived of), in the aftermath of the Holocaust it becomes appropriate to ask whether anti-Jewish interpretations might be the result of interpretive choices which already are anti-Jewish. This is what other scholars did.

Hermeneutics of Suspicion Toward Critical Interpretations

When a hermeneutic of suspicion is primarily directed toward critical interpretations, rather than toward the New Testament texts, scholars suspect that any anti-Jewish interpretations of the New Testament misrepresent the teaching of the text because of inappropriate interpretive choices made on the basis of anti-Jewish ideological presuppositions. Whether or not these scholars work with the distinction between "what the text meant" and "what it means," for them anti-Jewish interpretations are incorrect representations of the textual evidence for two different though related reasons: either the Jewish background of the New Testament texts is not seriously taken into account; or inappropriate epistemological categories have been used to make sense of the text. Yet, in both cases, scholars presuppose with relatively conservative Christian believers that New Testament texts as authoritative Scriptures cannot involve anti-Jewish and anti-Semitic teachings—as such a teaching is clearly morally untenable.

The first group of scholars can be represented by Joseph Bonsirven, S.J., W. D. Davies, Otto Betz, Krister Stendahl and, more recently, Robin Scroggs and E. P. Sanders.[17] Each of them underscores that the New Testament must be interpreted in terms of its Jewish context, at first primarily because of diachronic concerns regarding the history of traditions, then because of synchronic concerns regarding

Jewish and Early Christian religious systems.[18] Furthermore, following the History of Religions school, each insists that the Jewish documents be interpreted on their own terms, rather than from the distorted polemical perspective of the early Christian literature—as was too often the case with Paul Billerbeck.[19] This amounts to saying that critical interpretations must use Jewish categories to make sense of New Testament texts.

Other scholars carried this point further by implicitly or explicitly seeking to correct anti–Jewish interpretations through close attention to the categories used to make sense of New Testament texts, so as to ascertain that they actually are categories that belong to these texts. This is what I have tried to do in my structural interpretations of Paul's letters and of the Gospel according to Matthew,[20] by seeking to elucidate the basic system of "convictions" or semantic categories that structured Paul's and Matthew's respective faith and teaching. In short, I conclude that when these texts are interpreted in terms of the semantic categories inscribed in them neither Paul's nor Matthew's fundamental religious teaching is anti–Jewish.[21] Using different methods, Amy–Jill Levine reaches similar general conclusions regarding the Gospel according to Matthew through her elucidation of central semantic categories concerning Matthew's view of "sacred history."[22] She shows that sacred history is to be understood in terms of both a temporal and a social axis, rather than simply in terms of a temporal axis.[23] Then, through a careful examination of the social and ethnic dimensions of key passages of Matthew's Gospel, it becomes clear that this Gospel presents a polemic of Jesus against religious and political leaders, rather than against "the Jews."[24]

In sum, these critical studies (in this section) confirm and specify our conclusions regarding the first set of examples (in the previous section). They clarify the role of two specific interpretive processes: the choices of intertexts [25] and of epistemological categories, in terms of which one makes sense of the text. While each of these scholars would insist that the choices of intertexts and/or of epistemological categories were exclusively made through legitimacy judgments regarding textual and intertextual evidence,[26] it is difficult to deny that ideological concerns for anti-Jewish teachings also played a role in these choices, although possibly a subconscious one. The decision to take into account rather than to ignore Jewish literature as an intertext or to focus upon certain thematic categories (e.g., religious leadership as distinguished from the rest of the Jewish people)[27] clearly reflects a post-Holocaust concern (related to value judgments) in the very process of making sense of the text (through epistemology judgments).

Beyond the previous conclusions, through the focus of their hermeneutics of suspicion upon the interpretations themselves, the studies noted in this section suggest, although not without ambivalence, that ideology and "the religious" play a role in interpretation. As a component of the interpreter's ideology, anti-Judaism (and anti-Judaism) involves caricaturing other people's religious beliefs and practices by considering them in terms of one's own beliefs and practices, rather than in their own terms. Consequently, in order to avoid generating anti-Jewish interpretations, these studies affirm and respect the otherness of other people's religions—a critical practice of the History of Religions. It is quite appropriate to reject anti-Jewish ideologies. Yet, these studies implicitly or explicitly deny the role of an ideology in their own interpretations, as if the description of the otherness of the religious teaching of a text (be it Jewish or Christian text) was not necessarily done from a certain perspective or context. Thus, at the very point where these studies acknowledge that ideology plays a role in interpretation it is exclusively cast in a negative light, as something that good interpreters should transcend.

Actually, these interpretations implicitly respect, and thus are structured by, certain convictions frequently found among ordinary Christian believers; namely, the twofold conviction that according to which the New Testament texts have scriptural authority and that anti-Judaism is incompatible with Christianity. Affirming and respecting contemporary interpreters' convictions is consistent with affirming and respecting the convictions of a religious text, as above. This affirmation of contemporary interpreters' convictions is quite appropriate. This raises the question: Why should it not be an intrinsic part of biblical criticism?

One-Dimensional Practices and the Denial of Their Ideological Character

The effort of assessing the ways in which our biblical interpretations affect Jewish communities or individuals—an important ethical commitment—has begun to redefine the task and scope of biblical criticism in significant ways. It has contributed to the challenging of any notion of a clear distinction between detached critical studies of "what the text meant" and engaged hermeneutical studies of "what the text means." Yet much uncertainty regarding the role of ideology in critical interpretation remians, because much uncertainty regarding the relationship between detached and engaged practices of biblical criticism and thus between textual determinacy and indeterminacy remains. Two *Semeia* volumes devoted to this question reflect this lack of consensus.[28] These uncertainties raise central issues which need to be addressed, but also suggest that our critical practice needs to be envisioned from a very different perspective.

As I noted ten years ago, despite all our good intentions and our valiant efforts as Christian European–American scholars, critical studies of the New Testament such as those mentioned above do not succeed in preventing anti–Semitic readings and, in surreptitious ways, might even promote them.[29] This is due, I have suggested, to the "one–dimensional" character of these critical interpretations.[30] Whether it courageously confronts the dark side of New Testament texts or seeks to correct illegitimate interpretations and whatever sophisticated hermeneutical theory its methodology might involve, *in practice* each of these interpretations seeks to establish the (detached, single, universal) true meaning of the text.[31] They deny the role that interests, concerns, cultural contexts play in critical interpretations as in any other interpretation, and thus are "one-dimensional" according to the ideology of what Herbert Marcuse calls "advanced industrial societies."[32]

As a result, in each of the previous examples, the interpretation gives the appearance of encompassing the biblical text as a whole. Its conclusions about the teaching of the text are seemingly in smooth continuity with the text. Its positive or negative assessment of these conclusions and their implications appear natural: Who would not be revolted by anti-Judaism? Who would not be relieved to discover that after all a text is not anti-Jewish? Because of these well-intentioned efforts, *in practice* each of these interpretations presents "what the text is and says" as a self-contained text-object, as if it had not been constructed out of textual fragments and by smoothing out the rough edges and filling in the cracks. The interpretation presents "the meaningful teaching" of the text as a speech-act addressed to an original, historically given audience, as if it had not shaped the text by making sense of its polyvalent semantic features in terms of specific categories. The interpretation presents this teaching of the text as directly "meaningful for our lives" in a specific context, as if its presentation were not designed to manipulate our sense of value, our interests, and our concerns. In sum, these one-dimensional critical interpretations are problematic because *in practice* they fail to make explicit the interpretive processes involved in their articulation, including the role that ideologies play in constructing, shaping, and designing them.

The problem is not that ideologies play a role in our critical interpretations. According to Louis Althusser's definition, far from being a false consciousness, an "ideology represents the imaginary relationship of individuals to their real conditions of existence," which has "the function...of 'constituting' concrete individuals as subjects."[33] From this definition it is clear that no interpreter (as subject/agent of an interpretive practice) can develop an interpretation apart from an ideology. As Belsey underscores, "ideology is not an optional extra"; it is "the very condition of our experience in the world."[34] Therefore, in common sense interpretations, the role of ideology remains unconscious, unquestioned, taken for granted, and these interpretations are "obvious" and "natural." This, in itself, is to be expected. A problem arises when criticism denies the role of ideology in interpretations (and then is shaped by "the ideology of no ideology,"[35] instead of making it explicit.[36]

In such cases, biblical criticism is not truly critical. However when the practice of biblical criticism includes an assessment of the ways in which it affects Jewish communities, it can become critical. It cannot avoid exposing the role of ideology in common sense "anti-Jewish-interpretations-of-New-Testament-texts-as-authoritative-Scriptural-teaching." Then, it has to recognize that as long as it fails to acknowledge the role of ideology in its own interpretations, it is in no position to expose that of other readings. Thus despite our efforts to eradicate these repulsive readings, we reinforce the convictions of these common sense Christian readers that their interpretations are indeed obvious, natural, unquestionable, and authoritative. Why would these readers want to substitute for their "obviously right" interpretation (from their ideological perspective) a scholarly, detached, critical interpretation that seems (still from their perspective) "arbitrary," since it is not what the text obviously teaches, or that seems "biased and wrong," since it is in contradiction with what they see as authoritative? We sould not be surprised by this response. This is how common sense readers see our critical interpretations when we deny the role of ideology in our own readings or simply when we strive to be ideology-free. Indeed, we often reinforce their convictions that they should hold on to their anti-Jewish interpretation as authoritative teaching.

Making explicit the interpretive processes, including the role of ideologies, involved *in our own critical interpretations* is the way out of this dilemma. It is what ethical accountability in biblical interpretation requires from us.[37] But as I have emphasized, the implementation of this ethical obligation in our critical practices involves more than a self-conscious decision to devise a new methodology.[38] Since interpretive processes are normally taken for granted, obvious, natural—in brief, ideologically grounded—making them explicit, questioning their self-evidence, revealing their constructed character amounts to practicing biblical criticism according to another ideology.[39] As has been repeatedly said, this shift in practice involves a "shift in paradigm." According to Althusser's definition of ideology, this transformation is best described as a shift of "the imaginary relationship of individuals to their real conditions of existence." For believers, this kind of shift occurs in experiences of the holy as *mysterium tremendum.* In present secular European-American culture, one of the very rare collective experiences of the *tremendum* [40] is the Holocaust—even if it is a "*tremendum* of the abyss" [41]—provided of course that we stop long enough to meditate before it.

Redefining the Task and Scope of Biblical Criticism From the Perspective of the Holocaust

Assessing the ways in which critical biblical interpretations affect Jewish communities redefines the task of biblical criticism by revealing that critical <u>thinking</u> must account for the <u>Unthinkable</u>, the <u>tremendum</u> of the abyss, and consequently for the mysterious otherness of biblical texts and of their diverse interpretations.

Half a century afterward, it is awkward to have to acknowledge that, together with most Christian biblical scholars, I still grope for the implications of the Holocaust for our work. This delayed response is to be expected.[42] It takes time to come to the realization that these implications can only be envisioned when we accept that we actually need to stop our activism and, instead, meditate before the *Shoah,* the desolation,[43] abandon ourselves to the pain of this unthinkable horror, and consider our critical practices through the *tremendum* of the abyss. It takes time to realize that the *Shoah* is an earthquake of apocalyptic magnitude, which has shaken the very foundations of morality [44] and consequently of any praxis, including the practice of biblical criticism. [45] It takes even more time to recognize and to concede that critical biblical studies are close to the epicenter of this apocalyptic earthquake.

When one finally acknowledges that the earth shook, the rocks were split, and the veil of history was torn apart, [46] it becomes plainer that Christian biblical interpretations, an essential part of Christian moral teaching, are laced with anti-Judaism and share responsibility for the lethal anti-Judaism that engendered the death-camps—as the above mentioned studies have already recognized. It also becomes plainer that through our work we, Christian biblical scholars, [47] have contributed and continue to contribute to making the Crucified One the center of the cataclysm that engulfed European Jewry, as is poignantly represented in Marc Chagall's *White Crucifixion.* [48] During the entire period prior to and during the Holocaust, critical biblical studies, which because of their *Wissenschaft* had progressively become respected and influential, remained silent in splendid scientific detachment. *The sorrow and the pity* [49] experienced in the presence of "the desolation" of the *Shoah* teach us that detachment—be it for the sake of objectivity, for the pursuit of other duties, or because of indifference—is never neutral. Whenever and wherever anti-Judaism and anti-Judaism are fueled by Christian biblical interpretations—unfortunately, almost always and everywhere in Western cultures— detachment in critical biblical studies becomes an accomplice of this unthinkable crime.

Sorrow and pity permeate the hermeneutic of suspicion that we must adopt as we examine our practices as European-American biblical scholars because, at least in our contexts, critical biblical studies and Holocaust are closely intertwined. Our noblest endeavors contribute to generate what we execrate (See Romans 7:15-19). Unfortunately, this hellish vision of our work as critical biblical scholars is not a nightmare from which we will wake to a more pleasant reality. The unthinkable reality of the killing of six million men, women and children, each with his or her personal anguished face,[50] clings to Western critical biblical studies. The stench of death [51] seems to emanate, as we have seen, not only from the New Testament texts, their christologies [52] and theologies,[53] but also from the very core of critical biblical scholarship, namely its reading practices that condone the complicity of silence. The Holocaust radically challenges our critical practices and the very conception of criticism we hold as European-American Christian biblical scholars.

Denying Neither Engagement Nor Disengagement in Biblical Criticism: Meditating Before the Shoah

The radical implications of the Holocaust for biblical criticism begin to appear as soon as one remembers the broken glass of its beginning. *Kristallnacht* "testifies to a deeper breaking of basic human continuities." [54] When they are suspect of pursuing "what Hitler tried to accomplish—no more Jews," our one-dimensional interpretations and their smooth continuity break apart. We, scholars who use approaches born in Europe, must reexamine all aspects of our critical practice.

Most generally, the Holocaust demands both disengagement and engagement in scholarship. Against neo-Nazis who would deny that the Holocaust took place, a disengaged critical study that establishes its factualness is ever necessary. Yet, engagement is also necessary, since lack of engagement was the complicity that empowered the perpetrators. In the aftermath of the Holocaust, neither disengagement nor engagement can be excluded from critical biblical studies. When held together, both detached exegesis and engaged hermeneutics are transformed. They cannot be viewed as opposites; they are complementary processes in every act of interpretation; engagement and *disengagement* engender each other.[55]

Disengagement is necessary in order to recognize that anti-Jewish and anti-Semitic interpretations of New

Testament texts do accurately reflect something which is found in the texts—there are anti-Jewish features in these texts. But, as Daniel Boyarin underscores regarding Galatians 3:10-4:7, these texts are not simply anti-Jewish; they are both anti-Jewish and not anti-Jewish.[56] They give rise to interpretations which are anti-Jewish, but also to interpretations which are not anti-Jewish.

After *Kristallnacht*, disengagement requires from us not only to affirm the reality of the evidence (as that which has the power to affect readers) but also to question the continuity we perceive in the evidence by making explicit the legitimacy judgments through which we construct the text (what the text is) and its subject matter (what the text says). We follow the approach by which Peter Haas elucidates the constructed character of the various histories that nevertheless establish the factualness of the Holocaust.[57]

In this mode, disengagement presupposes engagement and calls for further engagement. The *Kristallnacht* breaking of the unified text-object studied with disengagement reveals that it is constructed by choosing certain features in a polyvalent text—that it presupposes engagement. Since there are several potential text-objects, any interpretation calls for engagement. In each case, we interpreters choose one constructed text-object among several potential ones because it makes sense in our cultural context (epistemology judgment) and because in a given situation it is particularly valuable for us, *pro nobis* (value judgment). In turn such *pro nobis* engagements in concrete life-situations require us to raise questions concerning the way people are affected by our interpretations. Then, despite the Western penchant toward individualism, my interpretation is never simply for me (*pro me*); it is also for others, who are affected by it and participate in it because their interests and values contribute to the basis for my interpretive choices.

Advocacy scholars have long claimed that engagement, contextualization and value judgments are components of any interpretation, including critical ones. But meditating before the Holocaust reveals in a particularly compelling way the significance and implications of the denials involved in a "detached" one-dimensional practice of biblical criticism that claims to be disengaged. Denying that disengagement is necessarily intertwined with engagement, description with contextualization, legitimacy judgments with epistemology and value judgments is not merely to deny unavoidable steps in the the interpretive process but also to deny that our historical situation demands engagement—that critical thought should be accountable for its social consequences.

Denial, suppression, repression, alienation transform the denied reality into a monster that destroys self and society. From Paul (Rom. 1:18-32) to the neo-marxist re-interpretations of Freud,[58] we have learned this is what happens when one denies a reality close to the core of human existence. Then we have to wonder: Is this how our well-intentioned, critical, biblical interpretations become dangerous, hellish? In such cases, is the reality that we are denying closely related to the core of our existence? Looking at our critical practices from the perspective of the Holocaust, we begin to can suspect that it is. After all, this denial, fueled by an obsession for the one-dimensional "security" of a detached, single, universally true interpretation, disavows our place in the interpretation, the *pro me* and *pro nobis* significance of the biblical text, the transforming power of the text upon us. It is therefore a denial of that which transcends us in the text and in the interpretation. When this reality of the core of our existence is denied, suppressed, repressed, it comes back and haunts us as a devouring monster. A monster such as the dragon spitting fire toward the little girl it will devour that can be seen in the self-portrait of one of the 15,000 children from the Prague ghetto drawn at the Theresienstadt camp in the days preceding her deportation to a death-*Lager*.

The questions are: What is, more specifically, this reality at the core of human experience that we deny in our practices? And How can we avoid denying it? As we pursue our mediation, we can hope that the *Shoah* will reveal to us this mysterious reality and how we can and should approach it. Then, the task and the scope of biblical criticism will be transformed.

Thinking the Unthinkable
and Accounting for the Holy:
Meditating Before the Shoah

Arthur Cohen locates himself within the realm of the Holocaust, as an insider with a clear sense of its boundaries: the rabbinic tradition as Jewish reality; the Christian tradition; and the end of religious tradition, as proclaimed by the radical secular interpreters of the Holocaust.[59] He describes his project thus: "I take boundaries as boundaries. What lies before me is the undertaking of making clearer what takes place within their confines."[60] What takes place within these boundaries, he concludes, is the contemporary Jewish experience of the *tremendum.*

The unavoidable struggle for meaning within these confines—how can one "live with it"?[61]—takes the form of theological reflections. This mode of critical analysis is chosen with the full awareness of

> the inadequacy of theology – the fact that its object can be formulated but never grasped, that its language approaches its object but can never exhaust it, that beyond every formulation of theological language the mystery of the living God remains.[62]

Theological reflections are uniquely fitting, because the Holocaust as *tremendum* can be "formulated but never grasped" or exhausted, because "beyond every formulation" its mystery remains. A theological language that keeps in mind its inadequacy is alone appropriate for an experience of the Holy as *mysterium tremendum,* even if it is the *tremendum* of the abyss.

The Holocaust can only be expressed in theological language even as it constantly reveals the limits of such language, which cannot encompass it. As such the Holocaust gives us, in this secular age, an experience of the Holy. "We of the modern age [who] are no longer able to deal with the Holy, cannot perceive it, or authenticate it"[63] can once again perceive, authenticate, and deal with the Holy, and be shaken to our foundations by it, even though it is an inverted *tremendum.* The death camps are the *tremendum* despite this inversion, as Cohen insists:

> I call the death camps the *tremendum,* for it is the monument of a meaningless inversion of life to an orgiastic celebration of death, to a psychosexual and pathological degeneracy unparalleled and unfathomable to any person bonded to life.[64]

The *tremendum* is a caesura, a rupture in Jewish history which unlike the Christian caesura "emerge[s] from below, a verticality as infernal as incarnation may be divine."[65]

Because "the *tremendum* marks an end" which "augurs a beginning,"[66] it calls into question the continuity with past and future. Yet the traditions are not excluded; they are transfigured. "The challenge of the *tremendum* to Judaism is not that traditional reality cannot survive the scrutiny of its teaching...but rather that its view of its own depths will be found shallow, insufficiently deep and flexible enough to compass and contain the *tremendum.*"[67] Thus, all that can be done is to build a bridge above the abyss. This bridge must be built with the material at hand in the history of Jewish tradition; hermeneutics of retrieval, as David Tracy notes in the "Foreword."[68] Yet, the very construction of this bridge makes the abyss ever visible. Thus, for Cohen, a hermeneutic of suspicion is in order, as he examines each piece of the tradition against the background of the *tremendum.* The ever present and mysterious abyss exposes the inadequacy of these traditions, their shallowness and their lack of flexibility; it is futile to think that any tradition could encompass and master the *tremendum.* Indeed, the *Shoah* brings to light that it is fundamentally wrong to claim that any tradition—and thus also any biblical text and *a fortiori* any given interpretation of it—could encompass and master the *tremendum,* whether it is the "transcending" *tremendum* of divine mystery or the "subscending" *tremendum* of the abysmal mystery (Tracy's vocabulary).[69] Before the awful mystery of the *Shoah,* the Jewish philosopher is freed from the temptation to absolutize either traditions or thinking and reason—their limitations are plain.

These traditions (and by extension, these biblical texts and their interpretations) can nevertheless become excellent building material for constructing a bridge over the abyss, *provided that their limitations remain exposed by the Shoah.* The Holocaust painfully reveals that the lack of recognition, the denial, or the suppression of the limitations of the sacred traditions (as well as of biblical texts and of their interpretations) is a fundamental source of evil. The abyss, "the meaningless inversion of life," occurs and is perpetuated when the human is infinitized; when death is denied by "build[ing] a mountain of corpses to the divinity of the dead, to placate death by the magic of endless murder." [70] The abyss also occurs, for instance, when the ultimate is confused with the final; when the *tremendum* is viewed as final, something it is not, although "it is ultimate because it comprehends and articulates all negativity and contradiction;" [71] when "what is taken as God's speech" (in the Bible) is viewed as final, although it "is really always [hu]man's hearing," thus ultimate; when God is taken as the final "strategist of our historical condition," although God as ultimate is "the mystery of our futurity." [72]

In sum, from the inside, Cohen underscores that the *tremendum* of the abyss is rooted in the thoughtlessness that fails to account for the constructed character of all that we perceive as significant. Thus he opens his theological reflections by observing that the Holocaust belongs together with "confounded" thinking, since it is unthinkable.

> Thinking and the death camps are incommensurable. The procedures of thought and the ways of knowing are confounded. It is to think the unthinkable—an enterprise that is not alone contradictory but hopeless—for thought entails as much a moral hope (that it may be triumphant, mastering its object, dissolving the difficulties, containing and elucidating the conundrum) as it is the investment of skill and dispassion in a methodic procedure.[73]

Redefining
the Task of Biblical Criticism
in a Post-Holocaust Perspective

These brief quotations and selected reflections by Cohen, an insider, are but a few of the many insights that his work offers to us, outsiders, who seek to forge a meaningful connection to the Holocaust, without trivializing and reducing its scandal.[74] Yet these are enough to reveal the glaring gap in the practice of biblical criticism by Christian European-American scholars: *our critical interpretations do NOT account for the Holy as <u>tremendum</u>.* This is the reality of the core of human experience that our interpretations deny with dire consequences.

As people "of the modern age [who] are no longer able to deal with the Holy, cannot perceive it, or authenticate it,"[75] by ourselves we have no clue regarding how a practice of biblical criticism could account for the Holy. When this issue is raised we revert to the debate regarding disengagement and engagement, as we ponder how to deal with the Holy as *mysterium tremendum et fascinans* that we relegate to the general domain of "feelings."[76] How could we account for something which is beyond our grasp and merely felt?

But Cohen resolves our confusion. Accounting for the Holy does not mean encompassing it. This is why one can think the Unthinkable. Accounting for the Holy involves acknowledging the inadequacy of language, and thus the inadequacy of all interpretations.

Thus the first lesson from Cohen is that we, European-American biblical scholars, must acknowledge that we are commonly driven by the false confidence that there is nothing beyond the reach of critical thought. Following Cohen we can denounce the triumphalism of critical thought in biblical studies that posits as its task "mastering its object, dissolving the difficulties, containing and elucidating the conundrum." All the one-dimensional quest implied in this view of critical thinking breaks into pieces against the Holocaust.

Consequently, we can no longer trust that biblical criticism will overcome all obstacles and triumphantly master the biblical texts and their significance. This is not a loss, but a gain.

Acknowledging the inability of biblical criticism to encompass the Holy is not a matter of abandoning positivistic illusions and of confessing that our critical interpretations merely have relative legitimacy, since they "must be seen as claiming only a greater or a lesser degree of probability and as always open to revision." [77] We have done this for a long time, without abandoning the false confidence that there is nothing beyond the reach of this non-positivist critical thought.

Similarly, it is not a matter of denying any usefulness to biblical criticism, because all interpretations are inadequate, because we are unable to establish with certainty the significance of biblical texts, and thus because of a subjective relativism none can be viewed as more authoritative than another. For Cohen, as for Fackenheim, giving up the possibility of meaningful thinking and becoming nihilist would be "to hand Hitler yet another, posthumous victory." [78] In the same way that the Holocaust does not deny the value of the Jewish traditions simply because it has shown them unable to encompass the Holy, so we cannot deny the traditions of biblical criticism.

Rather, when our critical interpretations acknowledge their inadequacy, at last they fully perform their task by making explicit the presence of the Holy. Indeed, by making explicit that they are totally unable to get hold of and encompass the *tremendum*, our interpretations also take note of, and thus account for, the presence of the *tremendum*, instead of ignoring it, denying it, or suppressing it. It is by such an acknowledgment that Cohen thoughtfully accounts for the Unthinkable as Unthinkable, as *tremendum*.

But, concretely, what does this mean for our practice of biblical criticism as Christian European-Americans? Obviously, a general, blanket acknowledgment of the inadequacy of our interpretations is not what is called for. (In such a case, Cohen's book would have ended with its first page!) Each of our specific interpretations needs to make explicit the points where it loses grip, where it can no longer stay in control, where it encounters issues that it cannot resolve or elucidate. Yet, the boundaries set around the sacred space of the Holy[79] by the limitations of our critical interpretations must still be authenticated. We might point to the inadequacies of our interpretations that are due to a lack of skill, a methodological flaw, or simply to laziness.

Once again we, secular modern people, need to turn toward the Holocaust to learn how to perceive and authenticate the place of the Holy in critical biblical interpretations.

Much could be said here without clarifying anything for those who have not yet been confronted by the Holocaust, who have not yet been forced by it to stop painfully silent, shaken to the core because nothing makes sense anymore, who have not yet found themselves meditating before the pointless suffering of the *Shoah*. Yet for those who have had this experience, my evocation of Cohen's description of the Jewish experience of the *Shoah* as *tremendum* should be sufficient to point out where Christian European-American biblical scholars can expect to encounter the *tremendum*.

First, the biblical texts as religious texts account for experiences of the *tremendum*. This does not mean that our critical interpretations should seek to elucidate their "religious content"—the Word of God as a fixed teaching from God. Meditating before the *Shoah* makes it clear that biblical texts cannot contain the *tremendum* any more than any other text. Nevertheless, a biblical text as a religious text accounts for the *tremendum*; re-presents the powerful and transforming experience its encounter was for its author; remains marked by it; and is "ultimate" (rather than "infinite," as Cohen undersores). In other words, the text is Word of God because it brings its readers into the presence of the *tremendum*, an encounter with a transforming power.

The author's as well as the readers' experiences of the *tremendum*—which cannot be expected to coincide with each other—are always beyond that which is presented by the text. No experience of the *tremendum* can ever be encompassed, mastered or controlled. Yet biblical criticism should not exclude these experiences of the *tremendum*. One of its primary tasks is to account for them.

A Practice of Biblical Study that Needs the Perspective of Jewish Communities to Be Critical

When it is agreed that our task as Christian biblical scholars includes accounting for the mysterious presence of the *tremendum* toward which the text points. Difficulties arise when we seek to envision how to proceed.

In our meditation before the Holocaust, we have learned from Cohen that practicing this aspect of biblical criticism—accounting for the *tremendum*—involves acknowledging that our interpretations cannot encompass the *tremendum*, the sacred, the Holy that is re-presented by the text. But, such an acknowledgment is not in itself a critical practice.

Does this mean that we should envision a critical practice that would allow us to get hold of something about the *tremendum*, the sacred, the Holy, and then acknowledge that the interpretations that result from such a practice do not encompass its object, the *tremendum*? This was my first impulse. In order to carry out this additional task, biblical criticism should identify as many of the characteristics of the experience(s) of the *tremendum* represented by the text as possible, for instance by using History of Religions tools, such as ritual analysis, [80] and by raising questions such as: What characterizes the *tremendum* represented by the text? Is it an experience of the "*tremendum* of the abyss"? An experience of "the *mysterium tremendum* of God"? Or any other experience of the *tremendum*?

This is what Lüdemann did by elucidating the "unholy in holy scriptures"; [81] and what Burnett did by elucidating the ideology of a biblical text. [82] Furthermore, with Burnett, we could elucidate the constructed character of this ideology, which is, after all the ideology of the implied author, constructed in order to manipulate the readers into adopting it for their daily lives. This seems a proper way of accounting for what has mysterious power upon and transcends the readers. In the aftermath of the Holocaust, such an hermeneutic of suspicion is appropriate. "Infinitizing" the finite—taking the constructed anti-Jewish theology and ideology of Matthew as complete and final authority—is an ever present danger. We have learned that if each experience of the *tremendum* is ultimate, none is "final." Thus we must underscore that the ideology of the text is nothing but a limited representation that cannot encompass the *tremendum* toward which it points.

But I had to conclude that all this would be an inappropriate practice of the redefined task of biblical criticism. As our preceding discussion of Lüdemann's and Burnett's works shows, the danger is always that, as one goes on and on in one's description of characteristics of the experience of the *tremendum* represented by the text, one feels more and more in control. As a consequence, one is on a path toward denial. Even when, as Burnett does, one points out the constructed character of the ideology proposed by the text (in order to empower readers to reject it), one forcefully affirms that one's interpretation is legitimate and thus that it "gets hold of and encompasses" primary characteristics of the experience of the *tremendum* represented by the text—its ideology "is" anti-Semitic; it "is" unholy. Then, as one fails to take into account that the religious, the ideological, the holy of the text is in fact the re-presentation of an experience of the *tremendum* that neither the text nor our interpretation can get hold of and encompass, because it is always beyond us, one quickly overlooks, neglects, forgets, suppresses, and denies the *tremendum* itself. Once again one ends up with a one-dimensional interpretation, denying this reality of the core of human existence in the New Testament texts, in one's own critical practice, and then, ultimately, in one's life. Once again one runs the risk of being haunted by a monster rising out of this denial.

The terrified and resigned face of a little girl before a fiery dragon at Theresienstadt demands from us, Christian European-American scholars, that our critical biblical interpretations of New Testament texts account for the Holy, the religious, the experiences of the *tremendum*, the ideologies of these texts—in sum, all that which elicit from Christian believers the confession: these texts are Scriptures, Canon, Word of God. Yet, knowing that we must do so is not enough. We still need to understand how to do it, by elucidating the conditions of possibility for doing it. Further meditations before the *Shoah* are required.

A way of insuring that a practice of biblical interpretation is critical and ethically responsible is to broaden its scope to include other readers. When we read *with* Others, especially with Others who belong to other religious communities, they reveal to us the specificity of our interpretation and awaken us to the surplus of meaning our interpretations cannot encompass. Reading New Testament texts (and other biblical texts) in the presence of the Jewish communities—as André LaCocque taught us to do—cannot but make us aware that these texts will always have a surplus of meaning that our interpretations cannot encompass, that we cannot know, because it remains ever beyond our reach. Then, our interpretations will account for the presence of the Holy even as they respect the variety of experiences of the *tremendum*. Then, our practices of interpretation will account for this dimension of the texts that we study, as a critical study should.

Endnotes

[1] Peter J. Haas, "What We Know Today That We Didn't Know Fifty Years Ago: Fifty Years of Holocaust Scholarship," *CCAR Journal: A Reform Jewish Quarterly* (Summer/Fall 1995): 5.

[2] Krister Stendahl, "Biblical Theology," in *The Interpreters Dictionary of the Bible*, vol. 1 (Nashville: Abingdon, 1962), 418-432. This is Stendahl's well known distinction between critical study regarding "what the text meant" and hermeneutics regarding "what the text means."

[3] Kendrick Grobel, "Interpretation, History and Principles of," in *The Interpreters Dictionary of the Bible*, vol. 2 (Nashville: Abingdon, 1962): 724.

[4] Ibid., 718-724.

[5] Van A. Harvey, *The Historian and the Believer: The Morality of Historical Knowledge and Christian Belief* (New York: Macmillan Company, 1966).

[6] Ibid., 164-203; John B. Cobb Jr. and James M. Robinson, eds., *The New Hermeneutic* (New York: Harper & Row, 1964).

[7] Hans-Georg Gadamer, *Wahrheit und Methode* (Tübingen: J. C. B. Mohr, 1960); and its English translation, *Truth and Method* (New York: Seabury Press, 1975).

[8] Samuel Sandmel, *Anti-Semitism in the New Testament?* (Philadelphia: Fortress, 1978); Alan T. Davies, ed., *Antisemitism and the Foundations of Christianity: Twelve Christian Theologians Explore the Development and Dynamics of Antisemitism within the Christian Tradition.* (New York: Paulist, 1979); Peter Richardson, David Granskou, and Stephen G. Wilson, eds., *Anti-Judaism in Early Christianity: V. 1. Paul and the Gospels — V. 2. Separation and Polemic* (Waterloo, Ontario, Canada: Wilfrid Laurier University Press, 1986).

[9] Gerd Lüdemann, *The Unholy in the Holy Scripture: The Dark Side of the Bible*, trans. J. Bowden (Louisville: Westminster/John Knox, 1997).

[10] Rosemary Ruether, *Faith and Fratricide: The Theological Roots of Anti-Semitism* (New York: Seabury Press, 1974); and, following her, most of the contributors to Davies, ed., *Antisemitism*, and Richardson et al., edss., *Anti-Judaism*.

[11] Lüdemann, 117-124.

[12] Fred W. Burnett, "Exposing the Anti-Jewish Ideology of Matthew's Implied Author: The Characterization of God as Father" in *Ideological Criticism of Biblical Texts, Semeia 59*, edited by David Jobling and Tina Pippin (Atlanta: Society of Biblical Literature, 1992), 156.

[13] Ibid., 174.

[14] For the distinction among "value judgments," "epistemology judgments," and "legitimacy judgments" as three distinct interpretive processes in each interpretation, see Daniel Patte, *Discipleship According to the Sermon on the Mount: Four Legitimate Readings, Four Plausible Views of Discipleship, and Their Relative Values* (Valley Forge, Pennsylvania: Trinity Press International, 1996), 11-28.

[15] Daniel Patte, *Ethics of Biblical Interpretation: A Reevaluation* (Louisville: Westminster/John Knox Press, 1995).

[16] Patte, *Discipleship*, 11-28.

[17] Joseph Bonsirven, S.J., *Exégèse rabbinique et exégèse paulinienne* (Paris: Beauchesne, 1939); idem, *Textes rabbiniques des deux premiers siècles chrétiens, pour servir à l'intelligence du Nouveau Testament* (Rome:

Pontificio Istituto Biblico, 1955); idem, *Palestinian Judaism in the time of Jesus Christ,* trans. William Wolf (New York: Holt, Rinehart and Winston, 1964); William David Davies, *The Setting of the Sermon on the Mount* (Cambridge: Cambridge University Press, 1966); idem, *Paul and Rabbinic Judaism: Some Rabbinic Elements in Pauline Theology* (New York: Harper & Row, 1967); Otto Betz, *Die Eschatologie in der Glaubensunterweisung* (Würzburg: Echter, 1965); idem, *What Do We Know about Jesus?,* trans. Margaret Kohl (London: S.C.M., 1968); Krister Stendahl, *The school of St. Matthew, and its use of the Old Testament. With a new introduction by the author* (Philadelphia, Fortress, 1968); idem, *Paul among Jews and Gentiles, and other essays* (Philadelphia: Fortress, 1976); Robin Scroggs, *The Last Adam: a Study in Pauline Anthropology* (Philadelphia: Fortress, 1966); and E. P. Sanders, *Paul and Palestinian Judaism: a Comparison of Patterns of Religion* (Philadelphia: Fortress, 1977).

[18] Sanders.

[19] Paul Billerbeck and Hermann L. Strack, *Kommentar zum Neuen Testament aus Talmud und Midrasch* (München: Beck.Billerbeck, 1922).

[20] Daniel Patte, *Paul's Faith and the Power of the Gospel* (Philadelphia: Fortress Press, 1983); idem, *The Gospel according to Matthew: A Structural Commentary on Matthew's Faith,* ([Philadelphia: Fortress Press, third printing, 1996] Valley Forge, Pennsylvania: Trinity Press International, 1987).

[21] Patte, *Paul's Faith,* 87-120; and idem, *Discipleship,* 358-396.

[22] Amy-Jill Levine, *The Social and Ethnic Dimensions of Matthean Salvation History* (Lewiston, New York: E. Mellen Press, 1988), 11.

[23] Ibid., 1-57, passim.

[24] One of Levine's main theses, summarized Ibid., 273-278; see also Anthony J. Saldarini, *Matthew's Christian-Jewish Community* (Chicago: University of Chicago Press, 1994).

[25] see George Aichele and Gary A. Phillips, *Intertextuality and the Bible, Semeia 69/70* (Atlanta: Scholars, 1995).

[26] I include myself , among the scholars who have such reactions, even though I believe we are now in a position to go beyond them. See my *Paul's Faith* and *Matthew.*

[27] see Levine; the same could be said about my choice of more abstract epistemological categories (e.g. typological patterns in Paul's letters [Patte, *Paul's Faith*] and how the will to act is established according to Matthew [Patte, *Matthew*]).

[28] Robert C. Culley and Robert B. Robinson, eds., *Textual Determinacy: Part One, Semeia 62* (Atlanta: Scholars Press, 1993); Robert B.

Robinson and Robert C. Culley, eds., *Textual Determinacy: Part Two, Semeia 71* (Atlanta: Scholars Press, 1995).

29 Daniel Patte, "Anti-Semitism in the New Testament: Confronting the Dark Side of Paul's and Matthew's Teaching." in *Chicago Theological Seminary Register* 78 (1988): 31-52.

30 As I further explain in Patte, *Ethics.*

31 This happens as the interpretation is developed and presented in order to convince its intended audience—including other scholars as well as, ultimately, people who hold anti-Jewish interpretations. In order to demonstrate its legitimacy, plausibility and validity, each of the above interpretations strives to ground its conclusions on solid textual evidence, to make sense of the text with explanations that account for all the textual features, and even to clarify its positive or negative implications for the relationship between Jews and Christians.

32 Herbert Marcuse, *One-Dimensional Man: Studies in the Ideology of Advanced Industrial Society* (Boston: Beacon, 1964), 12.

33 Louis Althusser, *Essays on Ideology* (London: Verso, 1984), 36, 45. For me, Althusser's definition of ideology makes sense, because it is a structuralist reformulation of the Marxist concept, because his definition can be applied to science, and thus to biblical criticism, and also because it can be related to the religious experience of the *tremendum.* For a critical analysis of Althusser's view, which also shows its relationship to Levi-Strauss's view of mythical structure, see Larrain, 154-164; see also Althusser, 130-211.

34 Catherine Belsey, *Critical Practice* ([Sixth printing, London and New York: Routledge, 1992] London and New York: Methuen, 1980), 5.

35 Fred Inglis, *Ideology and the Imagination* (London: Cambridge University Press, 1975), 55-58.

36 Belsey, 1-7; 124-146.

37 Elisabeth Schüssler Fiorenza, "The Ethics of Interpretation: De-Centering Biblical Scholarship," *Journal Of Biblical Literature,* 107 (1988): 3-17.

38 Patte, *Ethics.*

39 This new ideology will, of course, need to be made explicit.

40 I presuppose without further analysis that in this culture the experience of the *tremendum* is usually in individual spiritual experiences and that the Holocaust challenges this presupposition. On the complex issue of the experience of the *tremendum* in Western secular culture, see Gabriel Vahanian, *No Other God,* (New York: Braziller, 1966); idem, *L'utopie chrétienne* (Paris: Desclée de Brouwer, 1992), as well as his other books.

41 Arthur A.Cohen, *The Tremendum: A Theological Interpretation of the Holocaust* (New York: Crossroad, 1981).

42 Ibid., 2-3; Haas, "What We Know." Haas and Cohen provide similar explanations. Cohen's are more pertinent for my present concern. He explains this delay as he ponders the implications of the Holocaust for one's behavior by noting that it took one decade for the statistical accounting and historical description of the facts, one decade to provide in literature a "vivifying witness to the flesh of the dead and the mortal objectivity of the statistics" (for instance in Elie Wiesel's *Night*). During the third and fourth decades, the question of the meaning of the Holocaust could begin to be raised, with the increasing realization that this involves thinking the un-thinkable, the *mysterium tremendum*. Thus, it is not surprising that it is only during the fifth decade that one might be able to begin to think about implications.

43 The terms *Shoah* refers to the time of "desolation."

44 See Peter J. Haas, *Morality after Auschwitz : the Radical Challenge of the Nazi Ethic* (Philadelphia : Fortress, 1988). How could the foundation of morality not be shaken when the Holocaust is perpetrated by people — Nazis — whose actions conform to their ethical system, the Nazi Ethic.

45 I bring together insights gained from conversations with André LaCocque in 1996 and 1997.

46 Matthew 27:51; Enzo Traverso, *L'histoire déchirée: Essai sur Auschwitz et les intellectuels* (Paris: Cerf, 1996).

47 This comment also applies to scholars who, in Germany, resisted the rise of Nazism in their private lives, and today to those who deny the Christian character of their interpretations.

48 Art Institute of Chicago. See the description of this 1938 painting in terms of the Holocaust by Karl A. Plank, *Mother of the Wire Fence: Inside and Outside the Holocaust* (Louisville: Westminster/John Knox, 1994), 141-144.

49 As Marcel Ophuls has illustrated in his motion picture, *Le chagrin et la pitié.*

50 It is true that in the death camps, the killing was highly depersonalized in the gas-chambers. But as Browning in Christopher R. Browning, *Ordinary Men: Reserve Police Battalion 101 and the Final Solution in Poland* (New York: HarperCollins, 1992) has documented, about half of the six millions Jews were killed in a more personal way; they were gunned down with revolvers as well as machine guns; they were let to die of deprivation in ghettos or of exhaustion in labor camps. While the depersonalized, systemic character of evil in the Holocaust should not be forgotten, its personalized character must also be

accounted for. Then, the unthinkable horror of the Holocaust can be more directly perceived, in comparison to horrible tragedy occurring in our present—such as the Oklahoma City bombing and its 168 victims, whose stories fill the newspapers at the time I write (during the trial of the accused perpetrator). A few personal faces of victims of the Holocaust are the subject matter of Plank, *Mother of the Wire Fence*—see the faces in the photograph on which this book meditates (title page).

[51] As I continue to meditate on Chagall's *White Crucifixion*—the Crucified One as center of the Holocaust cataclysm—the ambivalence of our reading practices in critical biblical studies as applied to christological texts reminds me of Paul's observation that his Christian testimony was "read" in opposite ways by different people: "For we are the aroma of Christ…to the one a fragrance from death to death, to the other a fragrance from life to life" (2 Corinthians 2:15-16).

[52] Ruether, 246, *passim*.

[53] Burnett.

[54] Plank, 141.

[55] I use *"disengagement"* rather than "detachment," because the latter could be a process independent from "engagement."

[56] Daniel Boyarin, *A Radical Jew: Paul and the Politics of Identity* (Berkeley: University of California Press, 1994), 136-157. Boyarin's detailed discussion can be summarized by these concluding sentences: "Paul's hermeneutic of the Jews as signifier of the faithful body of Christians, of the Jews as the literal *kata sarka* of which Christians are the allegorical signified, *kata pneuma*, even if not the "origin of anti-Judaism,"certainly has effects in the world until this day. In other words, I argue that while Galatians is not an anti-Judaic text, its theory of the Jews nevertheless is one that is inimical to Jewish difference, indeed to all difference as such" (156). Note that I use "anti-Jewish" in the sense of Boyarin's "anti-Judaic" to designate a rejection of the Jews as Jewish believers and thus as a rejection of Judaism.

[57] Haas, "What We Know," 6-12. Haas surveys these histories from the monolithic descriptions of "the banality of evil" in an anonymous machinery of destruction (the bureaucratic evil of Adolph Eichmann and of the death camps, with a focus on the perpetrators' perspective; e.g., see Arendt) to the presentation of the *Shoah* as the result of a myriad of individual decisions (with a focus on the diverse experiences of the victims).

[58] see Patte, *Paul's Faith*, 256-277, 382.

[59] Arthur A.Cohen, *The Tremendum: A Theological Interpretation of the Holocaust* (New York: Crossroad, 1981), 57-58.

[60] Ibid., 58.

[61] Ibid., 3.

[62] Ibid., 61.

[63] Ibid., 18.

[64] Ibid., 19; see also 98.

[65] Ibid., 52-53.

[66] Ibid., 59.

[67] Ibid., 82.

[68] Ibid., x.

[69] Ibid., vii.

[70] Ibid., 19.

[71] Ibid., 49.

[72] Ibid., 97; see also Vahanian, *No Other God* and idem, *L'utopie chrétienne*

[73] Cohen, 1.

[74] Plank, 2.

[75] Cohen, 18.

[76] Rudolf Otto, *The Idea of the Holy: An inquiry into the non-rational factor in the idea of the divine and its relation to the rational*, trans. John W. Harvey (New York: Oxford University Press, 1923), quoted from the 1958 Galaxy Book edition, 41-49. This is true however one might translate *Gefühle.* For a sophisticated mapping out of this domain of "feelings, " see David R. Blumenthal, *Facing the Abusing God: A Theology of Protest* (Louisville: Westminster/John Knox, 1993), 23-31.

[77] Harvey, 14..

[78] Emil Fackenheim, *The Jewish Thought of Emil Fackenheim: A Reader*, ed. Michael L. Morgan (Detroit: Wayne State University Press, 1987), 159.

[79] See Cohen, 58.

[80] See Mark McVann, ed., *Transformations, Passages, and Processes: Ritual Approaches to Biblical Texts, Semeia 73* (Atlanta: Scholars, 1995).

[81] Lüdemann.

[82] Burnett.

Chapter 10

An Overlooked Double Entendre in Jonah 2:5

Shalom Paul

Professor LaCocque's analysis of the book of Jonah, *The Jonah Complex* (co-authored with his son, Pierre-Emmanuel LaCocque),[1] in which he combines his exegetical skills along with theological, hermeneutical, and psychological insights, is a significant contribution to the multi-dimensional interpretation of the prophet's message. Here I would like to offer one small literary note, which sheds additional light on one of the verses of the psalm in chapter two, aptly called a "musical pause" by LaCocque.[2] According to the psalm, Jonah, after having been tossed into the depths of the sea, exclaims: "You cast me into the depths, into the heart of the sea. The flood engulfed me. All your breakers and bellows swept over me" (vs. 4). "The waters closed in over me; the deep engulfed me. Weeds twined around my head" (vs. 6). In the intervening verse (vs. 5) we hear the desperate and despairing meditation of the drowning man: "I thought I was thrust (נגרשׁתי)out of your sight. Would I ever gaze again upon Your holy Temple?" This verse has been often compared to two similar ones: Ps 31:23, "Alarmed, I had thought, 'I am thrust out (נגרזתי) of your sight'"; and, even more appropriate thematically because of the water motif, Lam 3:54, "Waters flowed over my head; I said, 'I am lost' (נגזרתי)."

In Jonah, however, neither the root גרז nor גזר[3] is employed, but rather גרש. Though this verb, which means "to be thrust out, banished," fits the situation well, it should be noted that it also appears three other times in "maritime" contexts: Isa 57:20, "But the wicked are like the troubled (נגרש) sea, which cannot rest, whose waters toss up (ויגרשו)[4] mire and mud"; Amos 8:8, "Shall not the earth shake for this.... Shall it not all rise like the Nile and surge (ונגרשה) and subside like the Nile of Egypt?" And, as has been insightfully demonstrated by Blau, the verb in these latter two verses is not to be connected with גרש,[5] but rather is derived from a homonymous root describing the tossing, swirling, and surging of the sea.[6] So, too, the substantive in Ezek 27:21: "And the outcry of your pilots, the billows (מגרשות) shall heave." Further attestation for its occurrence may be adduced from the Hodayot Hymns from Qumran.[7]

> 1QH II (= X):12-13:
> "The assembly of the wicked is roused against me. They roar like the turbulence of the seas when their billows rage (בהרגש) and stir up (יגרישו)[8] mud and mire."
>
> 1QH III (= XI):32:
> "The schemers of the deep roar with the din of those stirring up (גורשי) mud."
>
> IQH VIII (= XVI):14-15:
> "But I had become the mockery of the raging torrents, which stir up (גרשו) their mire over me."

The verb is also found in rabbinic Hebrew; see Sifre, Deuteronomy 39; Yalqut Shim'oni 859: "You might suppose the (rain) water will stir up (גורסיו) the (fat) ground of the valley...." See also Midrash Alpha–Beta de Rabbi 'Aqiba, in: A. Jellinek, *Bet ha–Midrash,* vol. III (Jerusalem, 1938), p. 13 (Heb.), for the expression: "its waters stir up (מתגרשים) mud and mire."[9]

Now, then, we can better appreciate the clever *double entendre* of Jonah 2:5. The author has Jonah plaintively declare that he was "banished" (נגרשתי) from God's presence. But in the present context between vs. 4 (which describes his drowning in the "depths, into the heart of the sea. The flood engulfed me. All your breakers and bellows swept over me") and vs. 6 (which emphasizes the "waters" and "the deep"), his choice of this particular verb, whose homonymous root also connotes the turbulent undulation of waves tossing and turning, swirling and surging all about him, adds a poignant descriptive dimension to his distressful cry.

Notes

[1] André LaCocque and Pierre-E. LaCocque, *The Jonah Complex* (Atlanta: John Knox, 1981).

[2] It is not my intention to deal with the problem of the presence of the psalm here. The literary point made in this article is independent of the original or, most likely, secondary nature of the composition.

[3] For an analysis of these two roots and their respective renderings in the ancient translations, see L. Delekat, "Zum hebraïschen Wörterbuch," *Vetus Testamentum* 14 (1964): 11 -13.

[4] IQIs[a] has a variant reading in the *hithpa'el*, יתגרשו.

[5] *HAL*, vol. I, p. 196.

[6] J. Blau, "Uber Homonyme und angeblich Homonyme Wurzeln, I," *Vestus Testamentum* 6 (1956): 245-246, who also compares Arabic *bahr maÓgãr*, "an undulating sea." The correct meaning of this verb was already noted by Y. ibn Ganah, *Sepher Haschoraschim*, ed. W. Bacher (Berlin, 1896), 101 (Heb.), and by H. Yalon, in his review of E.L. Sukenik's *Dead Sea Scrolls*, in *Kiryath Sepher* 26 (1950): 246 (Heb.).

[7] It is obvious that all these references are influenced by the verse in Isaiah 57:20. The first references to the Hodayot passages are taken from J. Licht, *The Thanksgiving Scroll* (Jerusalem, 1957) (Heb.); the ones in parentheses are from F.G. Martinez, *The Dead Sea Scrolls Translated* (Leiden, 1994).

[8] Note the unique use of the *hiph'il* tense.

[9] Compare also Samaritan גרושה, "waves," in A.E. Cowley, *The Samaritan Liturgy* (Oxford, 1909), 262, 263.

Chapter 11

Christology After the Shoah

John T. Pawlikowski

The last several decades have witnessed a remarkable rethinking of Jesus' involvement with the Jewish community of his time. Some of that new research has concentrated on the roots of Jesus' spirituality and ministry in the Hebrew Scriptures and their reinterpretation in Second Temple Judaism. Scholars such as James Charlesworth and Anthony Saldarini have turned their attention to this dimension. Others have examined the basic statement of the relationship between Jews and Christians in light of Jesus' public ministry, death and resurrection. The scholar we honor in this *festschrift*, André LaCocque, has contributed important studies to this aspect of the question, especially his volume, *But As For Me*.[1] I have addressed both areas in several of my published works.[2]

In this contribution I would like to examine a dimension of Christological thinking that has not received a great deal of attention to date. I speak of the impact of the Holocaust on how we understand the meaning of the Christ Event as Christians. Some within the Christian community may find it strange to raise the issue at all. What possible connection can there be? My response in the first instance is that of Johannes Metz who has insisted, quite rightly I believe, that the Holocaust affects all theological perceptions, not only the theology of the Christian–Jewish relationship. Metz proposes three theses as indispensable for theological reflections: (1) "Christian theology after Auschwitz must...be guided by the insight that Christians can form and sufficiently understand their identity only in the face of Jews"; (2) "Because of Auschwitz, the statement 'Christians can only form and appropriately understand their identity in the face of the Jews' has been sharpened as follows: 'Christians can protect their identity only in front of and together with the history of the beliefs of the Jews'"; and (3) "Christian theology after Auschwitz must stress anew the Jewish dimension in Christian beliefs and must overcome the forced blocking out of the Jewish heritage within Christianity." [3]

And doing theology, "in the face of the Jews" after the Holocaust as Metz suggests, means understanding how Jews identify themselves today. There is little doubt that the Holocaust has come to serve as a central point of identity for many, if not most Jews, today despite many disagreements about its ultimate theological implications. And so a Christology developed in the light of Metz's theses cannot ignore the Holocaust as a pivotal reality.

One dimension of a post-Shoah Christology surely involves recapturing Jesus' Jewish roots. The "Aryanization" of Jesus that occurred in the writings of some German biblical scholars during the Nazi period coupled with the general theology of Jewish displacement from the covenant by the Church rampant in Christian theology since the Patristic era clearly contributed to Christian complicity with the Nazis. So the process begun by scholars such as Charlesworth, Saldarini, LaCocque and others after the Holocaust remains a moral imperative.

The Holocaust, however, was not merely the final and most ghastly chapter in the long history of Christian antisemitism. Though closely connected with that tradition in terms of popular support for the Nazi attack on the Jews and definitely the inspiration for some of the Nazi legislation affecting the Jewish community, the Holocaust was the result of a constellation of modern ideologies that went far beyond classical Christian antisemitism.

In the final analysis, the Holocaust marked a response, albeit a highly destructive one, to a new level of human self-awareness. The Nazis perceived that basic changes were underway in human consciousness. The impact of the new science and technology, with its underlying assumption of freedom, was beginning to provide the human community on a mass scale with a Promethean-type experience of escape from prior moral chains. People were starting to realize, however, dimly, an enhanced sense of dignity and autonomy far more extensive than most of Western Christian theology had previously conceded. Traditional theological concepts that had shaped much of the Christian moral perspective, notions such as divine punishment, hell, divine wrath, and providence, were losing some of the hold they had exercised over moral decision making since biblical times. Christian theology had tended to accentuate the omnipotence of God which in turn intensified the impotence of the human person and the rather inconsequential role played by the human community in maintaining the sustainability of the earth. The Nazis totally rejected this previous relationship. In fact, they were literally trying to turn it on its head.

The Holocaust thus inaugurated the beginning of a new era in human possibility over which hung the specter of either unprecedented destruction or unparalleled hope. With the rise of Nazism, the mass extermination of human life in a guiltless fashion became thinkable and technologically feasible. The door was now ajar for an era when dispassionate torture and the murder of millions could become not merely the act of a crazed despot, not just a desire for national security, not merely an irrational outbreak of xenophobic fear, but a calculated effort to reshape history supported by intellectual argumentation from the best and brightest minds in a society. It was an attempt, Emil Fackenheim has said, to wipe out the "divine image" in history. "The murder camp," Fackenheim insists, "was not an accidental by-product of the Nazi Empire. It was its essence." [4]

What emerges as a central reality from the study of the Holocaust is the Nazi effort to create the "superperson," to develop a truly liberated humanity, to be shared in only by a select group, namely, the Aryan race. This new humanity would be released from the moral restraints previously imposed by religious beliefs and would be capable of exerting virtually unlimited power in the shaping of the world and its inhabitants. In a somewhat indirect, though still powerful way, the Nazis had proclaimed the death of God as a guiding force in the governance of the universe.

In pursuit of their objective, the Nazis became convinced that all the "dregs of humanity" had to be eliminated or at least their influence on culture and human development significantly curtailed. The Jews fell into this "dregs" category first and foremost. They were classified as "vermin." The Nazis could not envision even a minimally useful role for Jews in the new society to which they planned to give birth. In addition, there existed a "sacral" mandate for persecuting Jews which did not obtain for other victim groups. While there may be some parallels for the Gypsy community, there is still a formidable difference between the two groups in this regard. While not endorsing Richard Rubenstein's use of the term "holy War" to describe the attack on the Jews, he is nonetheless quite on target in highlighting the "sacral" dimension of the attack on the Jews as a unique element.[5]

In stressing the special nature of the attack on the Jews, however, we should not lose sight of the other Nazi victims. New research is beginning to suggest a closer affinity between the Jews and other groups, especially Poles, Gypsies, people with disabilities and, to a degree, gay men and other sexual minorities.[6] Evidence has now surfaced that Nazi leaders such as Hitler, Himmler and General Hans Frank entertained the idea of total extermination, not merely subjugation, of Poles at some future date.[7] But the mass extermination of Jews became a reality and we should not blur the distinction between fact and possibility. Nonetheless, the extermination or subjugation, of the other victim groups under the rubric of humankind's ultimate purification assumes important theological significance. Regrettably the non-Jewish victims are generally ignored in most of the theological reflections on the Holocaust to date, whether by Christian or by Jewish scholars.[8]

The late Uriel Tal captured as well as anyone the basic theological challenge presented by the Holocaust. In his understanding, the so-called Final Solution had as its ultimate objective the total transformation of human values. Its stated intent was to liberate humanity from all previous moral ideals and codes. When the liberating process was complete, humanity once and for all would be rescued from the imprisonment of a God concept and its related notions of moral responsibility, redemption, sin, and revelation. Nazi ideology sought to transform theological ideas into exclusively anthropological and political concepts. In Tal's interpretation of the Holocaust, for the Nazis, "God becomes man in a political sense as a member of the Aryan race whose highest representative on earth is the Fuhrer." [9]

Tal's research led him to conclude that this new Nazi consciousness emerged only gradually in the decades following World War I. Its roots, however, were somewhat earlier. It was undeniably related to the general process of social secularization that had been transforming Germany since the latter part of the nineteenth century. Its philosophic parents included the deists, the French encyclopedists, Feuerbach, the Young Hegelians, and the evolutionary thinkers in concert with the developing corps of scientists, who through their many new discoveries were creating the impression that a triumphant material civilization was on the verge of dawning in Western Europe. In the end, Tal argued, "these intellectual and social movements struck a responsive chord in a rebellious generation, altered the traditional views of God, man, and society, and ultimately led to the pseudo-religious, pseudomessianic movement of Nazism." [10]

Michael Ryan, looking at Nazism through a more explicitly theological lens than Tal, comes to somewhat similar conclusions. Working from an analysis of *Mein Kampf*, Ryan insists that the most striking dimension of the "salvation history" found in Hitler's thought was his willingness to confine humanity in an absolute manner to a time-bound existence. In the Hitlerian perspective, humankind must resign itself to the conditions of finitude. But this resignation is accompanied by the assertion of all-pervasive power for itself within these conditions. The end result of all this was the self-deification of Hitler who proclaimed himself the new

"Savior" of the German nation. It is this Hitlerian mind-set that allows us, in Ryan's judgement, to term *Mein Kampf* a "theological" treatise. In the final analysis, in Ryan's words, Hitler's wordview "amounted to the deliberate decision on the part of mass man to live within the limits of finitude without either the moral restraints or the hopes of traditional religion—in this case, Christianity." [11]

In light of the ideological dimensions of the Holocaust, including its pseudo-messianic aspects uncovered by scholars such as Tal and Ryan, the response to our original question of "Why Auschwitz?" in a discussion of Christology should now be clear. If Christology involves Messianism, if Christology involves an understanding of the divine-human encounter and its implications for human responsibility, as it does, then the challenge the Holocaust presents in these areas simply cannot be ignored.

What then might be an appropriate Christological response to the challenge of the Holocaust? I would begin negatively in a way. The first implication is that the Holocaust has made it immoral for Christians to maintain any Christology that is excessively triumphalistic or that finds the significance of the Christ Event in the displacement of the Jewish People from an ongoing covenantal relationship with God. Such "displacement Christologies," so strongly rooted in the patristic tradition, can no longer be regarded as authentic Christology either in academic theology or as a framework for Christian liturgy. Gregory Baum put the Holocaust's fundamental challenge to Christology very well when he wrote some years ago that

> Auschwitz...is an altogether special sign of the times, in which God empowers the Church to correct its past teaching, *including its central dogma*, to the extent that it distorts God's action in Christ and promotes human destruction.... The Holocaust acted out the Church's fantasy that the Jews were a non-people, that they had no place before God and that they should have disappeared long ago by accepting Christ. The Church is now summoned to a radical reformulation of its faith, free of ideological deformation, making God's act in Christ fully and without reserve a message for life rather than death.[12]

A number of Christian theologians, myself included, have attempted to respond to Baum's challenge. The responses can be generally classified as (1) a Christology of Divine Vulnerability and (2) a Christology of Witness. These two Christological approaches, which have many particular shadings, are not, it needs emphasizing, mutually exclusive. As I shall shortly explain, it is my growing conviction that both are required responses in light of the Holocaust.

Initial efforts at reflecting on the implications of the Holocaust for Christology led some theologians to emphasize a connection between Jesus' suffering on Calvary and the suffering endured by the Jewish People over the centuries, especially under the Nazis. Franklin Sherman, for example, sees in the cross of Christ "the symbol of the agonizing God." The only legitimate Christology after the Holocaust, for Sherman, is one rooted in a perspective that views the Christ Event as a further enhancement of divine participation in suffering. This theological outlook, first expressed in the prophetic tradition (especially by Jeremiah) and reaffirmed in Jewish scholarship by Abraham Heschel, should make Christians as followers of the Crucified One the first to identify with the sufferings of the Jewish People, especially during the Holocaust. For Sherman, Christ crucified becomes the symbol of the agonizing God. Sherman laments the fact that the cross has become a source of division rather than reconciliation between Jews and Christians throughout history. For, in fact, the cross points to a very Jewish reality—suffering and martyrdom—and should serve as a source of new unity between Christians and Jews.[13]

The Israeli Catholic scholar Marcel Dubois, O.P., interprets the meaning of Christology in the face of the Holocaust in ways that parallel the thought of Sherman. Dubois is acutely aware of the difficulty Christians confront in setting the reality of the Holocaust within the context of a theology of the cross. He likewise acknowledges that such a linkage may appear as an obscenity to many Jews whose sufferings during the Holocaust the Church helped to perpetuate. Yet, despite these difficulties, Dubois remains convinced it is the direction in which Christian theology is compelled to move:

In the person of the suffering servant there appears to take place
an effable change. Our vision of Jewish destiny and our understanding of the Holocaust in particular depend on our compassion;
the Calvary of the Jewish people, whose summit is the
Holocaust, can help us to understand a little better the mystery
of the Cross.[14]

Dubois also picks up on Sherman's notion of Jewish-
Christian unity in light of the Holocaust. From a faith
perspective, Dubois argues, the Christian can truly affirm
that Jesus fulfills Israel in her destiny of Suffering Servant
and that Israel, in her experience of solitude and anguish,
answers and represents without knowing it the mystery of
the Passion and the Cross. The challenge of the massive
human annihilation which the Holocaust ushered in stands
before both Jews and Christians:

> they have learnt to be united in compassion; they must now learn
> to be united in hope, the hope…of the people that believes in the
> victory of life and in the fidelity of God.[15]

Another prominent scholar in the Christian–Jewish
dialogue, Clemens Thoma, has also briefly addressed the
question of Christology and the Holocaust, following a path
reminiscent of Sherman and Dubois. He views the Holocaust
as rooted in an antisemitic ideology that was at root
anti–Christian as well. Hence Christian responsibility for
the Holocaust cannot be argued indiscriminately, though
Thoma does not hesitate to acknowledge that Christian
contempt for the Jews greatly facilitated the success of the
so–called Final Solution. His equation of Jesus' suffering and
that of the Jews seems even stronger that the linkage posited
by Sherman and Dubois. He writes:

> …a believing Christian should not find it so very difficult to
> interpret the sacrifice of the Jews during the Nazi terror. His
> thoughts should be turned toward Christ to whom these Jewish
> masses became alike, in sorrow and death. Auschwitz is the
> most monumental sign of our time for the intimate bond and
> unity between Jewish martyrs — who stand for all Jews — and the

crucified Christ, even though the Jews in question could not be aware of it.[16]

This note of a nexus in suffering between Jews and Christians through the Cross is sounded as well by Douglas Hall. His reflections on the Nazi period have left him convinced that only a theology of the cross can express the meaning of the Incarnation today. Only such an approach to Christology establishes the authentic divine–human link implied in the Word becoming flesh by highlighting the solidarity of God with suffering humanity. Such a Christological direction results in a soteriology of solidarity that posits the cross of Jesus as a point of fraternal union with the Jewish People, as well as with all who seek human liberation and peace.

For Hall, as for the other theologians we have examined, Jesus becomes a potential source of union rather than exclusion for Jews and Christians in the post–Holocaust era. In his view:

> the faith of Israel is incomprehensible unless one sees at its heart a suffering God whose solidarity with humanity is so abysmal that the "cross in the heart of God" (H. Wheeler Robinson) must always be incarnating itself in history. Reading the words of Elie Wiesel, one knows, as a Christian, that he bears this indelible resemblance to the people of Israel.[17]

Sherman, Dubois, Thoma and Hall must be said to have only skimmed the surface in terms of assessing the Holocaust's impact on Christology. The most substantive effort to date is to be found in the writings of Jürgen Moltmann. Moltmann's reflections on this question began after a visit to the Maidanek concentration camp near Lublin, Poland. As he began to wrestle with the implications of his visit to the camp, he found strength in the closing words of Elie Wiesel's book *Night*: "Where is God? .... He hangs there from the gallows..." From there Moltmann goes on to interpret the Holocaust as the most dramatic revelation thus far of the basic meaning of the Christ event: God can save people, including Israel, because through the Cross participated in their very suffering. To theologize after the Holocaust would prove a futile enterprise in Moltmann's view,

> were not the *Sh'ma Israel* and the Lord's Prayer prayed in Auschwitz itself, were not God himself in Auschwitz, suffering with the martyred and murdered. Every other answer would be blasphemy. An absolute God would make us indifferent. The God of action and success would let us forget the dead, which we still cannot forget. God as nothingness would make the entire world into a concentration camp.[18]

What emerges for Moltmann from the experience of the Holocaust is a "theology of divine vulnerability" that has roots in Abraham Heschel's notion of *divine pathos*. He also argues that the idea of the suffering of God as the basic divine redemptive activity is consonant with rabbinic theology of the first century:

> The God who suffers in exile with Israel preserves the people from despair and fear. The realization of God's fellow-suffering impedes apathy, maintains sympathy for god in life, and holds hope for the future of God open.[19]

Moltmann adds that in rabbinic theology it is claimed that this suffering on the part of God is something he experiences at the very core of his being. God is not merely present where people are suffering; that suffering directly affects God. As Moltmann puts it, "God is not only involved in history; history is also in God himself." [20]

These Christian theological efforts at linking Jesus' suffering on the Cross with that of the Jews during the Holocaust have met with critical reaction in some quarters. I myself have some questions about its appropriateness as *the* Christological response to the Holocaust. For one, it tends to ignore Christian complicity in Jewish suffering during the Holocaust. From a more theological perspective, the Cross has always been described as a voluntary act on the part of God and Christ; the Cross can be understood in a redemptive fashion when seen as the culmination and the consequence of

Jesus' active ministry. Auschwitz was neither voluntary nor redemptive in any sense.

A. Roy Eckhardt has been one of the strongest critics of Moltmann's Christology in light of the Holocaust. For him ,there is no way we can honestly assert that millions of Jews were liberated from death or from any other suffering through the Crucifixion. It approaches blasphemy to make such acclaim in light of Christian involvement with Nazism. "What does it mean," he asks, "to tell the inmates of Buchenwald or Bergen-Belsen, as this Christian theologian does, that "through his suffering and death, the risen Christ brings "righteousness and life to the unrighteous and the dying? [21] For Eckardt, Moltmann simply claims too much for the sufferings of Christ. He also expresses concern that a Christology of "divine vulnerability" will lead to an exaggerated emphasis on weakness and divine protection whereas Jewish post-Holocaust theologians have emphasized the need for the judicious use of human power after the Holocaust.

Other criticism have come from scholars such as Frances Fiorenza (who argues for a concomitant stress on Jesus' resurrection) and from the Jewish scholar Eugene Borowitz. Moltmann's theology of divine vulnerability would also likely encounter some opposition from liberationist theologians, though Hall, who has sympathy for that perspective, also exhibits positive regard for Moltmann's Cross theology.

In my judgment the criticisms of Moltmann by Eckardt and others are considerably overdrawn. A Christology of the Cross is a meaningful response to the Holocaust, at least in terms of the notion of divine vulnerability, if it is integrated into a larger whole.

Any adequate Christology after the Holocaust must be directly related to more fundamental discussions about God in light of this experience. It must be related to the ideological and theological dimensions of the Holocaust that are uncovered by scholars such as Tal and Ryan. For me, the Holocaust has destroyed simplistic notions of a "commanding," all powerful God. But equally it has exposed our desperate need to retain a "compelling" God, *compelling* because we have experienced through symbolic encounter with God such healing and affirmation that buries any need to assert our humanity through the destructive, even deathly, use of human power.[22] As Vaclav Havel has noted, "as soon as man began considering himself the source of the highest meaning in the world and the measure of everything, the world began to lose its human dimension, and man began to lose control of it."[23] But if God is instead the measure, it is a God to whom we are drawn, rather than a God who imposes on us.

Understanding the ministry of Jesus as emerging from the heightened sense of divine–human intimacy that surfaced in Second Temple Judaism,[24] Christological statements made by the Church in reflection on that ministry can be seen as attempts to articulate a new sense of how profoundly humanity is imbedded in divinity. The ultimate significance of Christology so understood lies in its revelation of the grandeur of the human as a necessary corrective to the demeaning paternalism that often characterized the sense of the divine–human relationship in the past. In this sense a major component of all authentic Christology is theological anthropology. Martin Luther understood this in *The Freedom of the Christian Man*. And Gregory Baum has stressed that in his first papal encyclical Pope John Paul II presented human dignity as integral to Christological doctrine.[25]

In my view the fear and paternalism associated in the past with the statement of the divine–human relationship were at least partially responsible for the attempt by the Nazis to produce a total reversal of human meaning, as Tal has described it. Incarnational Christology can help the human person understand that he or she shares in the very life and existence of God. The human person remains creature; the gulf between humanity in people and humanity in the Godhead has not been totally obliterated. But it is also clear that a direct link exists; the two humanities can touch. The human struggle for self-identity vis-a-vis the Creator God, the source of the misuse of human power in the past, has come to an end in principle, though its full realization still lies ahead. In this sense we can truly affirm that Christ continues to bring humankind salvation in its root meaning—*wholeness*.

With a proper understanding of the meaning of the Christ Event men and women can be healed, they can finally overcome the primal desire to supplant the Creator in power and in status that lay at the heart of the Holocaust. Critical to this awareness is a sense of God's self-imposed limitation manifested in the cross. This is where Moltmann's theology can make a significant contribution. The notion of "divine vulnerability" can become a powerful Christological symbol to remind us that one need not exercise power, control and dominance to be "godly." It also shows that God is simply not desirous of absorbing humanity totally back into divine being, but rather affirming its eternal distinctiveness. That is the ultimate message of the resurrection, rather than the triumphalistic interpretations given the event that A. Roy Eckardt and others have rightly criticized in light of the Holocaust. Douglas Hall takes a position in the same vein when he writes that

> Whatever emphasis may be called for in the context where faith is *con*fessed, the *pro*fession of the faith always must entail the courage to affirm the reality of that which negates while at the same time insisting upon the gracious possibility of negating the negation. The profession of faith must do this because precisely the core of that upon which the disciple community mediates is a gospel which declares that the great negation by which creaturely life is continuously threatened has been entered into and is being overcome by a God who, by personally submitting to the aboriginal Nothingness, mollifies its power over us.[26]

But let me underline that if the notion of "divine vulnerability" is to serve in the above way it must be disassociated from direct linkages to Jewish sufferings above all, as well as the sufferings of other victims of the Nazis. From a theological perspective Jesus' suffering must be regarded as voluntary and redeeming. No such claims can be made in good conscience for the sufferings endured by Nazi victims. And on the human level, it is difficult to compare the depth of sufferings endured by the Gypsies, Poles, and disabled, gays, and others with that of Jesus, as painful as it might have been.

What I am claiming is that the Holocaust represents at one and the same time the ultimate expression of human freedom and evil—the two are intimately linked. The Holocaust as the ultimate assertion of human freedom from God in our time may in fact prove the beginning of the final resolution of the conflict between freedom and evil. When humanity finally recognizes the destruction it can produce in totally rejecting dependence on its Creator, as it did in the Holocaust, when it perceives that such rejection is a perversion and not an affirmation of human freedom, a new stage in human consciousness may be dawning. We may finally be coming to grips with evil at its roots. The power of evil will wane only when humankind develops along with a profound sense of the dignity it enjoys because of its direct links to God a corresponding sense of humility occasioned by a searching encounter with the devastation it is capable of producing when left to its own wits. A sense of profound humility evoked by the experience of the healing power present in the ultimate Creator of human power—this is crucial. On this point of humility as a critical response to the Holocaust, I join with Stanley Hauerwas in his reflections on the Holocaust even though we part company on several implications of the event.[27]

While the relationship between post-Holocaust human consciousness and Christology remains central to the question at hand, I now recognize that it does not exhaust the issue. Here is where the beginning reflections by several Christian scholars are to the point.

David Tracy and Elizabeth Schüssler Fiorenza have argued that, while Christian theologians in the modern period have begun to come to grips with historical consciousness, their approach remains inadequate. They insist that Christian theology cannot fully re-enter history until it faces up to the challenge of the Holocaust. Few Christian theologians measure up to this standard. Christian theologians, in their view:

> Have developed a theological hermeneutics where the subject-matter — the event itself — is once again allowed to rule in

theological hermeneutic. They have recognized the *Sach-Kritik* that the eschatological event itself demands. But they have too seldom returned to history—the real, concrete thing where events like the Holocaust happen.[28]

Johannes Metz is one among several Christian theologians who has taken the Tracy–Schüssler Fiorenza challenge to heart. Metz has emphasized that post–Holocaust Christology needs to have discipleship at its very core. "This kind of Christology," he says,

> is not primarily formed in a subjectless concept and system, but in discipleship stories. This kind of Christology does not bear casually, but fundamentally narrative features. This Christology of discipleship stands against a Christianity which interprets itself as a bourgeois religion; it opposes the idea that Christianity is totally at home in the bourgeois world. This Christology of discipleship also stands against that kind of Christianity which considers itself as a kind of religion of victors—with a surplus of answers and a corresponding lack of passionate questions in the being-on-the way. The Christology of discipleship makes it clear that Christianity, too, ahead of all system knowledge contains a narrative and remembrance knowledge.[29]

In his volume *Christian Theology after the Shoah*, James Moore proposes a Christological path that bears similarities to that presented by Metz. He, too, highlights the importance of narrative Christology in light of the holocaust. For him the central determinative theme for any authentic Christology of witness must be *resistance* within a general theology of discipleship. The rescuer becomes a prime example of true belief in the message of Christ. Any "redemptive" emphasis in Christology must always "be tied to the historical reality of any point in time, dismissing all efforts to thoroughly spiritualize the notion of redemption."[30]

Elizabeth Schüssler Fiorenza and Rebecca Chopp, both of whom have concerned themselves with the liberating dimensions of theology, offer general reflections on post–Holocaust faith which carry implications for Christological statements. Schüssler Fiorenza insists that we cannot speak of the suffering in its political particularity alone. "The ideological catchword was 'Untermensch,' the less than human, the subhuman being."[31]

Nazism for Schüssler Fiorenza represented an extreme example of the Western capitalistic form of patriarchy with origins in Aristotelian philosophy and subsequent mediation through Christian theology. The same ancient philosophical system, imported into Christian theology by Thomas Aquinas and others, that first subjugated women as people with a "subhuman" nature combined with religiously rooted bigotry and a new bio-theology to produce the Nazi cataclysm throughout Europe. Overcoming biblical and theological anti-Judaism, so closely identified with classical Christological statements, thus becomes the first step according to Schüssler Fiorenza in the complicated, rather wrenching process of cleansing Western society of its patriarchal basis.

Rebecca Chopp lays particular stress on the profound connection she perceives between Holocaust literature and liberation theology, a relationship she terms unique among Western religious writings. Both perspectives in her judgment create the need for a fundamental reconceptualization of Christian theology. Christianity is now forced to grapple not merely with individual suffering, but even more with suffering on a mass scale. Liberation theology and Holocaust literature both confront Christian theology with the question "who is the human subject that suffers history?"[32]

Chopp goes on to add that both liberation theology and Holocaust literature force us to understand history not merely in terms of abstract notions of evolution or process but primarily in terms of the suffering realities of that history caused by various forms of human exploitation. The history that now must be the basis of theological reflections is not abstract history, but the history of human victims. And the voices and the memories of the tortured, the forgotten, and the dead must become primary resources for Christian anthropology. And, while Chopp does not explicitly articulate this position, one could surmise that she would identify with the direction taken by Schüssler Fiorenza, namely, that biblical anti-Judaism with its inevitable dehumanization of concrete Jewish persons opened the way for Jewish suffering in the Holocaust and for the experiences of suffereing under imperialist colonialism to which liberation theology has been responding.

Clearly the emphasis by Rebecca Chopp, Johannes Metz and others on person-centered theology, on a theology that directly relates to the victims of current history, is very much to the point as I now understand the significance of Holocaust. Christology needs to become more than a theoretical affirmation of human dignity. The late Frantz Fanon's critique of abstract philosophical humanism in the midst of colonist exploitation in his preface to *The Wretched of the Earth* speaks to this in a decisive way. Pope John Paul's plea for a Christology that affirms human dignity in *Redemptor Hominis* must become the impetus for a concrete manifestation of that belief through identification with, and support of, the victims of oppression through personal and political means. This will enhance the dignity not only of the victim, but also of the person who reaches out. Donald Dietrich is quite right when he argues that "the Holocaust has reemphasized the need to highlight the person as *the* central factor in the social order to counterbalance state power."[33] Only in this way can we root out the instinctive patriarchal impulse that elevates power over mutuality in relationships, only in this way can we guarantee that the misuse of technological capacity is neutralized. In this sense there is a profound connection between the two basic forms of post-Holocaust Christology. For the new human consciousness rooted in an understanding of *divine vulnerability* will insure that a Christology of witness does not fall into the trap of service in the name of power rather than service in the name of genuine human dignity.

In this approach to Christology the emphasis on Jesus' sufferings on the cross surely has a place. But this suffering must not be seen in isolation from his public ministry. For it is the period of public ministry in which Jesus often went out of his way to identify with, and personally affirm, the social outcasts of his time that gives significance to his experience on the cross. His continual affirmation of human dignity in very concrete ways is what brought him a death sentence.

In his volume, *Moralizing Cultures,*[34] Vytautas Kavolis argues that while the sacred will continue to impact culture it will do so in a different way. Kavolis speaks of a movement towards the "humanization of morality." This movement involves a fundamental shift from the dominance of abstract principles requiring adherence whatever the consequences to a more directly practical concern with the reduction of human suffering and the enhancement of nondestructive capacities within humanity. For this to continue in a socially constructive way, we require moral leaders as much as, perhaps more, than abstract principle.

Applying Kavolis' perspective to Chistology after the Holocaust we can say that Jesus' own ministry becomes one such example of moral leadership. But so does the witness of the countless martyrs, whether in the Holocaust itself or subsequently, who have embodied Christology in concrete acts on behalf of the oppressed. In this sense the narrative of the rescuers during the Holocaust may now be seen as a central Christological resource. The personal, and even communal "cleansing"" of human consciousness from the temptations towards the destructive use of enhanced human power is a necessary first step in the humanization of morality. But the process cannot stop there. If reflection on the Holocaust leaves us merely with a Christology of divine vulnerability and does not bring us to a Christology of witness we have failed in our basic responsibility as post-Holocaust Christians.

Endnotes

1 André LaCocque, *But As For Me: The Question of Election and God's People* (Atlanta: John Knox Press, 1979).

2 See John T. Pawlikowski, *Christ in the Light of the Christian-Jewish Dialogue* (New York: Paulist Press, 1982); "Ein Bund oder zwei Bünde?" *Theologische Quartalschrift* 176 (1996): 325-340.

3 Johannes Baptist Metz, "Facing the Jews: Christian Theology After Auschwitz," in *The Holocaust as Interruption*, Concilium 175, edited by Elisabeth Schüssler Fiorenza and David Tracy (Edinburgh: T. & T. Clark, 1984), 43-52.

4 Emil Fackenheim, *The Jewish Return into History* (New York: Schocken Books, 1978), 246.

5 See *What Kind of God: Essays in Honor of Richard L. Rubenstein*, edited by Betty Rogers Rubenstein and Michael Berenbaum, Studies in the Shoah, Vol. 11 (Lanham, MD: University Press of America, 1995). Also see Richard L. Rubenstein "Holy Wars and Ethnic Cleansing: Report on Research in Progress" in *The Uses and Abuses of Knowledge*, edited by Henry F. Knight and Marcia Sachs Littell, Studies in the Shoah, Vol. 17 (Lanham, Maryland, 1997), 349-378.

6 See *A Mosaic of Victims: Non-Jews Persecuted and Murdered by the Nazis*, ed. Michael Berenbaum (New York: New York University Press, 1990); Richard C. Lucas, *Forgotten Holocaust: The Poles Under German Occupation 1939-1944* (Lexington: The University Press of Kentucky, 1986); Henry Friedlander, *The Origins of Nazi Genocide: From Euthanasia to the Final Solution* (Chapel Hill: University of North Carolina Press, 1995); and Gunter Grau, *Hidden Holocaust? Gay and Lesbian Persecution in Germany, 1933-45*, with a contribution by Claudia Schoppmann (New York: Cassell, 1995).

7 See Janusaz Gumkowski and Kazimierz Lesczynski, *Poland Under Nazi Occupation* (Warsaw: Polonia Publishing House, 1961), 59; and Karol Pospieszalski, *Polska pod Niemieckim Prawem* (Psnan: Wyoawnictwo Instytutu Zachodniego, 1946), 189.

8 See John T. Pawlikowski, "Uniqueness and Universality in the Holocaust: Some Ethical Reflections," in *Biblical and Humane: A Festschrift for John F. Priest*, edited by Linda Bennett Elder, David L. Barr and Elizabeth Struthers Malbon (Atlanta: Scholars Press, 1996), 275-289.

[9] Uriel Tal, "Forms of Pseudo-Religion in the German *Kulturbereich* Prior to the Holocaust," *Immanuel* 3 (Winter 1973-74): 6.

[10] Uriel Tal, *Christians and Jews in Germany: Religion, Politics and Ideology in the Second Reich 1870-1914* (Ithaca, New York: Cornell University Press, 1975), 302-303.

[11] See Michael Ryan, "Hitler's Challenge to Churches: A Theological-Political Analysis of *Mein Kampf*," in *The German Church Struggle and the Holocaust*, edited by Franklin H. Littell and Hubert G. Locke (Detroit: Wayne State University Press, 1974), 160-161.

[12] Gregory Baum, "Catholic Dogma after Auschwitz," in *Antisemitism and the Foundations of Christianity*, ed. Alan Davis (New York: Paulist Press. 1979), 142.

[13] Franklin Sherman, "Speaking of God After Auschwitz," *Worldview* 17 (1974): 29. See also Sherman's essay on the same theme in *Speaking of God Toda,.* edited by Paul D. Opsahl and Marc H. Tanenbaum, (Philadelphia: Fortress, 1974).

[14] Marcel Dubois, "Christian Reflections on the Holocaust," SIDIC 7:2 (1974): 15.

[15] Ibid., 15.

[16] Clemens Thoma, *A Christian Theology of Judaism* (New York: Paulist, 1977), 159; also see, 3.

[17] Douglas Hall, "Rethinking Christ," in *Antisemitism and the Foundations of Christianity*, 183. Also see idem, *God and Human Suffering: An Exercise in the Theology of the Cross* (Minneapolis: Augsburg, 1986), and idem, *Professing the Faith: Christian Theology in a North American Context* (Minneapolis: Fortress, 1993).

[18] Jürgen Moltmann, "The Crucified God," *Theology Today* 32 (April 1974): 9. Also see idem, *Jesus Christ for Today's World* (Minneapolis: Fortress, 1993). Also see Ziva Amishai-Maisew, "Christological Symbolism of the Holocaust," *Holocaust and Genocide Studies*, 3:4 (1988): 451-481.

[19] Moltmann, "The Crucified God," 13.

[20] Ibid., 13.

[21] A. Roy Eckardt, "Christians and Jews: Along a Theological Frontier," *Encounter* 40:2 (Spring 1979): 102.

22 See John T. Pawlikowski, "The Holocaust: Its Impact on Christian Thought and Ethics," in *New Perspectives on the Holocaust*, ed. Rochelle L. Millen (New York: New York University Press, 1996), 344-361.

23 Vaclav Havel, *Disturbing the Peace: A Conversation with Karel Hvizdala*, tran. Paul Wilson (New York: Alfred A. Knopf. 1990), 11.

24 See John T. Pawlikowski, *Jesus and the Theology of Israel* (Wilmington, Delaware: Michael Glazier, 1989).

25 Gregory Baum, "The First Papal Encyclical," *The Eucumenist* 17 (May/June 1979): 55.

26 Hall, *Professing the Faith*, 79.

27 Stanley Hauerwas, "Jews and Christians Among the Nations," *Cross Currents* (Spring 1981): 34; also see idem, "Resurrection, the Holocaust, and Forgiveness: A Sermon for Eastertime," in *Removing Anti-Judaism from the Pulpit*, edited by Howard Clark Kee and Irwin J. Borowsky (Philadelphia: American Interfaith Institute and Crossroad, 1996), 113-120.

28 Elisabeth Schüssler Fiorenza and David Tracy, "The Holocaust as Interruption and the Christian Return Into History," in *The Holocaust as Interruption*, 84-85.

29 Johannes Baptist Metz, "Facing the Jews: Christian Theology After Auschwitz, in *The Holocaust as Interruption*, 32.

30 James F. Moore, *Christian Theology after the Shoah*. Studies in the Shoah, Vol. 7 (Lanham, Maryland: University Press of America, 1993), 146.

31 Elisabeth Schüssler Fiorenza and David Tracy, "The Holocaust as Interruption," in *The Holocaust as Interruption*, 86.

32 Rebecca Chopp, "The Interruption of the Forgotten," in *The Holocaust as Interruption*, 20.

33 Donald J. Dietrich, *God and Humanity in Auschwitz: Jewish-Christian Relations and Sanctioned Murder* (New Brunswick: Transaction Publishers, 1995), 269.

34 Vytautas Kavolis. *Moralizing Cultures* (Lanham, Maryland: University Press of America, 1993).

Chapter 12

Fides Quaerens Intellectum: Biblical Antecedents?

Paul Ricoeur

Translated by David Pellauer

The Anselmian Argument can be seen as occupying a strategic position on the long trajectory that originate with the biblical scriptures, both Jewish and Christian, and continues through Kant's refutation of "ontological proof" properly speaking, and, beyond Kant, to Nietzsche's proclamation of the "death of God." According to this perspective, it is plausible to say that if we start from the end point we can gain not only an over-arching view of the whole length of this trajectory, but also we can grasp the dynamism that animated the kind of thinking produced along the way to its supposed exhaustion. On the other hand, it is perhaps by starting from this announced exhaustion that we may undertake a new thoughtful dialog with the biblical sources situated before the argument itself. This is, in a broad sense, the working hypothesis that governs my inquiry.[1] This inquiry will not take up the second part of the trajectory I have referred to, the subsequent destiny of the Anselmian argument from Descartes to Kant, and from Kant to Nietzsche. Instead, I shall limit myself to the biblical sources of the Anselmian argument. However, I take it for granted that, in this very limited investigation, we shall never lose sight of the subsequent destiny of this argument, which, in bringing its descendants to ruin, may have opened the way to new interpretations buried in what had been their provenance.

The Naming of God According to Saint Anselm

Three features of Anselm's argument refer us back to its Hebraic sources. The first one has to do with the dimension of invocation that frames his argument. We read in chapter II of the *Proslogion*: "And so, Lord, do thou, who dost give understanding to faith, give me, so far as thou knowest it to be profitable, to understand [*ut...intelligam*] that thou art as we believe; and that thou art that which we believe. And, indeed, we believe that thou art a being than which nothing greater can be conceived [*credimus te esse aliquid quo nihil maius cogitari potest*]."[2] Both the French and the English translations of this invocation have a "thou" five times where in the Latin text it only appears once explicitly, but where it is implied in the four verbs in the second person, as well as in the vocative *domine*. We may say without fear that the argument will become a proof when it will have broken its ties to this invocation that contains it. Yet it is also by way of this invocation that this argument remains attached to biblical faith, whose energy it prolongs. Indeed, the invocation consists in asking for an understanding of faith, which in advance recognizes itself to be placed under the sign of a gift.

Second feature: it is expected that this understanding will "recognize"—if we follow the apt French translation of *intelligere* by Michel Corbin—what is is already implicit in faith.[3] The sought for argument, despite the independence that will be claimed for it, thus remains bound to the contents of faith by a relation that we may call one of approximation. What is it a question of recognizing? This: "that thou art *as* we believe; and that thou art *that which* we believe." The recognition (or approximation) at issue here bears directly on being, but under the guise of a verb conjugated in the second person, and thus in harmony with the thou of the invocation. Hence, we can suspect a second time that the argument will become a proof when the verb "being," released from the second person, will be turned into a substantialized infinitive, wholly neutral as regards grammatical persons. In this way it will be prepared for all the reinterpretations inspired by Greek ontology, which is not aware of the "thou art."

Third feature: the understanding of faith, as recognition and approximation, becomes an argument, hence a movement of thinking aimed at the autonomy of a proof, once the equation is posited between the name called upon—God—bound to the invocation, and a predicated name, where the someone becomes something: "that thou art that which [*aliquid*], etc." Anselm suggests that this passage from someone to something is in some way already the object of faith ("we believe that...") and that the understanding of faith consists in unfolding this *nexus* of someone and something; in recognizing it, but in such a way that recognition becomes by itself a proof. Do we not read in the Preface: "I began to ask myself whether there might be found a single argument which would require no other for its proof [*ad se probandum*] than itself alone; and alone would suffice to demonstrate [*et solum ad astruendum*] that God truly exists [*quia deus here est*]."[4]

It is in this sense that Anselm's argument constitutes a strategic point along the trajectory referred to earlier. On the one hand, as contained in the invocation, it remains dependent; on the other hand, as aiming at autonomy ("a single argument which would require no other for its proof"), it leaves the orbit of the invocation and undertakes a solitary course, which will be precisely that of "proofs for the existence of God" by reason alone. How are we to account for this over-determination of an argument that presents itself as both the recognition of a content of the faith that precedes it (and which in a way constitutes its preunderstanding) and as a proof sufficient to itself alone?

Two answers can be invoked here: the continuity presumed by the first status conferred on the argument is made possible by a prior conceptual reflection and analysis that means we are not dealing here with a bare faith, if I may put it this way, that reason undertakes to understand, to recognize, but with an already interpreted faith, already bearing rational significations. What then would understanding prove and demonstrate? Not just that "God truly exists," but also that he "is a supreme [*summum*] Good requiring nothing else, which all other things require for their existence and well-being; and whatever we believe regarding the divine Being."[5]   What is "believed" has already to a significant degree been thought about, and this has happened following a certain conceptual tradition that is indicated by the four segments of what is predicated of God: supreme good, having need of no other, which all other things require for their being, and for their well-being. In short, Anselm's argument does not connect directly back to biblical faith. It draws upon a secular basis of thought, which had up to that time remained within the bounds of faith, but which, for the first time, seeks to be autonomous, without for all that denying its dependence on the invocation that asks to receive such understanding—therefore such autonomy—as a gift.[6]

Here is where the continuity between faith and the understanding of faith is compensated for by an interruptive effect produced by the fool who says in his heart "there is no God" (Psalm 14:1, 53:1, Romans 3:10-12). This interruptive effect is so powerful that it motivates the dialogue of the believer with himself, when he asks whether, like every sinner, he has not "lost that for which he was made."[7]

Yet despite this irruption of someone who is a stranger to faith, a minimal understanding with him is presupposed, namely: "this very fool, when he hears of this being of which I speak—a being than which nothing greater can be conceived—understands [*intelligit*] what he hears, and what he understands is in his understanding; although he does not understand [*intelligit*] it to exist."[8] It is the discourse addressed to the fool that calls for the signification "a being than which nothing greater can be conceived" to be isolated twice over: from the invocation, on the one hand, and from the affirmation of existence, on the other. Hence it will be a question for Anselm whether if we return to a point before his argumentative apparatus we do not reach a point where invocation and affirmation of existence are inseparable. Yet the fool is there constraining him to carry to the noetic plane the predicative name that faith confesses, and which will henceforth be posited apart from any connection to the invoked Thou and the sought for actuality: "for, it is one thing for an object to be in the understanding, and another to understand that the object exists."[9] Here is the point from which the argument that God cannot be conceived not to exist (Chap. III) unfolds. This argument consists in demonstrating that this separating of the noetic sense from existence is not thinkable. It puts back together what the fool's discourse had claimed to set apart. This is what we read at the end of *Proslogion* IV: "For, God is that than which a greater cannot be conceived. And he who thoroughly understands this, assuredly understands that this being so truly exists, that not even in concept can it be non-existent. Therefore, he who understands that God so exists, cannot conceive that he does not exist." The predicative name (that than which nothing greater can be conceived) has again become a proper name. God, that is, the one who is invoked, and the subject and predicate are once again fused. The argument consists, therefore, in reuniting what was already united for faith, and that the fool's discourse had claimed to dissociate, at the price of an absurdity. If faith had united invocation, noetic denomination, and existence, the argument would have nothing to "recognize." But it is the fool who, in dissociating the sequence, returns its plenitude of meaning to God's name. Thus, in this way, it is the fool who makes the argument necessary,[10] but within the limits of an argument by *reductio ad absurdum* that, unlike the ontological proof, lacks its own compelling force.

What follows, especially the end of the *Proslogion* confirms this. Chapters V to XII enrich the *quid* and *quod* of the argument, in terms of the dimensions of a faith that has already been identified and interpreted. "What are thou, then, Lord God, than whom nothing greater can be conceived?" (Chap. V). The answer is to be found in chapter XII: "But undoubtedly, whatever thou art, thou art through nothing else than thyself. Therefore, thou art the very life whereby thou livest; and the wisdom wherewith thou art wise; and the very goodness whereby thou art good *to the righteous and the wicked*; and so of other like attributes." What is pronounced here is the identity of the subject (thou) and the predicates designating those goods, intended by human *desire*, but apprehended in their supereminence. This identification of subject and predicate provides the sense of the proposition "whatever thou art, thou art through nothing else than thyself." At this stage, the understanding that sets into play the conceptual difference between "being through oneself" and "being through another thing" cannot be discerned from the invocation. It is in this sense that it is the recognition of the contents of faith. And it is from this enrichment that follows what Corbin calls the second name: "a being greater than can be conceived." Now the naming of God implies the negation by transcendence of every desired good, which beings who are not God have only through some other thing "Hast thou found what thou didst seek, my soul? Thou has found him to be a being which is the highest of all beings [*eum esse quiddam summum omnium*], a being than which nothing better [*quo nihil melius*] can be conceived; that this being is life itself, light, wisdom, goodness, eternal blessedness and blessed eternity; and that it is everywhere and always."[11] What does this second name add to the first name? Essentially, the relation to the desire that underlies the dynamic of seeking and finding. And this desire has as its goal the goods here enumerated (life, light, etc.). The second name designates what is excessive in relation to what is desirable, just as the first name designated what is excessive in relation to what is thinkable. However, to the extent that thinking is seeking, hence desire, the second name envelops the first name. And, with this, we understand retrospectively how the argument in chapters II and IV works. It is limited to denying that what faith takes as united can be dissociated: thou, the supereminent goods, existence. The argument creates nothing; it denies that the separation of the invoked

God and the predicates that make up the predicative name, united to the divine thou, is thinkable.

Hence we must next seek the biblical source for this work of naming.

Two questions will govern what I shall call our step backwards: 1) What, in the proclamation of the name, holds together a) the invocation of the divine thou, b) naming properly speaking (that is, the predicative assertion of those eminent qualities capable of being taken for the antecedent of the *quo nihil majus* of the first name and the *quo nihil melius* of the second name *cogitari potest*), and c) the assertion of existence? 2) What, in human desire, in human thought, in short, in the quest that joins desire and thinking, provides an audience for the word of the fool who "says in his heart, there is no God"? In other words, what dynamism drives the invocation to the argument?

The Biblical Source

God's Self-Presentation

In the faith of the Hebrew Bible, invocation, naming, and the assertion of existence are in principle inseparable. This is due to the fact that in the thought world and discourse of the Hebrew Bible, the invocation is itself preceded by what exegesis characterizes as God's self-presentation, to which the human invocation responds. A divine "I" announces himself, renderingj unnecessary any invocation, naming, or assertion of existence.

From Self-Presentation to Invocation

Let us begin with the briefest of such instances of God's self-presentation, Leviticus 18:5 and 21: "I [am] Jahweh." According to Zimmerli, this formula expresses the full presence in person of Jahweh in his word.[12] In relation to the commandments that the repeated formula frames, it functions first as an authorization, then as a signature. This formula is the shortest one we can conceive. Yet, at the same time that its plenitude lies in its very brevity, it calls for, following another remark of Zimmerli, "development and a subsequent explication." Here is an initial development. In the same context we read: "I [am] Jahweh, your God" (or: "me Jahweh I [am] your God"). In presenting himself, Jahweh bears witness to himself at the same time as the object of a certain form of human recognition. The possessive form—your God, my God—recalls that Jahweh never presented himself to Israel in any other way than as the God of his people. The covenant, about which I shall have more to say below, is thereby associated with God's very name. And from this initial development comes the opening of our formula to a process of explication that is principally narrative and prescriptive in form. "It is me Jahweh, your God, who brought you out of the house of Egypt, out of the house of slavery. You shall have no other gods besides me" (Exodus 20:2-3). Then follows the Decalogue. The relative narrative—"me...who brought you"—followed by the primary commandment makes for a predicative assertion immediately joined to the self-presentation. As for the exclusive demand inscribed in the first commandment, it too goes as one with this initial development of the "I [am] Jahweh" in the clause "your God."[13] The relative narrative includes in the Name the whole narrative of the Exodus, at the same time that the great commandment links the whole Decalogue to this Name. Thus, on the basis of "I [am] Jahweh," the initiative belongs to the "I" who announces himself as the source of history and ethics. The invocation that responds to him comes second.

From Invocation to Naming

The narrative clause and what we can call the legislative clause, which unfold the "I [am] Jahweh," constitute in turn the core of the naming of God. Let us understand here by naming the attribution of a predicate having the value of a proper name. We will speak of predicative naming in order to distinguish it from what we can call appellative naming (El Shadda, YHWH). Anselm's naming follows from this predicative naming, proper to the Hebrew Bible. For him, as in the Bible, the predicative naming adheres at this point to the appellative naming, in that it calls upon the same object in its invocation: "Thou who..." Here then we have the seed for the Anselmian name—as name one or name two—in the biblical domain.

For the Hebrew Bible, the name/predicate is above all else the Unique One. The key text here is the one known, in Hebraic literature, under the name of the *shema* (*shema* means: Listen! in the imperative mode): "Hear, O Israel: Jahweh our God [is] the one Jahweh" (Deuteronomy 6:4). In this text, the proclamation in the third person—Jahweh [is]—is equivalent to the self-presentation we have been discussing.[14] This declaration of oneness is immediately followed by the great commandment that, here again, is literally one with it: "You shall love Jahweh your God with all your heart, with all your soul, and with all your might." Throughout something exclusive is attested to: just as the one Jahweh excludes the other gods, a total love excludes any sharing with other objects of love.[15] We may disagree about whether existence is refused to other gods by this proclamation of oneness. In fact, the accent is not on the ontological status of idols, but on the undivided devotion due to Jahweh. Indeed, we need to take the entire sequence of Deuteronomy 6:4–19 as a whole: keep these words "engraved in your heart," "recite them to your children," remember the tradition of the Exodus ("take care that you do not forget..."), remain confident in the promise that has no guarantee. The whole counts as a (predicative) naming of God.[16] This naming, like God's self-presentation, is indivisibly ethical ("you shall love...") and narrative ("remember..."). In this sense, it unfolds predicatively the confession of the divine oneness that, itself, responds to the call "Hear, O Israel."

This then is the distant source of the Name according to Anselm: "than which nothing greater..."—"than which nothing better...." In effect, the ethical and narrative unfolding of the confession of oneness can be taken as the seed for the declaration of supereminence attested to by the Name according to Anselm. But this declaration remains without a guarantee. We shall ask below whether it leaves a place for something like an argument by means of which the understanding adds the surety of its "recognition." Before doing so, however, let us continue our investigation into the biblical sources.

From Naming to the Attestation of Existence

The third step is the one most filled with obstacles. It has to do with the existential import of invocation and of naming. Do we find on the biblical plane any indication that an ontological problematic, in our sense, as heirs of the Greeks, belongs to the development of the appellative and the predicative name? The texts we have so far considered—"I [am] Jahweh" and "Hear, O Israel, your God [is] One"—do not allow us to decide this question, inasmuch as Hebrew does not have a copula form for being, and therefore does not permit the shift from being as copula to being taken absolutely. At most, we can say that the self-presentation of God does not allow us to dissociate, as Anselm proposes to his antagonist, the fool, the noetic sense, included in the naming, from its existential sense, become extra-noetic. In this regard, we can risk saying that the self-presentation is equivalent to a self-monstration. And the faithful respond to this by an invocation that, on its side, allows for no slippage between what would be merely thought and what is attested as truly existing. The question simply does not arise. Thus we have seen the *shema* proclaiming the oneness of God unfolding in an ethical-narrative dimension. This unfolding stands for an attestation of existence in the applicable sense. Indeed, the evocation of past deliverances, in Deuteronomy 6:4-19, gives rise to, on the side of the receiver of the message, an assumed, faultless belief in the past actuality of those events that the faithful are enjoined to remember. The ethical efficacy of the commandment, joined to the power of the injunction "Hear, O Israel," is no less than what we might call the narrative efficacy from which it is inseparable. Still, in the absence of any critical reflection on the truth of the past and on the authority of the supreme legislator, the ontological question simply does not arise as a critical question.

Someone may object to these reticent comments that the Hebrew Bible includes at least one assertion about the being of God that cannot be overlooked. This assertion, of course, is the one found in Exodus 3:14, which contains the verb being two times: *eyer asher eyeh.* The Septuagint translates this enigmatic formula by *ego eimi ho on;* the Vulgate has *ego sum qui sum;* and in French one would like to use *je suis celui qui suis* [I am the one who am], but the grammar imposes *je suis celui qui est* [I am the one who is]. To this affirmation of exclusive identity seems to be joined that of a plenitude of identity with an ontological overtone. Is not a bridge thereby set up between the language of faith and that of Greek philosophy, authorizing Etienne Gilson, for example, to speak in this regard of a "biblical metaphysics"?[17] That the verb being is obstinately used twice in the first person in 3:14, then a third time in the continuation of this text, which I shall consider below in terms of its literary unity, should place on guard against too rapid an assimilation of the Hebrew "I am" and the Greek *einai.* In this regard, Anselm still has one foot in the biblical camp, inasmuch as he preserves the second person in an affirmation that is also an invocation: "we believe that thou art a being than which nothing greater can be conceived." That, in Exodus 3:14, the verb is conjugated in the first person, to the exclusion of any slippage from the "I am" to a substantialized infinitive "being," invites us to ask if the verb being, extracted from the "I am," has the same sense as the one presupposed by the Anselmian argument and already filtered through a long onto-theological tradition, where the Hebrew origin had already been interpreted in terms of the Greek ontology of being.

In order to reply to this perplexity it is important, following most Old Testament exegeses,[18] to replace the famous formula in the context from which it is too readily detached, namely, the narrative of the call of Moses (Exodus 3:1–4:7).[19]

This narrative is itself preceded by the vision of the burning bush from which comes God's call, "Moses, Moses," to which Moses replies, "here I am." This response of Moses already stands as the recognition of a presence that is all the more imperious in that it is marked by the "great spectacle" (3:3) of the burning bush that is not consumed. The history of his call could end there. But this is not the case. Called,

Moses objects to his calling five times. A first time: "who am I to…" And God replies: "I will be with you." Is not this reassurance sufficient? No. Moses again objects: "But if [the children of Israel] ask what is his name [the name of the God of the fathers who sends the prophet], what will I answer them?" It is to this objection that the famous *eyeh asher eyeh* replies. The place of the "I am the one who am" (or "who is") is therefore in no way immaterial if we are to make sense of this formula. It is important that the Revelation of the Name—which is the way this fragment is usually referred to—replies to an objection that itself is one segment in a call narrative.

In this regard, what follows is not less important than what had preceded it. Indeed, it is surprising to see that the "I am" becomes the subject of the verb that in fact utters the sending of Moses: "Thus you shall address yourself to the children of Israel: 'I am has sent me to you.'" The predicative name "I am" has become an appellative name. This is not all. A bit further on, the name Jahweh is placed in the same grammatical position as the third "I am": "you shall speak thus to the children of Israel: Jahweh, the God of your fathers…has sent me to you. This is the name I shall bear forever, by which you will call on me in future generations." Here two features cannot be neglected. First, the fact that the "I am the one who am" (or "who is") is part of the response to an objection on the part of the called prophet. Next, the fact that the third "I am," set in the subject position, hence as an appellative name, leads toward the ultimate appellation, the tetragrammon YHWH.[20]

Certainly, the narrative framing of the "I am the one who am" does not attenuate the force belonging to this formula, concerning which we can legitimately affirm that it exceeds the framework of the game of question and answer that serves in a way as the setting for this jewel. Yet this very excess suggests that the redoubled (even tripled) *eyeh* creates an exceptional hermeneutic situation, namely, the opening to a plurality of interpretations of the verb, being, itself. Precisely because the formula exceeds its context, its meaning becomes inseparable from its *Wirkungsgeschichte*, its history of effects, in the sense of effects of reading. In this regard, the Aristotelian-Thomistic interpretation is just one of these interpretations, that which has determined Western metaphysics. And Anselm's argument can be seen as one marker along the way of this interpretation. But if, as I suggested in the introduction to this essay, we consider the whole trajectory for which the ontological argument, from Descartes to Kant, is just one segment, and if we follow this trajectory up to the anti-kerygma of Nietzsche: "God is dead," then we can ask if other interpretive possibilities have not been covered over by the one that triumphed, beginning with the Septuagint translation, where the second *eyeh*, translated as *ho on*, is divested of the first person formulation that it has in common with the first *eyeh*, the redoubling of the "I am" engendering a kind of indeterminate proposition. This is why we may expect from a hermeneutics that stays closer to the text and to its framework, not some lost univocity which perhaps never existed, but precisely a plurivocity; namely, an indetermination that gives the formula the shock value of an enigma. In this regard, attempted alternative translations are especially interesting. I would like to recall that of Buber and Rosenzweig, which substitutes *Werden* (becoming) for *Sein* (being). But perhaps interpretation has to go beyond a simple word by word translation and needs to explore other semantic fields; that of efficacy, for example. (Thus, in German *Wirksamkeit* remains related to *Wirklichkeit*, which preserves the root *wirken*, to work, to operate, to be active. In this way, we take into account the active, operative aspect of the divine presence.) Or perhaps that of fidelity, implied in the structure of the covenant, which I shall discuss below. In any case, what was said earlier about the connection between the divine self-presentation and the memory of past liberations and a firm confidence in new, as yet unannounced deliverances suggests this connection between efficacy and fidelity.

What is essential is: 1) not to base the Hebrew "I am" on a signification of *being* that would oppose it to mere thinking, to subjective cognition. There is no need to fuse essence and existence, for the distinction between them is foreign to

Hebrew "thinking." 2) To preserve a plurivocity of the verb that we translate, for lack of anything better, by "is." 3) To hold in reserve the hypothesis that the response, concerning which we have said that it exceeds the question and the whole situation constituted by a call narrative, is not after all a response, but rather a way of *retreat* into the incognito, something that would exile the so-called response into something outside the text. Between the guarantee of the sending, which encloses the formula within the call narrative, and the dissimulation of the Name, which marks the excess of the response in relation to its narrative framework, we perhaps need not choose, but rather hold these two limit-interpretations as the two extremities of the space of variation offered to the hermeneutics of the divine Name.[21]

Another way of marking the divergence between the Hebrew "I am" and the Greek "being" would be to emphasize the more ethical than ontological function of the revelation of the Name. From this point of view, we must lose not sight of the quite specific function that the revelation of the Name exercises in the call narrative, namely, that of guaranteeing Moses's mission. Even if, once again, the formula goes beyond this function, which is still tributary to the narrative framework, it remains that this formula is a mandate that designates itself as existing, that is, as efficacious. It would then be the objection that provides the occasion for this response that holds the metaphysics of the Name within the ethical orbit of the mandate. It is fundamentally a question of removing the ambiguity that weighs on the mission (true or false prophet?) through a formula whose existential charge cannot be denied, but whose function as authenticating is even more obvious. The reality of God sets its seal of authenticity on Moses's mission. Even if we insist on the excess of meaning in this formula in relation to its function within the framework of the prophetic mission, we must say not only that the Greek "being" can be said in different ways, but also that there exists a non-Greek way of saying it, even several such ways that remain to be explored beyond any alleged "end of metaphysics." As Brevard Childs puts it, we must not break the connection between "self-disclosure" and a "call for commitment." Therefore we have to maintain the "I am who am" (or "who is") between two limits: a simple expansion of the formulas to authenticate the mandate in the call narratives, and the opening through the verb "being" of a space of plurivocity other than the one explored by the Greeks, culminating in the divine incognito that stands over against the authentifying function.[22]

What are we to conclude if not that the conjunction with Greek ontology is a part of the history of the reading of Exodus 3:14, and that it is the totality of the destiny of this reading that today is presented to our critical evaluation?

The Biblical Source

Self-Presentation and Contestation

Now we come to the other side of the problem formulated at the end of my brief comments on the Anselmian argument. What, in biblical faith, might tilt the invocation toward an argument capable of claiming its autonomy in relation to this faith that it is supposed to "recognize," and thereby to set itself up as a proof that finds its demonstrative force within itself?

At first glance, the self-presentation of God seems to cut short any such claim to autonomy. That God only reveals himself in calling, in recalling his past accompanying of his people, in signing his commandments with his Name, would seem to leave no place for a slippage at the heart of the self-presentation that is in the same movement a self-attestation.

However, this is not the case if we consider the faith of the Old Testament. Paradoxically, it is the self-presentation as such that calls for a human complement capable of covering the whole range that runs from invocation to contestation.

A human complement: the Hebrew Bible knows nothing of a God in and for himself. It only knows a God encountering human beings and even creation as a whole. The biblical God, as many have emphasized, is a relational God, which will justify Luther's subsequent thesis that the object of theology is not God, but God and humanity. The inclusion of humanity in God's self-presentation was already apparent in the first formula we have considered: "I am Jahweh" is immediately developed as "I am Jahweh, your God" (or: "me Jahweh am your God").[23] God allows himself to be apprehended only as the God of his people, and these people are known to God only as the people of God. The narrative clause and the ethical clause of what I have called the predicative naming of God bring the human component even ·closer to the God's self-presentation.

The expected response on the side of this human component is surely the invocation. The "thou" of invocation is the only response to the "I" of self-presentation, the "thou" in which we have recognized the *incipit* of the Anselmian argument. However this responsive invocation is just the limit form of a dramatic relation that the Hebrew bible explores in all its potentialities. The narrative clause, which prolongs the "I am Jahweh, your God," sums up a history of deliverance that is not stripped of suffering, complaints, even of rebellion. In this regard, Robert Alter suggests that the biblical narrative as a whole proceeds from the confrontation between a divine, ineluctable plan and a human reluctance that paradoxically temporalizes it.[24] And what does the imperative clause say? Would there be any sense in proscribing false gods and false cults if the spontaneous movement of the heart and the will were not the idolatry that Amos and Hosea call "prostitution" and that the deuteronomic chroniclers denounce as an "abomination"?

The Hebrews have an expression to convey the God/humanity relation into which the whole span of human replies, running from invocation to confrontation, is inscribed. This relation is the covenant, for which many exegetes find an antecedent, even a model, in the Hittite treaties between a suzerain and a vassal.[25] Two points here are important for our discussion. If the covenant stabilizes the bipolar relation constitutive of Israel's faith, it remains an asymmetric relation, in which the suzerain declares his sovereignty even while granting his protection' whereas the submissive, yet contracting party promises obedience. If it is true that the covenant, when compared to the unequal Hittite type of treaties, is far from an instance of simple capitulation, it is also true that it includes resources for protest, even for accusation, hence a power of reply inscribed in the very asymmetry of the relationship. These seeds of discordance are expressed in the theme of the trial that God holds of humanity, especially through the mouths of the prophets, but they are expressed as well in the trial humanity holds of God, a trial that culminates in the book of Job. Yes, God is on trial by his people and they are on trial by God. The questioning that will subsequently serve as the antecedents for the call for intelligibility inscribed in the Anselmian *fides quaerens intellectum* can be derived from this contestation implicitly in the covenantal relation.

The "Objection" to the Call

We can find a symptom of this quarrel with God already in the narrative of the call of Moses. This symptom is Moses's objection to his call, to which responds precisely the redoubled "I am." The narrative in Exodus 3-4 takes care to dramatize this objection in a five-stage crescendo, which cannot be reduced to the effects of the narrative art, however much this text constitutes an admirable example of the biblical art of narration.[26] Here we find all the ingredients for a dissociation in the relationship between the sender and the one sent and, in the background, between the self-presentation and the obedient response.

The Lamentation

The turning point in the curve outlined in the objection, ending in the words of the fool to which Anselm undertakes to reply, is constituted by the lament that in the psalms—a common treasure of the Jewish and Christian communities—constitues the opposite pole of the song of praise.

We may see in this pair—lamentation/song of praise—the most basic dialecticalization of the invocation. For the lamentation is still—or also—an invocation: "how long O Lord!" An elementary logic might incline us to consider the song of praise as the only legitimate response called for by God's self-presentation. We might also be tempted to take recalcitrance, that is, sin, as the only dissonance in the bipolar relationship between God and humanity. However the lament gives a voice to one who has undergone evil that is not reducible to the simple confession of evil committed, that is, to the language of penitence.

In fact, evil as undergone brings into play another dimension than that of the human historical condition, especially if this is reduced—wrongly—to just the "history of salvation" (the well-known *Heilsgeschichte* of exegesis and Old Testament theology). This other dimension is that of creation considered on a cosmic scale. The lament, in effect, is the cry that expresses the rending that affects every part of the creature as such, beyond the person of the covenant, beyond that of history, beyond even that of the *Heilsgeschichte*.

What do we gain by referring at this point to the lament of the creature? This: I said above that the biblical God is a relational God. Now the first relation—at least the one that the biblical canon puts at the head of the scriptures—is that of creation: "In the beginning God created..." This relation is first to the extent that the Bible ignores everything that might apply to a time before creation and, to this extent, every assertion about God considered in isolation. (Given the interpretation we have considered so far, this comment even holds for the "I am the one who is.") The Bible knows God only as related to his people, to humanity, to the whole of creation.[27]

The relation of creation considered in itself includes a dissonant element in principle that we may sum up as the persistence of evil. A speculative theology, claiming to speak of God in himself, "before" or "apart" from creation, may delay the confrontation with the problem posed by the persistence of evil and turn it into a separated chapter from any consideration of the divine perfections. A relational approach, on the contrary, has to think together and at the same time of creation and the persistence of evil.[28]

We can quickly see the consequences of this state of affairs for our inquiry concerning the biblical antecedents of

Anselm's argument. Anselm could focus his argument on the supereminent aspects of God taken as God. Biblical humanity, which can only be considered in terms of a relational schema, whether it is a question of the history of salvation or of the history of creation, cannot adjourn to some later stage its discourse on the problem of evil. Here the question of omnipotence finds itself posed simultaneously with the "I am the one who is."

It may be objected that the so-called priestly narrative of creation, which we read in Genesis 1, culminates in the contemplation of divine response, after God has set like a seal on creation the "yes" of approbation expressed in the admirable "God saw everything he had made and it was good" (Genesis 1:13). How, then, can there be any basis for complaint in creation, apart from humanity's "subsequent" sin? Is there anything other than evil committed? And is not evil undergone just retribution for evil committed? Far from being alien to our investigation, this question is related to whether the predicative name of God can be stated as "perfect being," as will be the case with Descartes, or as "greater than can be conceived," as in Anselm's second name. It is easy to see that it is the argument in its claim to the status of being a proof that is at issue, in its very starting point. The fragility of what will become the ontological argument does not lie perhaps only in the "deduction" of existence from essence, but in the equation between God and the highest good, which decides the divine nature, the predicative name of God. If it is true that the authors of the creation narratives are unaware of the concept of creation *ex nihilo.* Indeed, if they preserve, in their admiration for sovereignty, fear and trembling in the face of a drama, a combat, that not only has always had chaos as its enemy, but which is never done with its adverse forces, then the Old Testament discourse on creation throws up a positive obstacle to the idea of a perfect being, and even to that of a unique locus of highest goods.

That the lament of the creature is organically part of the relational God/creature structure can be read even in the biblical creation narratives. Even in its mildest form, the one we read in the first chapter of Genesis (and that the scribes responsible for the establishment of the canon meant to honor by putting there), creation is a drama where the initial vulnerability to chaos allows us to anticipate the fragility of the created order. So the glory of creation and lamentation in the face of the persistence of evil go together throughout the Hebrew Bible.[29] It is easy to understand why. It is during periods of distress, principally during the time of the exile, that the hope for return and for restoration finds a foundation in creation *in illo tempora*, as a victory over adverse forces. The celebration of victory and the experience of the violence of history constitute the two sides of a single confession of faith. In this sense, the lamentation is the existential context for recalling the mythic victory. An abyss exists that will never be closed between the liturgical affirmation of the sovereignty of God and the everyday experience of the persistence of evil. The psalms bear witness to this, where the faithful one naively recalls God to remember his victories and his ancient promises (Psalm 74). The sovereignty of God is thus the immemorial recall of an "ancient" creation, when it is not reported as a future beyond human mastery, thanks to the eschatological representation of a final, complete victory (as can already be seen in the little Apocalypse in Isaiah 25, called the "messianic banquet"). Affliction can be taken to be transitory, nonetheless it occupies the whole field of "historical" experience. We cannot overemphasize therefore the unmediated juxtaposition, in the Hebrew Bible, of the liturgical and hymnic affirmation of the omnipotence of God and the confession of the persistence of evil, a confession that is itself raised to the lyrical plane of the lamentation. The relation of the full sovereignty of God to the end of time only underscores the dissonance between the proclamation of omnipotence and the confession of the "terror of history." It is this counterpoint, in the form of a dialectic without resolution, that prevents the establishment of the equation of the God of Abraham, Isaac, and Jacob with the idea of perfection assumed by the Anselmian argument, and, later, by the different variations of the ontological argument. To do so we would have to be able to think God in himself, hence to subtract him from the drama of creation, which continues to be confronted with the confession of the persistence of evil. The biblical God cannot be thought apart from the work by which he brings about a fragile order, centered on a habitable earth, itself submitted to human governance prey to malfeasance and unjust suffering. Everything happens as if God were not yet God.[30]

Contestation

At the other extremity of the range of human replies that the structure of the covenant makes possible appears that contestation that adjoins without losing itself in the words of the fool who says in his heart: "no, there is no God."

Contestation indicates the nonservile character of the consent of the human party in the great covenant between God, his people, humanity, and creation. It takes on several different guises in the Hebrew Bible. The prophet's objection to the call that convokes him is already an attenuated form. The lamentation, in turn, sometimes rises to the level of a reproach, as when the complainant addresses himself to Jahweh as to a forgetful God, even a sleeping God—a complaint that many of those deported to Babylon and many of the conquered who remained during the time of the exile could not avoid joining to their cries of distress: "How long Lord...wake up! Wake up, as in past generations" (Isaiah 51:9).

A further step along the pathway of contestation is taken when a figure debates with God, even defies God, as we find illustrated in the supplication that Abraham addresses to God who is about to destroy Sodom and Gomorrah: "Abraham stood again before Jahweh. He drew near and said: are you really going to sweep away the righteous along with the sinner? Suppose there are fifty righteous in the city. Are you really going to destroy them and will you not pardon the city for the fifty righteous who are within it? Far be it from you to do such a thing! To slay the righteous along with the sinner, so that the righteous will be treated like the sinner. Far be it from you! Will the judge of all the earth not do what is just?" (Genesis 18:23–25).[31] Everything takes place as though Abraham challenges God to act according to the same model of justice that God imposes on humans. We may even say that Abraham argues with God, as if the future theological debate wherein the unlimited freedom of God as regards every logical and ethical norm is opposed to the identification of God and the norms he cannot transgress were already laid out by this sequence. The Bible does not formulate this debate in abstract terms. Instead it takes its stand at the heart of a dramatic dialogue between God and a human being where this human being questions God, to the point of calling him into question.[32]

It is against this background that we can situate the book of Job, where obedience, the independence of critical judgment, and the sovereignty of God clash without any conceptual resolution. This is not the place to examine this book in detail. I shall limit myself to the aspect of inconclusive dialectic that, in my opinion, prevents us from thinking of God apart from his twofold relation with humanity and with the whole of creation. The framework for the "testing," according to the terms of the prologue, is burst apart by the body of the poem—chapters 3–37 are undoubtedly of a literary origin distinct from the Prologue to which we find them attached. The controversy here is pushed to the point of accusing an unjust and cruel God. In demolishing the ideology of retribution, for which every evil undergone is the punishment for some evil committed, Job lays bare the scandal of unjust suffering, without which it is not possible to think about God, so long as we preserve the relational structure that binds together God, humanity, and the world, as seems to be the case throughout the Hebrew bible. In this sense, it has been said that the book of Job marks the extreme point of the crisis of the covenant. Hence it is stupefying to hear Jahweh, in the prose epilogue to the book, declare that Job alone has "spoken rightly" of God (Job 42:7). The difficulty for the exegete is to perceive the unity of meaning that holds the text in its final state together. In chapters 38–41, God, speaking from the depths of the whirlwind, does not respond to the accusation of injustice, but instead sets the totality of human experience—including unjust suffering and no doubt the legitimate protest of the suffering righteous—within the vast framework of a repetition of the cosmogony. "Where were you when I laid the foundations of the world?" (38:23–7). God, it almost seems, is not responding here to the Job of the Prologue, but to a Prometheus who dissimulates his *hubris* in his accusation and his insolence of comparing himself to God.[33] God does not answer the man, he discomfits him. It is the Abraham of the binding of Isaac more than the Abraham who pleads for the remaining righteous of Sodom and Gomorrah who can be heard in the final words of the conquered hero: "And Jahweh called to Job and said to him: Will the adversary of Shaddai yield? Is the one who censors God going to reply? and Job answered Jahweh: I have spoken thoughtlessly; what will I answer you? Instead I cover my mouth with my hand. I spoke once…I shall not do so again; twice…I shall add nothing" (50:1–5).[34]

To the withdrawal of God into the unfathomable secret of the creator in majesty corresponds the withdrawal of Job into the silence of the non-question: "Thus I take back my words, I repent with dust and ashes" (42:6). In this double withdrawal, the human being's complaint seems lost from view, even forgotten.

It was necessary no doubt to go so far as Job's contestation, and even more so up to its ambiguous denouement, to perceive the obstacle that a fundamentally relational approach, where not only is God never named in himself and for himself, but where he always appears as the *other* of a dramatic confrontation, constitutes in relation to a predicative naming of God, where the only things stated are the supereminent predicates. The main mediation that the Hebrew Bible proposes, then, is not to be sought on the side of Wisdom, which, through the mouth of Job, "confuses the counsels [of Jahweh] by meaningless proposals" (42:3), as if the point of wisdom were the word of the fool. This mediation appears instead to be that of a practical obedience, itself divided between mute submission and open disputation. The Anselmian argument may thus be interpreted as an attempt to reopen on a theoretical and speculative plane the debate that Wisdom—at least that expressed in the book of Job—seems to have led to a dead end. But the price to pay for this audacious enterprise seems to be the following. For the relational conception of God, with all its dramatic implications, is substituted an abstract concept in which the predicates of supereminence, which are alone retained from the predicative naming of God, find themselves dissociated from the counterpoint of a perhaps incomplete creation, or in any case from a creation marked by the persistence of evil. An inconclusive dialectic, scanned by the alternation of praise and lamentation, thus finds itself broken in the excess of the cry: "how long, Jahweh, will you forget me? To what end?" (Psalm 13:2)—an excess that exceeds itself only in the words of the fool: "No more God!" (Psalm 14:1).

Endnotes

[1] My position is close to that of Eberhard Jungel, *God as the Mystery of the World: On the Foundation of the Theology of the Crucified One in the Dispute Between Theism and Atheism,* trans. Darrell L. Guder (Grand Rapids: Eerdmans, 1983).

[2] *St. Anselm: Basic Writings,* trans. S. N. Deane (LaSalle, Ilinois: Open Court, 1962), 7.

[3] See Anselme de Canterbury, *Oeuvres,* vol. 1: *Monologion, Prosologion,* trans. Michel Corbin, S.J. (Paris: Cerf, 1986), 15.

[4] St. Anselm: Basic Writings, p. 1

[5] Ibid.

[6] Corbin indicates this work of the concept in what he designates as the second name: "thou concerning whom nothing better can be thought." See his introduction to his translation of the *Prosologion* in *Anselme de Canterbury,* 209-24.

[7] Corbin takes chapters XIV and XV of the *Proslogion* to be "the geometrical center of this work" (Ibid., 209).

[8] *St. Anselm: Basic Writings,* 7.

[9] Ibid.

[10] In the language of Boetius, which Anselm draws upon, an argument is a proposition "capable of deciding among the alternatives that are born from the diversity of human opinions" (*Anselme de Canterbury,* 210).

[11] *St. Anselm: Basic Writings*, 20.

[12] Walter Zimmerli, "Ich bin Jahwe," in *Gottes Offenbarung*, edited by Walter Zimmerli (Munich: Kaiser, 1963), 11-40. See also Karl Elliger, "Ich bin der Herr—euer Gott," in *Theologie als Glabenswagnis* (Hamburg: Furche, 1954), 9-34. According to Zimmerli, "Des Ich Jahwes wird aus dem Munde J. selber horbar gemacht." It does not matter for us that, from a historical point of view, the self-presentation, which we read in a written text, should take the place of an oral self-presentation, included in some regular ritual, where God would have taken the voice of a priest as his spokesperson, or where, to put it another way, the priest would have spoken in the name of Jahweh. For a canonical reading, such as that of Brevard Childs, *Introduction to the Old Testament as Scripture* (Philadelphia: Fortress Press, 1979), which I shall return to below, all that matters are that the texts have been received into the canon, with the signification they receive from being located therein.

[13] Another text, which exegesis attributes to the Priestly source (P) can be also be cited in this context, Exodus 6:2f.: "God also spoke to Moses and said to him: 'I [am] Jahweh. I made my self manifest to Abraham, Isaac, and Jacob under the name El Shadda, but I did not make myself known to them under my name Jahweh.'"

[14] From the point of view of the literary structure, someone is recounting what Moses said: "Hear, O Israel." The well-known "Jahweh is one" is pronounced, in the third person, as the content of this injunction. Next comes, in the imperative mode, the ethical tenor of this proclamation: "You shall love Jahweh, your God..."

[15] This bipolarity (proclamation of oneness/commandment to love) is strongly emphasized in Raymond Brown's commentary on the Exodus in *The Book of Deuteronomy: Introduction and Commentary* (Collegeville, Minnesota: The Liturgical Press, 1965), 41-43.

[16] See also Deuteronomy 11:13-21, Numbers 15:37-41. We may refer here also to Rashi's commentary: "Hear, O Israel, the Lord is our God, the Lord is One." *Commentary*: The Lord who is our God now and not the God of *other* nations, will become the One Lord as it is said in Wisdom 3:9: "then I shall change the tongue of peoples into a pure tongue so that they call upon the Name of the Lord"; and as it is said in Zechariah 14:9: "in that day, the Lord will be One and his Name will be One." YOU SHALL LOVE. Accomplish his words through love. He who acts through love does not resemble the one who acts out of fear. He who serves his master out of fear, when this latter

tyrannizes him, will leave his master and go away. *With all your heart:* with your two penchants. Another explanation: let not your heart be divided as regards God. *With all your soul:* even if he takes your life. *With all your might:* with all your money. There are those who love money more than themselves…. Another explanation: with all the measure by which he measures you, be this a good measure or one that chastises. And thus David said (Psalm 116:13 and 3): "I shall lift up the cup of salvation…. If I suffer distress and anguish, I shall call on the name of the Lord." And what is this love? That *his words…be….* By this means, you can know the Holy, Blessed be He, and take up his ways (from *Commentaire de Rachi au "Pentateuque,"* bad. du rabbinat francais [Paris: Fondation S. Levi, 1975]).

[17] Etienne Gilson, *L'Esprit de la Philosophie Medievale* (Paris: Vrin, 1954), 50-52. Regarding the philosophical and theological interpretations of Exodus 3:14, see Alain de Libera and Emilie Zum Brunn, *Celui qui est: interpretations Juives et Chretinennes d'Exode III 14* (Paris: Cerf, 1986); *Dieu et l'Etre, Exegeses d'Exode III, 14 et de Coran XX, 11-24* (Paris: Etudes Augustiniennes, n.d.). See also, D. Bourg et al., *L'Etre et Dieu,* Travaux du C.E.R.I.T. (Paris: Cerf, 1986).

[18] Certain exegetes (Zimmerli, Habel, and others) have underscored the structural kinship between the narrative of the call of Moses and other narratives about the call of the prophets (e.g. Jeremiah 1; Judges 6; Isaiah 6). The schema is something like the following: confrontation (here, the burning bush), an introductory speech (here the call: "Moses, Moses" and the response "here I am"), the call properly speaking (here 3:10: "Now go"), then the objection, to which we shall return when we see the trace of a human recalcitrance in the great conversation between God and man. It is to one of the objections that the "I am the one who am" replies. Finally, comes the word of reassurance (here repeated following the crescendo in Moses' objections).

[19] See Brevard Childs, "The Call of Moses," in his *The Book of Exodus: A Critical, Theological Commentary* (Philadelphia: Westminster, 1974), 47-89.

[20] Werner H. Schmidt, *Der Iawename und Ex. III 14,* places the accent of his exegesis on the progressive construction of the name Jahweh, which, we ought not to forget, becomes the *Rufnahme,* "the name I shall bear forever, by which you will call on me in future generations" (3:15). If we follow this exegetical line, 3:14 gives the meaning of the name Jahweh, by describing the third person in terms of the first person.

21 Enigmas are not lacking even in the immediate context. Why is this question about God's name lent to the people? Have they forgotten the God of the fathers, or is he nameless? Are they seeking a new Name or meaning? And, if this is the case, in what way does this validate Moses' mission? What is more, we have emphasized the threefold "I am." But the third occurrence provides the occasion for a substitution, the Tetragrammaton taking the place of the "I am" previously placed in the position of the grammatical subject of the verb "to send." Ought we then to go so far as to say that the series of "I am"s is there in order to prepare for the announcement of the Tetragrammaton, thanks to the grammatical kinship between the "I am" and a "he is" implied in one of the attested etymologies for the term Jahweh, which would be the verb "being" in the third person of the "incomplete" singular?

22 That an ontology distinct from the function of authentification could have been grafted to Exodus 3:14 is easy to understand. But this is just one interpretive path among others. Do we not read in second Isaiah 43:12-13: "and I am God, from eternity I am"? Childs suggests that the "ontological overtones" (83) virtually present in the formula of Exodus 3:14 may have found an initial expansion (which I would call proto-ontological) in the formula of Revelation 1:8, "he is, he was, and he is to come," and that this declaration could serve in turn as a bridge toward the Septuagint translation, which was already an interpretation and a creation of meaning. Philo, *Vita Moses*, 1.75, could be placed along this trajectory: "Say to them that I am the one who is, and that they can learn the difference between what is and what is not and…furthermore that no name can be properly applied to me to whom alone belongs existence." Here it is existence, by a kind of recoil effect, that renders the Name ineffable.

23 Zimmerli observes that the exclusive character of the possessive relation "your God" is opened by Ezekiel among others to the other nations: "You will recognize that I am Jahweh. The peoples will recognize that I am your God" (Ezekiel 38:23). As Zimmerli says, the brief *Selbsvorstellung* formula ("I am Jahweh"), through its very development, calls for an *Erkenntnisaussage* on the side of its human counterpart taken as a whole.

24 Robert Alter, *The Art of Biblical Narrative* (New York: Basic Books, 1983).

25 See Jon D. Levenson, *Creation and the Persistence of Evil: The Jewish Drama of Divine Omnipotence* (San Francisco: Harper and Row, 1985).

26 The first objection is still an objection of a lack of adequacy: who am I to undertake such a mission? The second, to which the "I am who am" responds, takes an oblique turn: if the children of Israel ask what is his name, what shall I answer them? The third takes as its pretext the people's possible nonrecognition of the one sent: "if they refuse to believe me and to listen to me and if they say: did Jahweh appear to you?" In other words, if they take me for a false prophet? The great contest between the prophets of Jahweh and those of Baal in the book of Kings comes to mind. In Exodus, the miracle of the staff that becomes a serpent for a brief moment, and then that of the leprous hand that becomes healthy again do not end the argument. There comes a fourth objection: "I am slow of speech and slow of tongue." The response to this is an affirmation of sovereignty that brings to mind the answers given in the book of Job: "who gave man a mouth with which to speak?" Then a fifth objection: "send someone else for this mission," which anticipates the defection of Jonah, fleeing in the opposite direction. And what do we read here? "Then Jahweh was angry with Moses." As for the splitting of the role between Moses and Aaron, which seems to put an end to the argument, this is heavy with future threats if one knows the episode of the golden calf that will divide Moses and Aaron.

27 I shall leave aside here any discussion bearing on the chronological priority of the preaching of the savior God over that of the creator God. This question has returned to prominence recently with the overthrowing of the chronology based on the classical theory of four sources. The only fixed point, it seems, is the proclamation of second Isaiah: only a God who created all things can change the course of history to the benefit of his captive people and thereby set the history of salvation into motion once again.

28 What follows owes much to the work of Levenson cited above.

29 Levenson notes that the Hebrew Bible does not know that notion of *creatio ex nihilo*, in the sense that was subsequently applied by Jewish, Christian, and Muslim theologians. In the first place, the Bible bears the traces, principally in Psalms and in Job, of myths similar to those of Babylon and Ugarit, where God fights against uncreated primordial powers, principally sea monsters. God comes out the winner, but chaos subsists. In this respect, the flood narrative, as a narrative of de-creation and re-creation, constitutes a valuable testimony concerning, on the one hand, the vulnerability of order, and, on the other hand, the connection between this order and the covenant. God's faithfulness, in promising never to destroy his creation again,

turns out to be the sole guarantee of order. Creation has become a corollary of the covenant. Psalm 104 gives an account of an intermediary stage between creation as combat and the creation with no opposition of Genesis 1. This is not a narrative, but rather the panorama of the splendors of creation. The abyss stills appears as menacing, but Leviathan appears as a work that "you form for your laughter" (v. 26). Creation, as in Job 38, consists in containing chaos within assigned limits, according to calculated measures. As for the narrative in Genesis 1, if chaos seems to be docile as concerns the order that is impressed upon it, following the mode of divisions and successive apportionings. nothing says that it is not primordial, as perhaps the shadows that the creative work makes alternate with the day convey. Levenson is perhaps correct to emphasize that the "rest" of the seventh day, in founding and sanctifying the sabbath, provides a human counterpart to the divine sabbath. And the sabbath itself is only a respite in the sequence of works and days, a liturgical pause where the contrast with bad times is once again underscored. Levenson boldly places his exegesis of the creation narratives under the sign of the subsequent speculations of certain Talmudists and of the Kabbala (38). We might ask whether this idea of an incomplete creation and perhaps, by a kind of recoil effect, of a God who is not yet God does not find an unexpected echo in the philosophy of Alfred North Whitehead.

[30] See Levenson, 38.

[31] What follows, of course, is: "Abraham continued: 'I am a fool to speak to my Lord, I who am dust and ashes. But perhaps of the fifty righteous, five are lacking. Will you, for the lack of five, make the whole city perish?' He answered, No, if fortyfive righteous are to be found there.' Abraham spoke up again and said: 'Suppose there are only forty.' And he answered: "I shall not do so, due to the forty."' From forty, Abraham passes to thirty, then to twenty, then to ten: "Let my Lord not become angry and I shall speak one last time: suppose there are ten to be found" and he answered: "I shall not destroy them, due to the ten" (Genesis 18:27-32). Levenson underscores the paradox so well indicated by Abraham's embarrassment ("I am a fool to speak to my Lord, I who am dust and ashes") — the paradox of a situation where it becomes both necessary and absurd to tell God what he ought to do.

[32] The paradox referred to in the previous note is redoubled if we oppose to this episode of Abraham's pleading that of the binding of Isaac, where Abraham urges submission to the divine command ("Here am

I" is pronounced two times!) to the point of being ready to sacrifice his son as a burnt offering. Genesis in reporting this scene, so often interpreted in literature and in works of art, puts it under the theme of the "test" (22:1). The end of this episode confirms this: "I now know that you fear God; you have not refused me your son, your only son" (22:12). Bringing these two episodes which have to do with the same character together, Levenson sees in them the two poles of the Jewish attitude to God: one forbids judging the inscrutable God, the other is not afraid to argue with him. This spiritual dialectic, Levenson thinks, results from the nature of the covenental relation, where the consent of the contracting human being is both preserved and surpassed. It is this same spiritual dialectic that unfolds its variations in the narrative, legislative, and cosmogonic texts. Here is confirmed the idea put forth above that the myth of a combat at the origin of creation, in making room for the persistence of evil, indicates at the same time a space of obedience for human beings, where they express their collaboration in the creation.

[33] See Levenson, 155.

[34] After Jahweh's second discourse, which shows Behemoth and Leviathan as submissive to him, Job makes this answer to Jahweh: "I know that you are all powerful: what you conceive, you can realize. I was the one who confused your counsels, by my meaningless proposals. I spoke without understanding of marvels that surpass me and that I am unaware of (Listen, let me speak, I am going to question you and you will instruct me). I knew you only through hearsay, but now my eyes have seen you. I take back my words, I repent with dust and with ashes" (42:1-6). The book of Job seems to be a result of the fact that the Hebrew Bible leaves argumentation and obedience juxtaposed (Levenson, 148-56).

Chapter 13

Genesis 1-5 as Matrix of Jesus' Mission

Wolfgang Roth

'...to complete the work of the one who sent me' (John 4:34)

How can the Johannine Jesus claim that his sender's work is incomplete? What is, to begin with, the nature of that work? And why does it stand in need of perfection? Further, in what way does the man from Nazareth bring to conclusion what was begun by that work?

Answers emerge when the narratives in Genesis 1-5 are seen as the primary foil for Jesus' mission. Had the creator of Paradise not identified to Adam and Eve among the trees the one whose fruit offers the gift of the knowledge of good and evil? Had he not, by pain of death, forbidden them to eat from it? And had he not, after the pair had attained the prohibited divine knowledge, removed them from the garden itself, though not from remembering it? Had this (preliminary) ending of the Paradise story not left the primal pair endowed with divine knowledge but without god-like life?

On further thought, does the story not suggest that what the Paradise creator had withheld from human grasp at that time, may at some other moment in the future be freely offered to those who do not claim it as their own? More, does the sequel story not portray Abel as first victim of the loss of Paradise? Does his innocently shed blood not mark him as one who does not requite the brother's hate in kind but who maintains another, earlier standard of action?

Leading questions all, to be sure! In the central part of the Johannine narrative (2:1–20:29), however answers are given through a sequence of six discourses, each highlighted by a 'sign' offered by Jesus. On closer inspection, these symbolic actions prove to correspond to successive themes in the creation story of Paradise. Through these signs, the Johannine Jesus transforms the original gifts of water, health, food, sight, life and spirit into transcendent gifts. More, the created Paradise offered only in part and incompletely, is now, through Jesus' mission and his friends' rebirth 'by water and the spirit,' offered in its divine fullness. In a word: Paradise Perfected.

This transfiguration of creation assumes the existence of two spheres, that of 'Eden/Paradise' (Genesis 2–4) and that of 'Kosmos' (Genesis 1 and 5). The Johannine compositions opens with the announcement of Jesus' mission as a heightened re-enactment of his mediatorial role in creation (1:1–18). The narration soon unfolds by a veiled blending of Abel's life and death into Jesus' mission and parabolically points to this understanding by using the enigmatic title 'Son of Man/Adam'—a hypothesis argued elsewhere.[1] The uniquely Johannine use of the term 'signs' with reference to their selection from Jesus' many deeds points to Genesis 1–5 as the primary scriptural matrix for the Johannine circles.

This unusual reading of Genesis 1–5 generates the Johannine narrative universe. Its storyline and its major figures, and their spatial and temporal positioning, are based on these two creation stories and on their immediate sequels. On the other hand, the Johannine Jesus narrative also seeks to reflect in its actual narrative execution the canon of Judaism at the time, that is, 'Moses and the Prophets.' Moreover, it is formulated in the light of its interaction with the competing conception of Jesus' mission put forward in Mark's and Matthew's narratives. In other words, its composition reflects the complexity of first century C.E. Judaism.

Given the work's figurative language and the exhortation of its central figure 'to search the Scriptures which bear witness to me' (John 16:25; 5:39), the following study is inductive in approach and explorative in nature. The extensive literature in Johannine studies cannot be discussed due to limitations of space. In addition, although my approach differs markedly from source and redaction criticism I do not have sufficient space for the required methodological discussion. Suffice it to note that the Johannine conceptualization of Jesus' mission is, in its literary entirety, born of an inherited anticipation of 'Paradise Made Perfect.' Thus, rather than positing sources and redactions as stages of a literary evolution, we approach the 'book of signs' as the seamless creation of a comprehensive vision.

In a manner of speaking, the proposed journey into understanding is comparable to the gradually changing response of Nicodemus to the claims of the Johannine Jesus. That Pharisee and "teacher of the Judeans" progresses from interested curiosity met by the master's stark instruction on spiritual rebirth through the cautious plea for fairness in his fellow Pharisees' treatment of Jesus to his indication that he had become a secret disciple (John 3:1–21; 7:45–52; 19:38–42). Jesus' word illustrates the point: "Everyone who has heard from the father and then preceded to study (the Scriptures in light of that divine call), does come to me" (John 6:45b).

The following study begins with the identification of 'the (six) works of the father,' understood as aspects of the one work with which his sender, his father, has entrusted him. Its completion is Jesus' mission. We will then show how these aspects correspond to the divine gifts of creation as laid out in the Paradise story. This leads to an exploration of two aspects of the Johannine narrative in light of its scriptural model: 'Eden versus Kosmos' and 'Love and Hate'. In conclusion, broader interpretive issues raised by our study as well as the relation of the Johannine narrative to 'Moses and the Prophets' will be briefly noted.

The Work(s) of Jesus and Their 'Witness'

After Jesus' conversation with the Samaritan woman at Jacob's well, his disciples encourage him to eat (John 4:31-38). When he responds that he has food to eat about which they do not know, they are puzzled and wonder whether somebody has brought him food. This prompts the master to deliver a brief lesson on the disciples' mission; they are sent to reap 'fruit toward the life of the age' (4:36). His opening words summarily refer to his own mission as the framework for that of his disciples: "My food is to do the will of the one who sent me and to complete his work" (4:34). What sustains Jesus in his task, beyond the physical nourishment about which his disciples are concerned, is carrying out the mission of someone whose identity is not disclosed by name. Here as elsewhere this One is defined as Jesus' sender and as his divine father. No wonder the disciples remain puzzled not only about who that divine figure actually is but also about his whereabouts and the actual nature of his work.

Jesus speaks once more about the 'work' given him to do, this time addressing his divine father (John 17:1-26). Now, shortly before his death in Jerusalem, that same work 'has been completed,' and the father is asked to glorify his son with 'the glory he had at his side before the Kosmos existed' (17:4-5). Apart from the requested glorification into a previous state of being to be explored below, we note the affirmation that Jesus' imminent death marks the finish of what began with his appearance among his people. Evidently, the Johannine writer understands the master's activity in its entirety as the work which, begun by his father, he was commissioned to finish.

The third passage in which the completion of the activity first undertaken by Jesus' father is the subject, occurs in the story of Jesus' healing of the man who had been ill for 38 years (John 5:1-47). After Judeans had challenged his claim that "my father is at work until now, and I am at work as well"

(5:17), he eventually adduces his 'witnesses' (5:30–47). In this connection he says, "I have a witness higher than that of John! After all, the works which the father told me to complete—the very works which I am doing, they bear witness concerning me that the father has sent me." (5:36) Here, however, reference is made to Jesus' works in the plural. In other words, while the father's and the son's activity is one work when seen in its entirety, it can also be seen as a series of individual works.

There are several references to Jesus' work(s) without the notion of his 'completing' what the father began. They show that Jesus' works are done by no one else but Jesus and that he thus stakes his credibility on them (John 15:24; 10:37–38). He can only do them because his father remains in him; when he does carry them out, they become evident as those actually done by his father (14:10; 9:3). Thus they are contrasted with those done in the name of the evil one; in fact, God's works have become visible so as to undo those of the devil (John 8:41; 1 John 3:8,12). The season for the appearance of God's works is now, while it is day (John 9:4; 7:3); moreover, the future will witness yet greater ones (5:20). These aspects of Jesus' works attest him as the one whom the father commissioned to bring to perfection what he began (10:25).

What exactly is the nature of these works? How does their variety exhibit unity? How do they fit into the frame of the father's and the son's one work?

Six Feasts - Six Sections - Seven Signs

Readers of John's Jesus narrative are told that what its storyteller presents is actually a selection from a much greater store of deeds of the master: "Jesus did many other signs in his disciples' presence. They are not put down in this booklet. These have been written up so that you are persuaded that Jesus is the anointed one, God's son, and that in this certainty you have, in his name, life" (John 20:30-31, see also 21:25). Why are Jesus' deeds here identified as 'signs'? And why are the first two of them expressly counted (2:11/4:54) so as to suggest to hearers that they continue counting? What is the principle according to which this selection of signs was made? More: How does this series of signs lead to "life"? And how is that 'life beyond life' mediated?

As for the Johannine 'Book of Signs' in its entirety, it is composed of a title-like postscript (20:30-31), an introduction which lays out John the Baptizer's mission as the divinely designated opening witness (1:1-51) and a conclusion which introduces Peter's mission after Jesus' departure (21:1-25). The core of the narrative (2:1-20:29) is made up of six narrative units. Each of these is related to a "festival (of the Judeans)," six in all. The period of activity spans three Passovers (2:11; 6:4; 11:55) and includes one (unnamed) festival between the first and second Passover (5:1) and two named ones between the second and third (Booths in 7:2 and Hanukah in 10:22).

As we will see shortly, these festival references serve as markers, identifying six instructional units. As such they mark, over the course of time stretching from before the first Passover to the fateful third Passover, progress in instruction. Take the two disciples of John the Baptizer who respond to their master's attestation of Jesus (John 1:35-39; 2:2; 6:66-71; 15:12-17): They move from being willing enquirers (before the first Passover) through being 'servant disciples' in Jesus' immediate company (for the ensuing two years) to eventually becoming 'Jesus' friends' and continuators of their master's mission beyond the latter's earthly sojourn.

Each of the units marked off from one another through the festival references (2:1-4:54; 5:1-47; 6:1-71; 7:1-10:21; 10:22-11:54; 11:55-20:29), is made up of two elements: (1) narration of a 'sign' (two in the first section) and, (2) thematically related to the nature of this sign, one or more instructional discourses, progressively ranging wider and wider in scope, in dialogical and/or monological mode. Thus 5:2-9a tells a sign: the healing of the man who had been 38 years in weakness. This is followed by Jesus' teaching about the significance of the sign, beginning with a dialog (quoted or related; 5:9b–18) and issuing into an extensive monologue about the mission given to him by his father (5:19–47).

The positioning of sign and discourse in relation to each other varies from unit to unit. However, the theme introduced by the sign provides conceptual coherence to each section. The signs of the first three are told at the section opening in order to provide the basis for the following discourse. On the other hand, the last two signs, those of the gift of life out of death and of 'divine spirit,' are respectively the climax of Jesus' wait until Lazarus' actual demise and of his farewell teachings of his disciples, followed by his death and appearances to his disciples.

Thus each 'sign' points to that work of Jesus which provides the unit with its organizing topic. In the following tabulation, Jesus is in each unit identified as giver of a gift that is acted out through a sign and explained through discursive instruction. We already noted that the first section has two expressly enumerated signs. This feature will briefly claim our attention below in the discussion of the relation of the Johannine portrayal of Jesus to that of Mark and Matthew.

	Sign	*Gift*
2:1–4:54	1. Water into Wine in Galilee	Living Water
	2. Healing in Galilee	Health Beyond Infirmity
5:1–47	3. Healing at Bethesda	Health Beyond Infirmity
6:1–71	4. Feeding of 5,000	Celestial Food
7:1–10:21	5. Opening Blind Eyes	Spiritual Discernment
10:22–11:54	6. Resurrecting Lazarus	Defeat of Death
11:55–20:29	7. Inbreathing Divine Spirit	Divine Spirit

Water - Health - Food - Discernment - Death - Spirit

These topics represent a canonical gift sequence. In the Johannine narratives each gift in turn is raised the plain of 'life beyond life,' or, in most translations, 'eternal life.' That life 'beyond' is defined both spatially and chronologically; it is lived within the Edenic/Paradise sphere, and it is lived already now as well as in any (past and) future. How is this transformation narratively developed in each of the six sections?

To begin with the first section (John 2:1-4:54), the supply of material water from Jacob's well to the Samaritan woman makes life for her and her family possible. However, what Jesus offers is water which will, in the language of Genesis 2:6, become within her 'a fountain of water springing forth unto the life beyond this life' (John 4:14). Her initial misunderstanding highlights the unexpected, the new in Jesus' offer.

Similarly, in the second section (John 5:1-47), the gift of wellness to a man infirm for 38 years is greater than health enjoyed from birth (5:6-9a). Thus he is given another chance to live 'well.' When Jesus then exhorts him "to sin no more lest worse befall" (5:14), he alludes to the prohibition announced to Adam in Paradise after he had been given life (Genesis 2:15-17).

As for the gift of sustenance, it is told in the third section (John 6:1-71), that while Moses fed Israel in the desert with daily manna, Jesus feeds the 5,000 with celestial manna, "the bread of life" (6:32-35). The notion of 'the bread of life' cannot but evoke in the hearers' mind the image of the 'tree of life' in Paradise and its forbidden nature then and there (Genesis 3:22-24), contrary to its God-given availability now through Jesus.

In the fourth section (John 7:1-10:21), Jesus' gift of sight to a congenitally blind man offers the ultimate discernment: belief in Jesus' identity as 'Son of Adam/Man' (9:35-38). Already alerted to the raising of the preceding Paradise gifts, one is reminded of the forbidden 'tree of knowing good and evil' as foil for the Johannine narration (Genesis 2:9, 15–17, 3:1–24). The blind man's coming to sight reverses the fateful result of Adam's and Eve's eating from that tree. In this case, the man's congenital blindness alludes to the notion of (an obedient) Adam's initial inability 'to know good and evil', that is, to be able to make the ultimate discernment and so to become 'like God' (Genesis 3:5,22). The Johannine heightening of the Genesis motif in fact inverts it: What in Paradise was withheld from human reach by divine decree, is now through divine initiative freely granted.

The fifth gift of John's Jesus, the overcoming of Lazarus death (John 11:1–54), is similarly an inversion. It alludes to the human fate of death, the result of Eve's and Adam's disobedience. The story is cast so as to make apparent Jesus' intention to effect its reversal. Thus he ensures that he does not arrive at Bethany until Lazarus is dead and buried (11:6–14). His ensuing conversation with Martha who had come out to meet him (11:17–27), raises the question of the resurrection, as Martha affirms, "on the last day." But Jesus' response both announces, yet still also veils, that that day has come and is now.

Jesus is aware that his ability to present this pen–ultimate gift is the ultimate test of his mission. Thus he expresses it in emotions: he "weeps" and twice he is "deeply distressed" (11:35,33,38)—emotions which the looming final test evokes. This is why the narration slows down, all the more so because it is recognized by witnesses as such (11:38–44). It is after the audible appeal to his father, made for the sake of those present, that he succeeds in reversing death, that very death which had reigned since Adam's and Eve's disobedience and which is symbolized by the creator's removal of Adam and Eve from access to the tree of life (Genesis 3:22, 19). As anticipated (John 7:4), this sign is rendered in public and causes the emnity which soon leads to his willingly accepted passion and death (11: 45–53; 13:10–11, 21–33; 18:2–14). His last word from the cross can thus not be an outcry of abandonment but of highest achievement: "It is completed" (19:28–30). In other words, the one sent to do his father's work and, as loyal son, to bring it to conclusion (4:34), has completed his mission.

In the last section (11:55-20:29), the final gift is that of 'holy spirit' (20:19-23). Edenic creation had been culminated in the creator's "breathing" life "in" to Adam's face when he had been formed in the garden on the last day of creation week (Genesis 2:7), thus constituting him and his descendants as living human beings. The spirit which Jesus "breathes in" (John 20:22) to the group of disciples gathered behind still closed doors on the first day of the week, turns that room into Paradise restored and makes the gathered disciples carriers and conveyors of 'life beyond life.' They are now "born of (living) water and (holy) spirit" (3:5), the ultimate qualification of discipleship that Jesus had identified in programmatic discourse directed to 'the teacher of the Judeans,' the Pharisee Nicodemus, who was on the road to becoming a secret disciple.

Why are Jesus' Six Works "Signs"?

If the sixfold motif sequence 'water, life, food, discernment, death, loss of Paradise' defining the Eden story provided the Johannine composition with the successive elements of its conceptualization of Jesus' mission, several questions raised above find their answer.

First, this thematic correlation is properly signaled by a selection from Jesus' many works; only these works may be called 'signs.' Now we understand that these works are pointers to the Eden story as the scriptural matrix of Jesus mission. By the same token, this selection recognizes other possibilities of 'selecting' Jesus' deeds in the service of other conceptualizations of the master's mission. Thus the Johannine perspective does not claim to be the only one possible. Rather, the Johannine heightening stands alongside comparable enhancements of scriptural models by other conceptualizations of Jesus' mission, by Mark and Matthew,

Thomas or Luke, Paul or the writer of the Letter to the Hebrews. In this connection we note that the Johannine composition identifies itself as 'a Book of Signs' (20:30-31) but never labels itself "gospel." The latter term is appropriately used only in connection with those Jesus narratives which use it in direct relation to their conceptualizations of Jesus' mission, that is, Mark and Matthew.

Secondly, the presentation of the six signs not only connects Jesus' task during his sojourn in the Kosmos directly with the divine work of creation as told in Genesis 2. It also implies that the original six day creative activity of the divine father has now, in the light of Jesus' enhancement of the original gifts of creation, been shown to stand in need of completion. Or, put inversely by Jesus, "My food is to do the will of the one who sent me and to complete his work." (4:34) By saying this, John's Jesus does not diminish his divine father; on the contrary, the father is and remains the one who gives the commandments to his son and to whom the latter turns with the request to be glorified, that is, confirmed as obedient even to willing acceptance of martyrdom (12:49; 17:5). He and the father "are one" (10:30).

Thirdly, as 'signs' pointing to Genesis 1-5 as a basic matrix of the Johannine conceptualization of Jesus' mission, they necessarily lead to an interpretation of the fourth New Testament Jesus narrative which makes the opening chapters of the First Testament its primary—though not its exclusive—frame of reference. Thus the commentator is led to place the Johannine unfolding of Jesus' mission into the spatial and temporal settings of Genesis 1-5 and cannot but read John's story with the major figures and the storyline of its scriptural model in mind. To illustrate this point, we will briefly explore 'Eden and Kosmos' as well as two defining forces in the storyline: 'Hate and Love'.

Eden versus Kosmos

When the departing Jesus comforts his own, he urges them not to be disturbed. Then he proceeds to speak of the place which he will prepare for them after his going away, "In my father's house are many places to stay..." (John 14:2). That place, where his friends will eventually join him, is obviously not located in the Kosmos but in another sphere, a domain where his father dwells. The spatial separation of the two realms is as evident as their interrelation with each other. Thus Jesus leaves that other sphere, his home and origin, and descends into the Kosmos. Upon the completion of the work his father sent him to do, he leaves the Kosmos and returns to that realm (16:28, see 13:1, 17:11). His friends had been promised to see "the heaven opened and messengers of God ascending from and descending upon the Son of Adam/Man" (1:51). In other words, while Jesus sojourns in the Kosmos, he remains in communication with that other realm.

The interrelation is also implied in terms of time. In the prayer to his father after the farewell to his friends, Jesus asks that his own go to join him in the place for which he is departing. This he requests so that they may behold his glory which his father gave him "because you loved me before the founding of the Kosmos" (17:24). In a similar fashion he asks earlier in the prayer that his father glorify him with the glory "which I had beside you before the Kosmos had come into being" (17:5). Moreover, the Kosmos not only has its beginning at a time when the other sphere was already in existence, it also comes to its end while the other realm continues to be: "The Kosmos passes away" because through Jesus' death it and its ruler have "come into judgment" (1 John 2:19; John 12:31).

Johannine Edenology/Cosmology evidently juxtaposes and contrasts the two realms because it interprets the opening chapters of Genesis as narrations relating to the two realm created by God: Eden/Paradise and Kosmos. This reading resembles a widely attested connection of Genesis 1-2 with a 'double decker universe.' For those who argue that the creation stories represent two ways of narrating one and the same creation, Genesis 2 specifies in vivid detail what Genesis 1 presents systematically and comprehensively; thus tensions between the two narratives are harmonized.

Still others read the two stories with reference not only to two created spheres but also to two competing, even mutually opposed creating agents.

Moreover, in the Johannine perspective the divine making of Eden's Paradise and of its guardian pair Adam/Eve with their sons Cain and Abel, is not only spatially separated from Kosmos, but also both ante-dates and post-dates it. This allows the writer to refer to what occurred "before the founding of the Kosmos." The Johannine appropriation of the creation stories suggests that there exist, as it were by scriptural definition, two separate created spheres. Their interactions in time and space are therefore also the temporal and spatial framework of Jesus' mission. By the same token, assertions made in the context of Johannine Edenology/Kosmology also have an ethical dimension.

Love and Hate

With these antithetical terms the ethic of the two spheres moves into focus. The attitude and actions of love ascribed to the celestial sphere are contrasted with the hate that the Kosmos shows to those who are not his own (John 15:18-19; 17:4; 1 John 3:13). Thus the Johannine Jesus begins his farewell speech with "the new commandment" of mutual love; love is the decisive mark of discipleship (John 13:34-35). On the other hand, the first Johannine letter makes the perfection of divine love among the followers a matter of obedience not to "a new commandment" but to "an old one which you have heard from the beginning" (1 John 2:3-7).

The discourse in 1 John 3:11-18 confirms that this ethical antithesis is a reflection of the Johannine reading of Genesis 1-5. The message to love one another has been heard "from the beginning," that is, in the first pages of the Scriptures. Hence it is the fratricide committed by Cain which supplies, by implication, the scriptural base for the argument. Since Cain murdered his brother, he is by definition one who hates his brother. In turn, his murderous act is evidence that the 'life beyond' is not his portion (see also 1 John 4:16b-21). By the same token, the victim of Cain's hate, demonstrated brotherly love by allowing himself to be treacherously dealt with by his brother.

Thus the love-hate ethic of the Johannine writings is derived from scriptural motifs found in Genesis 2:4b -4:16. As I have argued elsewhere, mutual love and hate are archetypally enacted by Abel and Cain, and in this enactment implicit obedience and defiance of the divine will became apparent in Paradise.[2] There it is proposed that the enigmatic designation 'Son of Adam / Man' is a veiled reference to Jesus as 'Abel Reincarnate.' The honoree of this collection has, in a response to that paper, raised relevant questions;[3] I plan to discuss those in a broader context elsewhere.

Finally, we note that this aspect of the love-hate ethic underlies the troublesome passage John 8:31-59 which tells how Judeans who had come to believe in Jesus are drawn into sharp controversy and eventually seek to stone him. There Jesus, in reaction to the Judeans' intention to kill him, first seeks to demonstrate the inconsistency of their behavior (8:39-42) and then precedes to attribute their destructive plans to their descent from Satan: "You are descended from the father, that is, the devil, and so you wish to carry out the desires of your father. That one has from the beginning been a murderer. He did not continue to take his stand in the (sphere of) truth because truth was not his share. When he utters deceit, he speaks out of his own (origins), because he is a liar, as also his father (is)" (8:44).

Evidently, the opponents of the Johannine Jesus are on the basis of their murderous nature judged to be descendants of Cain. When they lie and plan murder they act in keeping with the nature of their father who was born a manslayer, moreover, he was a liar as was his father. In other words, Cain was conceived by Eve with the devil when the latter, in the form of that snake, had his way with her. Moreover, this understanding of Cain's conception implies that of the two sons of Adam as described in Genesis 4:1-16, only Abel was originally conceived by Eve from Adam. Is he therefore 'only begotten'? We note that a similar reading of Genesis 3-4 underlies the instruction on hate and love in 1 John 3:10-18.

Conclusion

A fuller discussion of the manner in which the opening sections of Genesis supply a basic matrix of the Johannine portrayal of Jesus' mission must be left to a future, more comprehensive study. Suffice it to say here that Johannine teaching in its narrative form draws on that matrix by way of narrative design, while in its epistolary form it does so by way of allusion. Thus the Letters of John, which are propositional and hortatory in style, occasionally illustrate a point with a direct reference to a motif in Genesis 1-5. For instance, Cain's failure to observe the primal command of brotherly love is due to his evil works; after all, it is known that everybody who hates his brother is a murderer (1 John 3:11-18, see also 4:9 and 2:7). On the other hand, the Johannine Jesus narrative basically unfolds its storyline on the basis of Genesis 1-5, albeit parabolically in order to invite exploration through 'searching the Scriptures.'

The Johannine writers did of course not design and formulate their Jesus portrayal in a vacuum, that is, in exclusive interaction with Genesis 1-5. What other generative forces are at work in the composition of 'A Book of Signs'? We have already explored our writer's and audience's expectation horizon within which the Johannine writing is conceived. Secondly, there is the new situation which the loss of the Temple in 70 C.E. brought and which in different ways is addressed in each of the four New Testament Jesus narratives. Finally, there is the obligation to think and compose within the parameters that the canon of the period, 'Moses and the Prophets,' defines. We devote to each of these three points a brief discussion.

1. Early Jewish writers stood in a tradition of Scripture appropriation that they in part shared with other groups of first century C.E. Judaism but which in part

was also uniquely their own. The hermeneutic ranges represented by priestly Sadducees, lay Pharisees, Mosaic Samaritans, Galilean migrant prophets, allegorizing Hellenists, Scripture searching 'Healers,' Palestinian zealots, Zadoqite Dead Sea Covenanters and individual savants like Philo or Luke illustrate the point. Considerable variations were accepted but also debated within as well as between these groups, notably in haggadic activities relating to liturgies, storytelling, Scripture meditation, preaching and argument. Here and there groups of disciples following a teacher interacted with each other over the life time of their master and beyond, as the Schools of Hillel and Shammai illustrate.

The Jesus stories were also part of this activity. Individual 'evangelists' remained rooted in their hermeneutic and maximized or minimized aspects of Jesus' mission within their expectation horizons, doing so in part through interaction with or in response to other groups.

That each of the canonical Jesus narratives is the result of such interaction, is readily observable in the way in which the mission of John the Baptist as first witness and of Simon Peter as Jesus' lead follower are defined in the Jesus narratives. Especially the Johannine introduction (1:1-51) and conclusion (21:1-25) are shaped by interaction with (Petrine-Galilean / Pharisaic) portrayals of Jesus mission by Mark and Matthew. This issue cannot be pursued here, except in relation to the Johannine inclusion of the expressly numerated 'second sign', the distance healing of the royal officer's son of Capernaum (4:46-54). It is thematically a Galilean version of the immediately following third sign enacted in Jerusalem (5:2-9a) because, in both, restoration of health is the theme. Suffice it to note that aside from the Feeding of 5,000, this is the only deed of power that directly corresponds to power deeds that Matthew narrates (8:5-13, see also Luke 7:1-10).

The Johannine Jesus connects with this sign, by way of instruction, nothing more than his wearied recognition that "unless you see signs and wonders, you certainly don't come to faith" (John 4:48). It is the point narratively demonstrated by the risen Jesus with reference to doubting Thomas (John 20:24-29). In other words, the Johannine inclusion of the Matthean version of the healing of the officer's son serves to highlight, in contrast with its Matthean version, the at best limited value of 'signs and wonders.'

2. Since the destruction of the Temple in 70 C.E. is an important element in each of the canonical Jesus stories, their narrators sought to show how Jesus' mission is in fact a new chapter in the story of divine activity in Israel as well as among the seventy nations descended from Noah, the 'Gentiles.' The time span of one, at the most two generations after 70 C.E. was, as it were, the window of opportunity for doing so. Indeed, the two successor communities of biblical Israel took shape in that period: a Pharisaic-Rabbinic and a Patristic-Christian one, Synagogue and Church. Each of the canonical Jesus stories as well the emerging focus of early Judaism on Halacha soon to be codified in the Mishnah, also bear witness to the creativity which the (soon permanent) loss of the old center, the temple, brought. Had not several hundred years earlier the destruction of the Solomonic Temple already led to scriptural creativity and communal rebirth? Had not already then begun that searching in Scripture to which a psalmist invites with the prayer, "Take the veil from my eyes so that I may behold wondrous things found in your law!" (119:18)? The Johannine vision illustrates the point.

3. A final consideration brings us back to the Johannine Jesus story and its narrative execution. Its six sections not only are thematically based on a motif sequence of the Paradise story, they also conform in

their narrative execution to (the five fifths of the Law of) 'Moses and the Prophets,' the scriptural canon recognized in the first century C.E. generally and specifically in the Jesus stories of the New Testament (John 1:45, Mark 9:4-5, Matthew 5:17, Luke 24:27). I have in, an earlier paper, shown that the Johannine story, on the (surface) level of its narrative execution, supplies verbal cues which connect each section successively with 'The Prophets' and the five parts of 'Moses.' [4]

The reversion in the sequencing is striking. The Johannine story starts with the 'Prophets' as a correlating scriptural unit, and then has as the other corresponding units the fifth, fourth, third, second and first books of 'Moses'. This inversion procedure probably has antecedents in Hebrew Scripture and is attested in the writings of early Jewish and Christian groups.[5] As far as the Johannine 'Book of Signs' is concerned, the compositional inversion makes it possible to present Jesus' "breathing in" holy spirit as his final gift, heightening, both in terms of (surface) phrase choice and (basic) theme identity, the original creation of Genesis 2.

Read in the light of our findings, the story of changing water into wine at Cana (John 2:1-10) shows itself to be both preview and metaphoric summary of the Johannine narrative: Jesus turns 'six stone jars standing there ready for the purification rites of the Judeans,' filled at his order with the water (of the scriptures 'Moses and the Prophets'), into vessels now containing the 'wine' of his spiritual gifts, offered in the six sections of the Johannine Jesus story. Moreover, the master of ceremonies is surprised by the quality of the wine served last. This is why it is not merely the first of the signs, but the 'master sign.'

Endnotes

[1] Wolfgang Roth, "Jesus as the Son of Man: The Scriptural Identity of a Johannine Image," in *The Living Text. Essays in Honor of Ernest W. Saunders*, edited by Dennis E. Groh and Robert Jewett (Lanham: University Press of America, 1985), 11-26.

[2] Ibid.

[3] André LaCocque, "The Narrative Code of the Fourth Gospel: A Response to Wolfgang Roth," *Biblical Research* XXXII (1987): 31-33.

[4] For the argumentation see Wolfgang Roth, "Scripture Coding in the Fourth Gospel," *Biblica Research* XXXII (1987): 6-29 and compare the response by LaCocque, "Narrative Code."

[5] See LaCocque, "Narrative Code," 30-31.

Chapter 14

God of the Future

Herman Schaalman

It is well over a half century ago that the world shuddered to the full knowledge of the *shoa*. Some aspects and facts had been known selectively before war's end to a number of world leaders and a few others but the full weight of the horror broke over most of us only afterwards. The survivors themselves were usually most sparing in telling their tales. Many of them have died without revealing the shattering experiences suffered or witnessed in the camps. Many children and grandchildren know little of anything about those cataclysmic events through which their own kin passed.

As for the rest of humanity, some were totally disinterested—either ignorant of those dark happenings or overwhelmed by the weight of their own concerns. Others wanted to forget what had occurred either from profound guilt or from the seductive desire to forget the past and get on with the present and future. A few even went so far as to deny the facticity of the *shoa* either reducing it to cunning propaganda or seeking to render it to minor, even banal proportions. Still others sought to rob the *shoa* of its uniqueness by linking or comparing it to other atrocities committed and suffered the world over.

Even some Jews have questioned or rejected the uniqueness of those horrendous years or have complained about any central focus given to the *shoa* either now after all these years or, altogether, as an unwarranted deflection from other concerns.

Perhaps all of these reactions seen from certain angles or examined carefully can be understood to a degree, or attributed to and explained as well known human responses to overpowering facts and events. In their own surely unintended manner, however, they testify to the very uniqueness and power of the *shoa* which continues to call for additional and ever new ways of probing for its meanings and consequences.

To put it bluntly, the *shoa* is an event of a magnitude comparable to the covenantal revelation at Mt. Sinai; the pain, death and redemption associated with Golgotha; the need for revolutionary reconstructions after the loss of altar and sovereignty to the Romans. How can that be?

It centers on God. After the *shoa* there is an unavoidable need to reconsider the traditional formulations of God's being and, therefore, also of the traditional liturgical vocabulary.

Traditionally, in one form or another, whether explicitly or implicitly, God was depicted and spoken of as omnipotent. God was that supreme, unchallengeable power from Whom, through Whom, by Whom everything proceeded. All reality, all existence, all history were the immediate or mediate products of Divine Power. In its purest form this belief and proclamation of omnipotence allowed for no other cause for any effect in the universe and in human life. Sin, therefore, was the always ultimately futile attempt to thwart, contravene or evade divine omnipotence. It was believed always to be followed by punishment whether immediate or delayed.

This view of God has the unquestioned advantage of so ordering and structuring existence as to provide clearly definable guidelines and commandments. It wove an always reliable, secure armor-like vestment for human life, its decisions, crises and hopes. It was a most comforting, though at times uncomfortable harness directing humans from birth through life to death and beyond.

For many of us today this traditional view and belief is shattered by the *shoa*. If the *shoa* were the effect of an omnipotent divine cause then what could be the motivation for such causality? Is it sheer divine caprice? Is it, as traditionally assumed and historiographically noted, divine punishment for egregious human sins? Is it divine absence no matter how motivated, divine "hiding" or even divine indifference?

All of these explanations and more have been attempted to account for the event of the *shoa* in a world ruled by an omnipotent God. Every one of them fails. Some from sheer absurdity, others from the horrendous implications about God hidden or explicit in them. For many of us, these attempts to explain or justify God in relation to the *shoa* ring so hollow, or better obscene, as to become totally unacceptable. Nor is there any comfort or profit in retreating to a posture of total unquestioning submission by pleading ignorance of God's will and intentions and desperately seeking to resume a pre-*shoa* liturgic and theological life as though such a retreat could restore the earlier covenantal assurances, trust and relation.

The *shoa* shatters divine omnipotence for many Jews once and for all. If God willed or permitted the *shoa*, Jews are left in a bottomless void. And not Jews alone! Christians share this horror-filled stare into the abyss.

But what of omniscience? Is omniscience likewise doomed to irretrievable collapse? It is. What could omniscience possibly mean when it is decoupled from omnipotence? What value to believers can a God be who knows all but is either incapable or in principle unwilling to act on such totality of knowledge. It would merely be an interior event within God without any consequences for humans seeking for answers by which to live in divinely acceptable ways. Seen this way, omniscience is the ultimate isolation of God from human life and history, is the ultimate absence of God.

Neither omnipotence nor omniscience can furnish such insights into the *shoa* or offer such explanations as to enable a believer in God to remain faithful. Both are inadequate in principle. Both fail us and need to be discarded.

There is, however, another "omni" which does not share this fate. God's omnipresence can be asserted, indeed needs to be asserted. To put it differently: God was at Auschwitz, had to be there not as Ruler, not as Redeemer, not as Victor, but as Sufferer. God, as it were, was wounded in the *shoa*, suffered together with God's first covenant people. Only a God thus tragically involved and now needing us to help and heal, yes precisely, God, is tenable. Only such a God who needs me to love and pray and bring joy helps and strengthens the retrieval of faith and faithfulness after the enormity of the catastrophe. One million children under ten years of age stand between God and me, children whose parents and grandparents were not belligerents engaged in armed conflict, but were, therefore, in the truest and purest meaning of that word: innocents.

We should have known all along that God needed to be understood also as Sufferer. Biblical and rabbinic texts speak of it clearly. What else could explain God's reaction of expelling Adam and Eve from Eden were it not that God suffered a radical disappointment with this curious final item in the created order? What suffering must have occurred within God when barely called into being humanity proves judged to be so corrupt and evil that creation itself is ruptured? What a deep wound Torah reports was struck to God by our ancestors' cardinal sin at the Golden Calf prompting God in a nearly uncontrollable anger to wipe out the barely six weeks old new covenant partner, a catastrophe avoided only by Moses' adroit management of divine wrath? (Could God not have sent Moses down from the mountain a day or two sooner thus nipping in the bud the fateful disloyalty?) And what about Moses himself? One misstep, admittedly fundamental, and this most intimate companion, messenger and spokesman for God is punished mercilessly. No suffering for God here? Or what about the *shechinah* who weeping accompanies the exiles after the futile and destructive war against Rome?

Divine anger, divine retribution, God being so taken unawares, so surprised that God flares up, are these not unmistakable signs of an understanding of the nature of God that are incompatible with omnipotence and omniscience! Omniscience and Omnipotence are the fruits of the Greek philosophical search for the Absolute, an Absolute which is, therefore, in itself beyond human reach, beyond relation. The God of the Bible is fundamentally relational.

The God of the Bible is relational, interactive, tied to us as we are to God, mutually dependent, i.e. covenantal. For that is the meaning of the Covenant, a mutual bonding: "I will be your God and You will be My people." It is in a mysterious way a commitment by God, self-limiting, irrevocable but conditional for us and unconditional for God. It is equally binding, but not equally weighted. It is a gift of grace, a gift from that, to us, impenetrable aspect of God that makes God God and not human.

If omnipotence and omniscience are untenable because of and after the *shoa* the consequences are not only theological but liturgical as well. Our prayer vocabulary is in need of revision along with our theological ruminations. The words we speak to God in the moments of prayer both public and private, both prescribed or spontaneous need to reflect who we are, where we are in time and place. We and our prayer words need to be in total integrity. Much of tradition can remain usable, but much clearly not.

For example, in the Daily Prayer Book edited by the late Chief Rabbi of the British Empire, Joseph H. Hertz the well-known opening hymn "Yiadal" contains in the albeit poetic English translation the verse: "He knows and heeds the secret thoughts of man; He saw the end of all ere aught began." (Adam's?, Moses'?, yours?, mine?) Some verses of the equally often used *Adon olam*, again in poetic translation: "All strength is His... The cup of life whene'er I crave... Rest in the Lord in fearless calm." Or: "Happy are we! How goodly is our portion, how pleasant our lot, and how beautiful our heritage!" etc., etc.

In the modernized Prayer Book of the Reform movement: "You are Goodness: Your mercies never end; You are Compassion; Your love will never fail." etc., etc. Or the dreadful *unetane tokef*: "...on Rosh Hashana it is written, on Yom Kippur it is sealed: How many shall pass on, how many shall come to be; who shall live and who shall die; who shall perish by fire and who by water; who by sword and who by beast, etc., etc." These very small, random samples surely make the point that traditional language quite often becomes so remote if not alien as to lose its prayer power and for many of us its integrity. I have no ready solution except to seek or create substitute language and imagery, a task for gifted linguist, poets and liturgists, probably even preferably in concert.

The *shoa* because it is unique, beyond all comparisons, is thus a radical break with basic aspects of the tradition. It demands total reevaluation of much of the past including to be sure the entire conception of reward and punishment.

It is not only the *shoa* which confronts us with the necessity to rethink, and if possible reformulate some of our basic theological thought and liturgical language. Conditions created by the advancing edge of the human enterprise especially in the various fields of science equally compel us to thoughtful review. In particular, it is the perception of time which compels us to rethink some basic teachings and values of traditional religion. The change from the second to the third millennium in the Christian calendar makes such a review virtually unavoidable. Though the Christian reckoning of time has universal acceptance and usage the Jewish traditional counting of the existence of the world as five thousand seven hundred fifty eight does not absolve us of this task either.

Deeply embedded in the Judeo-Christian perception of time (to a lesser degree also in Islam) is a subtle but unavoidable pressure. Time is fleeting. Time is short, running out. Eschatology is a preferred preoccupation. The question of the "end of time," the *Kairos*, the right and proper time for ultimate fulfillment is asked frequently, sometimes urgently and answered variously. Some anticipate as the fulfillment of their most deeply held faith commitments the end of the world soon, even imminently. Many others though not swept along by such eschatological and apocalyptic expectations are none-the-less firmly committed to their eventual occurrence though not necessarily in the immediate future. In both traditions there is a powerful surge toward an end-time. In fact, salvation, redemption, the completion of the cyclical movement from the incomplete creation to its *shalom*, its unbroken, healed totality is a highly venerated and desired conclusion of the human enterprise. It is a long delayed but yearned for fulfillment. It is the *tikkun olam*, the completion and restoration of the flawed Beginning.

Yet all of these are based on a perception of time severely, even radically limited. Time, the most distinctive, unique human perception is considered to be ultimately, relatively short. A few thousand years at best. One Jewish story about the "right time" for the Messiah tells us that it is to occur within a Sabbath of Thousands. Just as traditionally, so incorporated in sacred texts, the universe was a three storied structure consisting of Heaven, Earth, and the Netherworld; as space was thus delimited, so was time. It was to run only for a predetermined, brief span. Many yearned and prayed to live at the moment when such an end-time would occur no matter how attained.

Do such perceptions still function for us? Are they still real and meaningful for us who learn that the Universe might be twelve to fifteen billion years old, our Earth about four billion years, and the sun with a calculated life of some six billion years more? Do we who learn that hominids might be four million years old still think of time in only thousands of years? Why are we led to reckon the extent of the human adventure in such puny numbers? Is it inconceivable for the human story to be told for another five million, fifty million, five hundred million years? If paleontology teaches of fossils hundreds of millions years old, why not we? And if this were not in principle impossible but, in fact, plausible and possible what happens to eschatology, to the "end of the world," the end of time?

Instead of thinking of ourselves as senescent and nearing an inescapable not far-off termination as humans we are barely out of our diapers, not even toddlers as yet in the future unfolding of life on Earth, of human life. Arrogantly we have judged people who lived three, four thousand years ago as primitives. In a few hundred years our descendants will, no doubt, look on us as their primitive forbears. If the current explosion in human exploration of both the macro- and micro-cosms continues, and it shows no sign of slowing but, on the contrary, of speeding up, then we despite our proud new knowledge will be seen rightly as mere beginners.

If this is our milieu, what happens to some of our basic faith statements and values? Will they not need to undergo review, rethinking, rearticulation? These are high-risk prospects and tasks, but at the same time full of the excitement of new visions, new ideas, new probings into the mystery of God, of reality, of us as humans.

We stand not only at the beginning of the new millennium. We stand at the threshold of seemingly limitless new possibilities, a joint search for enlarged meanings of wide open vistas into a future of which we had not dared to dream. We, people of faith, we who delve into the mystery of God, are called to raise our eyes way beyond the limited horizons which up to now confined us.

Here is a possibility of a future virtually beyond our imagination. It is a most enticing, invigorating prospect. God is not of the past only; God is primarily of the future, and so are we.

Chapter 15

Understanding Scripture and the Holocaust

Byron L. Sherwin

And so it happened that when they were young, the two brothers, Rabbi Elimelekh and Rabbi Zusya, who were destined to become great hasidic masters, wandered as beggars from town to town so that they could learn humility, and so that they could share in the experience of the *Shekhinah*—of God, whose presence is in exile in our world. Each day, they would arrive in a town, beg for their food and lodging, spend the night, and travel on the next morning. Never would they spend more or less than one night in each town.

One day they came to a certain town. Food and drink were given them, but they could neither eat nor drink. A place to sleep was provided, but they could not rest, for they felt a terrible sense of dread in that place. Neither of them could sleep through the night because of ghastly nightmares. And so, in the midst of the night, they left this town, where they had apprehended a sense of dread beyond the imaginable.[1] In Hebrew, this town was called *Ushpizin*; in Polish, *Oswiecim*. The Germans named it: *Auschwitz*.

When this hasidic tale was first told, 200 years before the Holocaust, no one could imagine what it was that caused Rabbi Elimelekh and Rabbi Zusya such a somber sense of foreboding. No one could imagine what it was that they apprehended. But, now we can. What they previsaged was what happened in that place, which has come to epitomize and to symbolize the event we now call the "Holocaust." The horror that invaded *their* imagination has now become *our* history.

Yet, Elimelekh of Lizensk and Zusya of Anipol were not the first Jews to previsage the Holocaust. Looking back at how Jews of former generations have understood the Scriptures, we see that they seem to have previsaged it as well. Consequently, when speaking about the Holocaust and our understanding of the Bible, we must focus upon two issues:

1. How has the Holocaust influenced the contemporary understanding of Scripture, especially the Jewish understanding of the biblical text?

2. How has Jewish tradition's understanding of Scripture influenced how we perceive the Holocaust?

Though this essay will address both of these issues, the focus here will be on the second—simply because it is usually neglected. A very pervasive view in the contemporary Jewish community is to see all of Jewish experience through the lens of the Holocaust.[2] But, what I want to suggest is the opposite; namely, to look at the Holocaust through the lens of Jewish tradition. As is discussed below, this approach accomplishes two things that the view of reducing Judaism and Jewish experience to the Holocaust cannot accomplish. First, it understands the Holocaust *within* the context of Jewish historical and theological self-understanding, rather than understanding all of Jewish experience and theology within the context of the Holocaust. Put another way, it refuses to reduce Judaism to the Holocaust, as is so often being done in the contemporary Jewish community. Secondly, it demonstrates the link between the Holocaust and the continuity of Jewish self-understanding, flowing from Scripture, through the ancient and medieval rabbinic writings, down to our own day. Before offering some examples of this approach, three preliminary observations need to be made.

First, a talmudic tradition teaches that everything is found in the Torah, that everything is anticipated in its text, that by a deep investigation of the text, we find a continuity between biblical figures and ourselves. We discover that the protagonists of the biblical drama are our contemporaries, that their problems are ours, that their experience is ours, that there is no real gap between them and us, that there is an inextricable interrelationship between the sacred texts of Judaism and the historical experiences of the Jewish people. The Jewish people and the text of the Hebrew Bible are inseparable. We simultaneously see historical events through the lens of the text while we read the text through the prism of historical events.

Second, contrary to popular opinion, Judaism is *not* the Hebrew Bible, but the Bible interpreted in and by post-Biblical Jewish tradition, what the Bible is taken to mean. When Jews look at the biblical text, they always see it through the corrective lens of traditional interpretation. What the text itself says is of penultimate importance to what tradition takes the text to mean. Consequently, when we place the Bible and the Holocaust in a single thought, they are joined by how we can discover foreshadowings, forebodings of the Holocaust in the lives of biblical personalities as interpreted by many generations of their descendants. It must therefore be stressed that while Jews and Christians both accept the Hebrew Scriptures as a shared spiritual inheritance, though they share a common text, they do *not* share a common meaning of the text. The text read is the same. The meaning extrapolated from the text often is different.

Third, there is a medieval Hebrew proverb that has enormously influenced how Jews have read the Scriptures: *Ma'asei avot, siman le-vanim;* "Events in the lives of our biblical forebears are signs to their future descendants." Put another way, it means that what happens to Jews in history is already previsaged by what happened to their biblical ancestors. With regard to the Holocaust it means that the

Holocaust is already anticipated in Scripture, that there is a continuity between the experience of the *avot* [the biblical forebears of the Jewish people] and the Holocaust experience.[3]

Having made these preliminary observations, let me move now to the biblical text itself. I want to focus on two biblical characters—Abraham and Isaac. But, before doing that, I want to discuss Job, and to explain why Job is *not* part of the Jewish discussion of the Holocaust and its convergence with understanding the biblical text.[4]

When the Holocaust and the Bible are mentioned together, the biblical personality and the biblical book that often first comes to mind is Job. The reasons seem obvious. First, because Job is the paradigmatically innocent victim of suffering in the biblical text. Second, because, more than any other biblical book, the Book of Job directly and forthrightly confronts the theological problem of undeserved suffering, the problem of *theodicy,* of why the good and the innocent suffer and of why the evil prosper in a world presumably governed by a God who is benevolent, powerful and just. Since the problem of theodicy is powerfully and poignantly raised by the Holocaust, one should expect that re-visioning the Bible through the prism of the Holocaust would focus our attention upon Job. But, such is *not* the case. Why?

As we look at traditional Jewish literature spawned by catastrophic events in Jewish history—the destruction of the Temples, the massacres during the Crusades, the expulsion from Spain, the Chmelnitzki massacres—to name a few, and as we look at the traditional Jewish literature written in response to the Holocaust, even in secular Hebrew and Yiddish Holocaust literature, there is little reference to Job. His experiences, while linked to the Holocaust very commonly by Christians, are not as often so linked by traditional Jews. Why? Perhaps because Job is *not* one of the *avot*. According to the dominant rabbinic traditions, Job was not a Jew. Therefore, the principle of *ma'asei avot siman le-vanim* does not apply to him. His experiences are not those of the Jewish people. As was already mentioned, Jews read the biblical text through the lens of interpretive tradition.

Who is Job, according to that tradition? According to a rabbinic tradition mentioned twice in the Talmud (*Sota* 11a, *Sanhedrin* 106a), Job was an advisor to Pharaoh. In fact, he was one of Pharaoh's top three advisors, the others being Balaam and Jethro.

One day, Pharaoh asked their advice on a new policy he was contemplating. This was the first genocidal plan of a ruler of a country, but not the last. Pharaoh's plan was systematically to annihilate the people of Israel, first by murdering each newborn son by drowning him in the river Nile.

The text tells us that each of Pharaoh's advisors reacted differently to the plan. Jethro courageously opposed it. For this, he was rewarded by becoming the grandfather of Moses' children. Balaam endorsed the genocidal scheme. For this, he was punished with death. Job remained silent, assenting to the plan with his silent apathy. For this, says the Talmud, he was punished with sufferings.

In this view, Job is not a paradigm for the suffering innocent victim of the Holocaust. Rather, Job is a paradigm for the apathetic gentile bystander during the Holocaust. He is an exemplar of the individual who could have prevented genocide from occurring, but who let it happen with his apathetic assent. Hence, as we look anew at the Book of Job through the prism of talmudic interpretation, as we look at Job and the Holocaust together, Job emerges not as a model of victimization, not as a paradigm for addressing the problem of theodicy, but as a paradigm of silent assent to evil, of not doing what he was able to do to thwart genocide. Job's experience cannot help us to confront the experience of the victims of genocide because his is not a *Jewish* experience; he is not one of the *avot.* Rather, his experience is related to that of those non-Jews during the Holocaust who could have interceded, but who did not.

Let us now move to Abraham, the first Jew. Again, we must look at the story of Abraham through the lens of rabbinic interpretation, through the interpretative filter of *midrash.* And, what do we find?

According to Genesis 12:1, Judaism begins with God's appearance to Abraham, commanding him to leave his birth place and to go on faith to a new land, a promised land. But, ask the rabbis: how did Abraham know who was speaking to him? There is no indication in the text before Genesis 12 that Abraham was even aware of the existence of God. All we know to that point is that Abraham lived in Ur of the Chaldeas. In Genesis 11, we hear of Abraham's father, Terach, to whom rabbinic legend gives the profession of an idol manufacturer in a land of idol worshippers.

Rabbinic legend attempts to fill this seeming gap in the biblical narrative by offering a series of *midrashim* describing how Abraham came to the gradual realization that there was one God, that the idols were not divine. Having come to this realization by his own intellectual investigations, Abraham was then able to respond to God's word when God reveals God's presence and will at the beginning of Genesis 12.[5]

Of the many rabbinic legends about Abraham's journey toward faith and his trials of faith, one is most poignant as we look back at it from our post-Holocaust vantage point. According to this legend, Abraham's rejection of the idolatry of his time and place evoked the ire of the king, none other than the evil king Nimrod, whose very name the talmudic rabbis related to the Hebrew word *mered* ("rebellion," i.e., rebellion against God). Nimrod first incarcerates Abraham in prison, trying to starve Abraham to death. Unsuccessful with that strategy, Nimrod applies more severe measures. He orders all of his subjects to bring wood to fuel a great fiery furnace that he had built for a single purpose—the immolation of Abraham. At the king's command, Abraham is cast into this fiery furnace. But, miraculously, Abraham survives this attempt on his life.[6] Thus, already here, at the very beginning of Jewish experience, we have the first Jew placed in a kind of ghetto to be starved to death and then cast into a fiery furnace, a crematorium, to be murdered. Yet, the life of his faith continues. *Ma'asei avot siman le-vanim.*

But, while Abraham, the first Jew, is the first victim of a ruler who wants to annihilate the faith of Abraham and the future progeny of Abraham by destroying the progenitor of the people of Israel, Nimrod is not the last ruler with genocidal plans. Abraham, the first Jew, the first victim of being cast into a crematorium, is also the first survivor of a plan of annihilation. All of this according to rabbinic legend. But, from the biblical text itself, it would seem that Isaac, Abraham's son, is the first victim of a holocaust, and the first holocaust survivor.

We are told that God orders Abraham to offer his son Isaac as a sacrifice, but not as any sacrifice—as an *olah,* a sacrifice that is completely consumed by fire (Gen. 22:2). The usual English translation for *olah* is "Holocaust." According to most Jewish interpretations of this text in Genesis 22, Abraham listens to an angel who comes to command him not to sacrifice Isaac. Isaac is spared and a ram is offered in Isaac's stead. Yet, there is another line of interpretation of this text found throughout Jewish literature.

According to this interpretation of the biblical text, Abraham does not listen to the angel. Indeed, the angel's coming is considered a test of Abraham's obedience to God.[7] Abraham received a command of God. How could such a command be countermanded by an angel? How can Abraham's trial of faith be complete unless he carries out his test, unless he actually sacrifices Isaac?

In this view, Abraham carries through with God's command. Isaac is killed and offered as an *olah,* as a sacrifice, as a holocaust. But, a few chapters later, Isaac marries Rebecca. How is this possible if Isaac had been killed? According to a midrash, God resurrected Isaac some years after his death, so that he can marry Rebecca, so that the history of Israel can continue.[8] Here, Isaac is the first victim of a holocaust and the first holocaust survivor. In this tale of his death and restoration, he becomes a paradigm for future generations, for future tragedies. *Ma'aseh avot siman le-vanim.* An example:

> Ask now and see, was there ever such a holocaust like this in human history? When were there ever hundreds and thousands of sacrifices in one day, each and every one of them like that of Isaac the son of Abraham.

> Oh the pure souls, the innocent lives, the innocent children slain
> and slaughtered. God, will you be silent in the face of such
> things?

This text is not from the literature of the European Holocaust, but from a penitential prayer written in response to the experience of a Jewish community in eleventh-century Germany during the Crusades.[9]

This understanding of the biblical text that has Isaac actually dying is already found in the Talmud (*Ta'anit* 16a). In a discussion of why ashes are placed on the heads of each participant in a public fast, one view is that this is done to remind us that we are dust and ashes. The other view is that this is done in remembrance of Isaac who was offered as an *olah* sacrifice, as a holocaust, and of whom nothing was left but ashes. Here, Isaac, like so many of his descendants during the Holocaust, is a Jew turned into smoke and ashes.

The tradition that has Isaac dying and being resurrected seems to have been consciously suppressed by rabbinic tradition itself, which is why it is not well known. One reason was because the reading of the story of Isaac as one of death and resurrection had been taken by Christians as an anticipation of the death and resurrection of Jesus. Already in the Epistle of Barnabas, Isaac is referred to as the prototype for the sufferings and trials of Jesus. The Church Fathers developed the idea that just as Isaac bore the wood for his sacrifice, and as Jesus bore his cross, so should each Christian bear his wood, her cross.

As is well known, classical Christianity interpreted the Hebrew Scriptures as an anticipation, as a prefiguration of the New Testament, and saw the life and passion of Jesus as being anticipated in the text of the Hebrew Bible. In medieval Jewish-Christian polemics, one of the critical claims each group hurled at the other was with regard to their alleged perversion of the meaning of the Scriptures. In these polemics, Jews rejected the Christian reading of the so-called "Old Testament" as an anticipation and foreshadowing of the New Testament. For this reason, the tradition that described Isaac's death and resurrection was suppressed by Jewish tradition itself. And yet, a version of the death/resurrection idea developed in the Jewish community in the aftermath of the Holocaust and with the birth of the State of Israel. In what has been called the "civil religion" of the Jewish people, the identification of the Holocaust with death and of the State of Israel with resurrection became common and popular.[10] Suddenly biblical and rabbinic texts were read anew as being a foreshadowing of the Holocaust/Israel scenario. Consider, for example, this obscure midrash that in our times has been generously quoted.

A verse in Psalms (20:2) reads: "The Lord will answer you in the day of trouble." The *Midrash on Psalms* (20:4) explains this verse by a parable:

> A father and son were journeying on a road. The son grew weary, and asked his father: *Heikhan he ha-medinah* [meaning, "when are we coming to the city," but literally—"where is the state."] The father replied, "Son, take this as a sign: when you see a cemetery know that the *medinah* is near." Likewise, God says to the people of Israel: When you experience great troubles, surely in that hour redemption is coming, for it is written, "the Lord will answer you in the day of trouble."

According to this text, seeing the cemetery is the prelude to seeing the state, death is the prelude to rebirth. This text is now often read as a previsaging of Israel as a divinely engineered rebirth after the devastation and death of the Holocaust. However, in my view, this interpretation raises immense theological problems. One such problem relates to the sacrifice of Isaac and to the use of the word "Holocaust." Holocaust means a sacrifice, an *olah.* Isaac was sacrificed at God's command. Does this mean that God desired *the* Holocaust? Does this mean that *the* Holocaust was God's will?

Though a number of Jewish thinkers, both Orthodox (like Joel Teitelbaum, the late Satmerer rebbe) and Reform Jewish theologians (like Ignatz Maybaum) have taken this view, not to mention non-Jews like the Moonies, I do not see how any responsible, compassionate person could maintain today that the Holocaust was an expression of the divine will, that it was a divine punishment for some sin. What cruel kind of God could desire the murder of so many people? What sin could justify the deaths of over a million innocent Jewish children? Furthermore, the view that God somehow caused Jewish rebirth with the State of Israel as a kind of recompense for the Holocaust, is equally theologically problematic. As Abraham Heschel has written, "The State of Israel is not an atonement. It would be blasphemy to regard it as a compensation."[11]

Two of the conclusions one can draw from this all too brief excursion into the theological implications of the Holocaust are:

1. That the term "Holocaust," because of its biblical meaning as a sacrifice, is the wrong term for Jews to use in referring to this event. It might be better advised to use the other (biblical) Hebrew term *Shoah* meaning "devastation," or, the more traditional Hebrew term that is also used in Yiddish—*hurban,* which that means destruction. *Hurban* is also used to refer to the destruction of the Temples, thereby giving the Holocaust event a place in the continuity of Jewish trauma and tragedy.

2. Jews need to spend more effort than they already have spent in developing theologies both with regard to the *Shoah* and with regard to the State of Israel. Such theologies must link classical Jewish thought with the meaning for Jews of these two experiences: namely, *Shoah* and Israel. It is now time to dispense with sloganism regarding these realities and move to the development of viable and authentic theologies.

The *Shoah* must not only affect how Jews read Scripture, but also how Jews relate to, understand, and observe their liturgy. For example, in the Passover *Haggadah,* there is the statement: "In every generation some have risen up against us to annihilate us, but the Holy One [i.e., God] always delivered us out of their hands." But, can Jews say this, can Jews believe this, after *Shoah?* I think not. Jews need not only to revisage but also to revise their post–*Shoah* liturgy to reflect and to articulate a post–*Shoah* theology.

A post–*Shoah* theology and liturgy must have their roots in classical sources. A link and a continuity between the theological problems of today and the theological literature that constitutes Jewish tradition must be forged. Consider this example that relates to the *Shoah* and the interpretation of Scripture.

As already has been stated, we cannot accept a theology that has God desire a genocide. But, when did the first genocide occur? According to Scripture, it was when Cain killed Abel. According to the Talmud (*Sanhedrin* 37a), each person *is* the human race in miniature. Murdering one person means murdering that person and all his or her future descendants. The Talmud reminds us that to kill Adam would have meant the genocide of the entire human race. "Adam" in Hebrew means human being. To murder "Adam" is to commit genocide. As Jean-Paul Sartre once said, "Every murder is a genocide."

The possibility of murder and genocide comes into history with the first human beings who were born—Cain and Abel. Cain kills Abel. Abel is at that time 25% of the world's population. Human history begins with murder, fratricide and genocide. And, already on the biblical text describing the murder of Abel, the talmudic rabbis raise the question that must be at the core of any Jewish theology of the *Shoah*. In midrash *Genesis Rabbah* (22:9), the following parable is brought by Rabbi Shimon bar Yohai to reflect on the murder of Abel by Cain. The text reads:

> Think of two gladiators wrestling before the king; had the king wished, he could have separated them. But he did not so desire, and one overcame the other and killed him, he [the victim] crying out [before he died], "Let my cause be pleaded before the king!"

Here, God is the Emperor, a co-conspirator in murder, in genocide. This midrashic text translates the verse, "The

blood of your brother [Abel] cries *to* Me from the earth"
(Gen. 4:10) as "The blood of your brother Abel cries *at* Me,
accusing Me [God] from the earth." In this view, God—like
Job, is portrayed as the apathetic bystander to genocide, to
Shoah. But, we also have another motif that bears mention
here, rooted in Scripture and developed in rabbinic literature.
This motif describes God as sharing in the suffering of the
victim. Here God is not a co-conspirator but a co-victim.[12]
It is from the dialectic of these two views, God as co-victim
and God as silent co-conspirator, that a post-*Shoah* theology
can emerge. In summation: not only must the *Shoah*
influence how we understand Scripture, but it must also compel
us to develop a traditionally rooted though contemporaneously
pertinent understanding of our relationship in the post-*Shoah*
world, not only to the Scriptures, not only to God, but to one
another as well.

During the course of his productive, effective and creative
career, André LaCocque has made a unique contribution to
the understanding and the application of Scripture to living in
the post-Shoah world, both for Christians and Jews. His
unusual mastery of Hebrew and Aramaic texts, his vast
knowledge of classical and modern Jewish and Christian
commentaries, and his uncanny ability to relate ancient texts
to modern psychological insights and to existential problems
have enriched the minds and hearts of his colleagues and of
the myriads of students he has taught during his illustrious
career. His leadership, as director of the Center for Jewish-
Christian Studies at Chicago Theological Seminary, helped to
pioneer Christian-Jewish dialogue and understanding,
grounded in a foundation of academic excellence. Always on
the cutting edge, his scholarship has opened many new doors
in the world of learning. Beginning in his native Belgium
during World War II, André LaCocque has lived what he has
studied and taught. His was one of a handful of families who
risked much to save Jewish lives during the Holocaust. After
coming to America, he continued to translate his convictions
into actions, his commitments into deeds. For these and for
many more reasons, I am pleased and singularly honored to
contribute this essay to this volume dedicated to the life and

work of my cherished colleague and precious friend, André LaCocque.

Endnotes

[1] Elie Wiesel, *Souls on Fire* (New York: Random House, 1972), 117-118.

[2] See Byron L. Sherwin, *Sparks Amidst the Ashes: The Spiritual Legacy of Polish Jewry* (New York: Oxford University Press, 1997), 83-87.

[3] Compare Emil Fackenheim, *The Jewish Bible After the Holocaust* (Bloomington, Indiana: Indiana University Press, 1990).

[4] Compare Martin Buber, *On Judaism*, ed. Nahum Glatzer (New York: Schocken Books: 1967), 224.

[5] On rabbinic legends regarding Nimrod, Terach and Abraham, see Louis Ginzberg, *The Legends of the Jews*, 6 vols. (Philadelphia: The Jewish Publication Society of America, 1925), vol. 1, 186-217; vol. 5, 209-225.

[6] Adolph Jellinek, "Ma'aseh Avraham," in ed. Adolph Jellinek, *Beit ha-Midrash*, , vol. 1 (Vienna, 1855), 25-34.

[7] Shalom Spiegel, *The Last Trial*, trans. Judah Goldin (Philadelphia: The Jewish Publication Society of America, 1967).

[8] Ibid., 6-7.

[9] Ibid., 19-20.

[10] See Jonathan Woocher, *Sacred Survival: The Civil Religion of American Jews* (Bloomington, IN: Indiana University Press, 1986), 131-136.

[11] Abraham Joshua Heschel, *Israel: An Echo of Eternity* (New York: Farrar, Straus and Giroux, 1967), 113.

[12] See Abraham Joshua Heschel, *The Prophets* (Philadelphia: The Jewish Publication Society of America, 1962), 221-232.

Publications by André LaCocque

Main Publications in English

But As For Me: The Question of Election for God's People. Atlanta: John Knox Press, 1979.

The Book of Daniel (Foreword by Paul Ricoeur). Atlanta: John Knox, and London: SPCK, 1979. [Exists also in French.]

The Jonah Complex (with Pierre E. LaCocque; foreword by Mircea Eliade). Atlanta: John Knox, 1981.

Daniel in His Time (Foreword by R. Martin-Achard). Columbia: University of South Carolina Press, 1998. [Exists also in French.]

Jonah: a Psycho-Religious Approach to the Prophet. Columbia: University of South Carolina Press, 1990. [Exists also in French.]

The Feminine Unconventional. Minneapolis: Fortress Press, 1990. [French translation: Subersives, "Lectio Divina" Paris, Cerf 1992.]

Commitment and Commemoration. [As editor.] Chicago: Exploration Press, 1994. [Proceedings of conferences organized by the CJCS.]

"The Book of Daniel," *International Bible Commentary*. Minneapolis: Liturgical Press, 1998. [Exists also in Spanish; will be translated into French, German, Russian, etc.]

A series of ca. 40 Maps for *IBC* [See preceding item.]

Thinking Biblically (with Paul Ricoeur). Chicago: University of Chicago Press, 1998. [Will also be in French in Paris: Le Seuil, 1998.]

Romance, She Wrote: A Hermeneutical Essay on Song of Songs. Harrisburg, Pennsylvania: Trinity International Press, 1998.

Daniel in His Time (translation into Korean). Seoul: The Christian Literature Society of Korea, 1999.

Articles and Collective Works
(since 1986)

"Torah-Nomos" in *The Life of the Covenant: The Challenge of Contemporary Judaism (Essays in Honor of Herman E. Schaalman)*. Edited by J.A. Edelheit. Chicago: Spertus College of Judaica Press, 1986, pp. 85-96.

"The Narrative Code of the Fourth Gospel: A Response to Wolfgang Roth" in *Papers of the Chicago Society of Biblical Research*. Vol. XXXII, 1987, pp. 30-41.

"Sin and Guilt" in *The Encyclopedia of Religion* vol. 13. Edited by Mircea Eliade. NewYork: Macmillan, 1987.

"Haman in the Book of Esther" in *Biblical and Other Studies*. Edited by Reuben Ahroni. *Hebrew Annual Review* vol. 11. Columbus, Ohio: Ohio State University Press, 1988.

Guest Editor, *Chicago Theological Seminary Register*, "Religious Pluralism—The Dialogue Between Jews and Christians" (66:1) 1986.

"In Memoriam Mircea Eliade," *Chicago Theological Seminary Register* (66:2) 1986.

Guest Editor, *Chicago Theological Seminary Register*, "The New Testament and Judaica/Judism" (68:1) 1988.

Guest Editor, *Chicago Theological Seminary Register*, "Muslim Women Scholars on Women" (83:1 and 2) 1993.

"The Socio-Spiritual Formative Milieu of the Daniel Apocalypse," *The Book of Daniel in the Light of New Findings*. A.S. van der Woude, ed., Bibliotheca Ephemeridum Theologicarum Lovaniensium, CVI. Leuven University Press: Peeters, 1993.

"The Land in D and P," *Dort ziehen Schiffe dahin...* (Beiträge zur Erforschung des Alten Testaments und des Antiken Judentums # 28), Collected Communications to the xiv[th] Congress of the IOSOT, Paris 1992. Edited by M. Augustin & K. D. Schunck, eds. Frankfurt/Berlin/Bern/New York/Paris/Vienna: Peter Lang, 1996.

"Joseph Son of Jacob" in *Homage to Perry LeFevre*. Chicago: Exploration Press, 1994.

"God after Auschwitz: A Contribution to Contemporary Theology" in *Journal of Ecumenical Studies*, Spring 1996.

"Job and Religion at Its Best" in *Biblical Interpretation*, 4:2, June 1996, 131-153.

"The Great Cry of Jesus in Matthew 27:50" in *Putting Body and Soul Together: Essays in Honor of Robin Scroggs*. Valley Forge: Trinity Press International, 1997, 138-164.

"The Book of Daniel" in *International Bible Commentary*. Minneapolis: The Liturgical Press, 1998. [To be translated into French, Spanish, Polish, etc.]

A Series of Historical Geographical Maps for the above-mentioned Commentary (as Map Editor), 1998.

"La Decalogue et les Codes royaux de l'Orient Ancien" in *Le Monde de la Bible*, No. 117, Mars–Avril, 1999, 31–32.

"The Different Versions of Esther " in *Biblical Interpretation 7*. Leiden: Brill, 1999, 301–22.

In Press:

"Le dernier cri de Jésus selon Matthieu 27:50," *EthR*, Montpellier, 2000.

"Allusions to Creation in Daniel 7" in eds. J. J. Collins and P. W. Flint. *The Book of Daniel: Composition and Reception*. Leiden: Brill, 1999.

"Genèse 29:31 – 30:24" in *Mélanges Albert Pury*. Geneva: Labor et Fides, 1999.

"Jesus' Hermeneutics of the Law: Rereading the Parable of the Good Samaritan" in *Festscrift Jacques Doukhan*. Andrews University Press, 2000.

Prinicpales Publications
en Francais

Le devenir de Dieu. Paris: Editions Universitaires, 1967.

Pérennité d'Israël. Genève: Labor et Fides, 1964.
Le livre de Daniel. Neuchatel-Paris: Delachaux et Niestlé, 1976.

"II Zacharie," *Aggée, Malachie, Zacharie.* "Commentaires de l'Ancien Testament" XIc, 2nd éd. Genève: Labor et Fides, 1981.

Daniel et son temps. Genève: Labor et Fides, 1983.

59 articles in *Dictionaire encyclopédique de la Bible.* Paris: Brepols, 1987.

Le complexe de Jonas. Paris: Cerf, 1989.

Subversives, Coll. "Lectio Divina" # 148. Paris: Cerf, 1992.

Penser la Bible, avec Paul Ricoeur. Paris: Seuil, 1998.

Sous Contrat (Under Contract):

Le livre de Ruth, Comm. de l'Ancien Testament. Geneva: Labor, 1998.

Le livre d'Esther, Comm. de l'Ancien Testament. Geneva: Labor, 1999.

"Le livre de Daniel," *IBC* (Voir liste en Anglais). Paris: Le Cerf.

Les Pirke Aboth et l'Evangile: Parallèles et Contrastes. Paris: Le Cerf.

Articles en Francais
(since 1989)

"Hamam dans le livre d'Esther," *Revue de Théologie et de Philosophie.* Lausanne/Switzerland, # 121 (1989), 307‑322.

"André Neher, en hommage," *Sens* # 143, Paris 1989, 411‑12.

"La Shulamite et les chars d'Aminadab: Un essai herméneutique sur Cant 6,12‑7, l" *Revue Biblique* 102:3, 1995, 330‑47.

"Le dernier cri de Jesus dans Matthieu 27:50," in *Etudes Theologiques et Religieuses.* Montpellier, 2000.

"Genèse 29:31 – 30:24" in *Mélanges Albert de Pury.* Geneva: Labor et Fides, 1999.